RAUCH'S PENNSYLVANIA DUTCH

HAND-BOOK: A BOOK FOR INSTRUCTION

METALMARK BOOKS

RAUCH'S

ENNSYLVANIA DUTCH

HAND-BOOK.

A Book for Instruction.

RAUCH'S

ENNSYLVANIA DEITSH

HOND-BOOCH.

En Booch for Inshtructa.

By E. H. RAUCH,

("Pit Schwæffelbrenner.")

MAUCH CHUNK, PA.:

E. H. RAUCH, PRINTER AND PUBLISHER.

1879.

PREFACE.

About the year 1870, I made up my mind to publish this book, with a view of affording practical and profitable instruction, especially for business men who are located among Pennsylvania Dutch speaking people, and also for the many thousands of native Pennsylvania girls and boys who attend the English public schools, and yet almost exclusively speak the Pennsylvania Dutch language at home and in the community.

I then commenced the work, and had gathered several thousand Pennsylvania Dutch words and arranged them alphabetically with translations. But then I discovered my entire incompetency for such a work, by reason of a lack of sufficient experience to make my spelling of words consistent and uniform. I became discouraged, and for the time abandoned the work.

Since then I have had ample experience, and believe I have very much improved and simplified the spelling, which is strictly according to English rules. The German rule would not be practical, because from eighteen to twenty per cent. of all the words commonly used in Pennsylvania Dutch are either English or a compound of English and German, and also because all the youth of our State is taught to read English, and comparitively but few receive any sort of German education. The English rule is therefore decidedly the best for this purpose. Any one who can read English, can also read Pennsylvania Dutch as I have it recorded, and give it, in nineteen out of twenty cases, the correct pronunciation. Therefore, I believe this book will be found specially practical and valuable as an instructor.

To read it, no study of orthography is at all necessary, because it is simply English. The *ch* is the only German sound, pronounced as *gh* in *Dougherty* or *Gallagher*.

As quite a number of newspapers devote portions of their space to Pennsylvania Dutch articles — generally humorous — a book of this kind will assure uniformity of spelling Pennsylvania Dutch words.

Whilst many of the writers, doubtless, will contend that the spelling of this or that word is defective, and whilst there will probably be errors and some inconsistencies, I am confident that, as a whole, this work will be pronounced a very good beginning — a healthy plant of a practical Pennsylvania Dutch literature.

It is not necessary to undertake a history of the Pennsylvania Dutch language. Indeed, I would not feel competent even if inclined to state it. Prof. S. S. Haldeman contends that it is the dialect of South Germany transplanted to Pennsylvania. Probably that is nearly correct. I would say it is the natural dialect begotten by the intermixture of English and German speaking people in the same community, and by that I mean all classes of Germans, and not merely those of South Germany. Be this as it may, Pennsylvania Dutch is a language, spoken not only by one-third of all the people of the great State of Pennsylvania, but also by thousands and hundreds of thousands of descendants of Pennsylvanians now located in Ohio, Indiana, Illinois, Wisconsin, Missouri, Kansas, Nebraska, Iowa, West Virginia, Northern Maryland, Tennessee, Texas and in some other localities. The language came into being as all other languages came, from natural causes.

Flattering myself that to some extent I have succeeded, after a number of years of experience and practice, in making a fair record of the Pennsylvania Dutch language, I respectfully submit my work for approval or rejection by an intelligent public.

E. H. Rauch.

(TRANSLATION.—IVVERSETZUNG.)

About 'm yohr 1870, hob ich my mind uf
gamaucht for 'n booch shreiva un publisha, fun
Pennsylvania Deitsh in English un English in
Pennsylvania Deitsh, mit der obsicht for practically un pruffitliche instructions gevva, abbor-
dich for bisness menner os in pletz woona fun
Pennsylvania Deitsh shwetzende leit, un aw for
de feela daussenda fun Pennsylvania boova un
maid os in de Englisha shoola gane un doch
sheer nix shwetza derhame un in der nochbershaft os Pennsylvania Deitsh.

Ich hob sellamohls de arwet aw g'fonga, un
hob a pawr daussend wardta g'sommelt un
arranged alphabetically. Awer ich hob aw ous
g'foona os ich noch net fit war for so'n job, weil
ich net de noatwendich un practical erfawrung
g'hot hob for de wardta shpella uf 'n regularer
un uniformer wæg. Ich bin mootlose warra, un
hob sellamohls de arwet uf gevva.

Sidder sellam hob ich feel erfawrung g'hot,
un my shpella is now orrick simple, according
tzu der Englisha rule. De Deitsh rule doots net
so goot, weil fun auchtzæ bis tzwansich per cent.
fun de wardta os for common g'used wærra in
Pennsylvania Deitsh, English sin, odder an mix-
ter fun English un Deitsh, un aw weil all de kinner in unserm Shtate larna English laisa, un

yusht 'n klainer dale fun eena krega enniche
sort fun Deitshe larnung. De English rule, dawrum, is by weitam de besht for des booch. Ennich ebber os English laisa g'larnt hut con aw
my Pennsylvania Deitsh laisa, un in ninetzain
ous tzwansich fella, recht ous shprecha. Ich
glawb os des booch specially goot is ols 'n
inshtructor, weil es gor kæ neie orthography is,
un brauch kæ shtudya—for es is im shpella common English. Der *ch* is der ainsicha Deitsh
sound, un wærd ous g'shprucha we *gh* im Englisha nawma *Dougherty.*

Weil ordlich feel tzeitunga plotz maucha for
Pennsylvanish Deitshe shticker — for common
humorish — an booch fun dar awrt wærd useful si, un feel wært, for 'n uniformer waeg tzu
shpella fore bringa. Feel fun de shreiver du'n ferleicht contenda os 's shpella fun dem un sellam
wardt besser si kent, un es con si os failer g'funna
wærra, awer ich bin confident os im gonsa wærd
des booch goot g'hasa—an g'soonty plons for 'n
practically Pennsylvania Deitshe literature.

Es is net noatwendich os ich unnernem 'n
history fun der Pennsylvania Deitch shproach
tzu gevva. Ich wær net amohl able sell tzu du
wann ich aw wet. Der Prof. S. S. Haldeman
bahawpt os de shproach is fun Seed Deitshlond
in Pennsylvania ei gaplonst. Sell is ferleicht so.

Ich date awer sawga es is de noddeerlich shproach
in existance cooma dorrich de fermixung fun
English un Deitsh shwetzende leit in der same
nochbershaft, un by sellam mane ich olly clossa
Deitshe, un net yusht de os fun seed Deitshlond
cooma sin.

Luss des awer si we's will, Pennsylvania
Deitsh is 'n shproach, g'shwetzt net yusht by ea
drittle fun de leit im grossa Shtate Pennsylvania,
awer aw by daussenda un hoonerta fun daussenda
Pennsylvanishe noch-coomer now in Ohio, Indiana, Illinois, Wisconsin, Missouri, Kansas, Nebraska, Iowa, West Virginia, Nordlich Maryland,
Tennessee, Texas, un in onnery pletz.   De
shproach is in existance cooma, fun noddeerliche
ursaucha. Un weil ich glawb os ich anyhow tzu'm
dale mich fit g'maucht hob, dorrich yohra fun
erfawrung un practice, der eck-shtæ tzu laiga for
'n practically Pennsylvania Deitshe literature, du
ich yetz my arwet fore 's intelligenta public for 's
awnemma un goot haisa, odder for 's weck
shmeisa un condemma.

E. H. RAUCH.

𝕰𝖓𝖌𝖑𝖎𝖘𝖍-𝕻𝖊𝖓𝖓𝖘𝖞𝖑𝖛𝖆𝖓𝖎𝖆 𝕯𝖚𝖙𝖈𝖍
TRANSLATION OF WORDS.

𝕰𝖓𝖌𝖑𝖎𝖘𝖍𝖊-𝕻𝖊𝖓𝖓𝖘𝖞𝖑𝖛𝖆𝖓𝖎𝖆 𝕯𝖊𝖎𝖙𝖘𝖍𝖊
IVVERSETZUNG FUN WARDTA.

Aback, tzurick.

Abandoned, ferlussa.

Abate, nochlussa.

Abatement, nochlussung.

Abbreviate, obkartza.

Abbreviation obkartzung

Abbreviated, obgakartz'd

Abdicate, ufgevva.

Abdomen, leib, bauch.

Abhor, obshei.

Abhorrent, obsheilich.

Ability, ability.

Able, able, g'shickt.

Abolish, abolish.

Abolished, abolished.

Abolishing, abolisha.

Abolition, abolition.

Abolitionist, abolitionist.

About, about, weaga.

Above, uvva, ivver.

Abreast, navanonner.

Abroad, im ouslond.

Abrupt, pletzlich.

Absent, aweck, net doh

Absentee, absentee.

Abstain, obshtæ.

Abstract, obtzoog.

Absurd, unfershtendich.

Absurdity, unfershtond.

Abundant, irverflissich.

Abuse, abuse.

Abused, abused.

Abusing, abusa.

Abusive, abusif.

Abut, awshtosa.

Abutment, awshtose.

Accept, accept.

Accepting, accepta.

Acceed, ferwillicha.

Access, tzugong.

Accident, unglick.

Accidental, unglicklich

Accumulate, tzunemma.

Accumulation, tzunawm

Account, rechnung, account.

Accountant, accountant.

Accountable, accountable

Accounted, account.
Accounting, accounta.
Accuse. ferklawg.
Accused, baklawg'd.
Accuser, baklaiger.
Accusing, baklawga.
Accustom, gewohnheit
Accustomed, gewohnd.
Ace, ace.
Ache, shmartz,
Aching, shmartza.
Achieve, ousfeera.
Achievement, ousfeerung
Acknowledge, g'shtæ,
  acknowledge.
Acknowledged, g'shton
  na, acknowledged.
Acorn, aichle,
Acquaint, bakonnt.
Acquaintance, bakonnta
Acquire, arlonga.
Acquit, fri-gevva.
Acre, ocker
Across, drivva, nivver.
Act, act.
Acted, g'act.
Acting, acta.
Active, actif.
Actor, acter.
Accute, cute.
Adage, shprich-wardt.
Adapt, awpossa.
Adaptation, auwendung.
Add, add.
Adding, adda.
Addition, addition.
Additional, additional.
Addict, g'waina.
Addicted, g'wained.
Address, address.
Addressing, addressa.

Addressed, addressed.
Adjourn, adjourn.
Adjourning, adjourna.
Adjourned, adjourned.
Adjournment, adjourn-
  ment.
Adhere, awclaiva.
Adherent, awhenker.
Adherence, awhong.
Adieu, farrywell.
Adjacent, naigsht.
Adjective, biwardt.
Adjoin, awshtose.
Adjoining, awshtosa.
Adjure, bashwaira.
Adjust, fix.
Adjusting, fixa.
Adjusted, g'fixed.
Administrator, admin-
  istrator.
Administer, administra.
Administration, ad-
  ministration.
Admire, admire.
Admiring, admira.
Admit, admit, gelta
  lussa.
Admission, admission.
Admittance, admittance.
Admitting, admitta.
Adopt, adopt.
Adopted, g'adopt.
Adopting, adopta.
Adoption, adoption.
Adult, gawoxner.
Adulterate. ferfelsh.
Adulterated, ferfelsh'd.
Adulterating, ferfelsha.
Adulteration, ferfelshung
Advance, fore-ous.
Advancing, advansa.

Advanced, ahead, gon-ga, advanced.
Advantage, fortle, advantage.
Advantage, fortlehoft.
Adverb, shwetzwardt.
Adversary, gaigner.
Adverse, tzuwidder.
Advert, aucht gevva.
Advertise, adferdise.
Advertising, adferdisa.
Advertised, adferdised.
Advertisement, adferdisement.
Advertiser, adferdiser.
Advice, advice, roat.
Advising, advisa, rota.
Advised, awgarota, advised.
Adviser, adviser, roatgevver.
Advocate, advocate.
Advocating, advocata.
Aeronaut, ballooner.
Afar, ous, weit, ob.
Affair, g'sheft, affair.
Affirm, affarm.
Affirming, affarma.
Affirmed, affarm'd.
Affirmative, affarmatif.
Affectionate, freindlich
Afflict, kronk. im troovel.
Affliction, troovel.
Afford, afford.
Affording, afforda.
Affray, shtreit, shlagerei.
Affront, awgriff, affront
Afoot, tzu foos.
Afore, tzufore.
Afraid, ongsht, bong.
After, dernoch, noch.

Afterwards, nochderhond
Again, widder.
Against, dergaiga.
Age, olt, elt, olter.
Aged, olt, elt.
Agent, agent.
Agency, agency.
Aggress, awgriff.
Aggressive, aggressif.
Agitate, agitate.
Agitating, agitata.
Agree, agree.
Agreeing, agreea.
Agreed, agreed.
Agreement, agreement
Agreeable, awganame.
Agriculture, baua.
Ago, tzeit-long, tzurick.
Agoing, im gong.
Ague, kalt fever.
Ahead, forwarts, ahead
Aid, hilf.
Aiding, helfa.
Aided, g'hulfa.
Aider, helfer.
Aim, tzeel.
Aiming, tzeela.
Air, looft.
Airy, looftich.
Alas, auch.
Alarm, larm.
Alderman, shquire.
Alien, ouslender.
Alike, gleich.
Alive, lavendich.
All, oll, olla, yeader, gons, oller.
Allege, bahawpt.
Alliance, bintniss.
Allow, arlawb.
Allowance, arlawbniss.

Allowed, arlawbt.
Allowing, arlauwa.
Almanac, collender.
Almighty, allmechtich.
Almost, sheer.
Alone, allæ.
Along, derbi, mit.
Aloud, loud.
Alms, almosa.
Aloft, noch, uvva.
Aloof, aweck.
Alphabet, alphabet.
Already, shun.
Also, aw, also.
Altar, altar.
Alter, ferenner.
Altered, ferennered.
Alteration, ferennerung.
Altering, ferennera.
Although, ubshun.
Altitude, haich, hai.
Altogether, olmitnon-
ner.
Always, immer.
Amalgamate, fermixa.
Amalgamation, amal-
gamation, fermixung
Amass, uf heifla.
Amaze, fershrecka.
Amenable, ontwartlich
Amend, amend.
Amending, amenda.
Amendment, amendment
Amiable, awganame.
Amid, unner, mitta
Amiss, failerhoft.
Amity, freindshoft.
Among, derbi, unner.
Amorous, ferleebt.
Amount, amount, sum.
Amounting, amounta.

Amuse, plesseera, un-
nerhalta.
An, ane, an.
Analogy, anelichkeit.
Ancestors, fore-eltra.
And, un.
Ancient, for olters.
Anecdote, shtory, an-
ecdote.
Anew, fun niam.
Angel, engle.
Anger, boseheit.
Angry, base.
Angling, fisha.
Angling-line, fish-line.
Angling-rod, fish-gad.
Animal, credoor.
Ankle, knechel.
Annex, annex.
Annexing, annexa.
Annexed, annexed.
Announce, announce.
Announcing, announsa
Announced, announced.
Announcement, a n -
nouncement.
Annual, yarelich.
Annul, fernichta.
Another, an onnerer.
Answer, ontwart.
Answered, g'answered,
g'ontwart.
Ant, awmouse.
Ants, awmice.
Anterior, elter, forhar.
Ante-room, fore-shtoob
Anvil, ombose.
Anxiety, engsht.
Anxious, engshtlich.
Any, ane, yader, en-
nich.

Apart, besides, forsich.
Apartment, shtoob.
Apostle, oppushtle.
Apothecary, obbadaik.
Aparatus, aparatus.
Apparel, claidung.
Apparent, awshinelich
Appeal, appeal.
Appealing, appeala.
Appealed, appealed.
Appear, arshine.
Appearance,arshinung
Appearing, arshina.
Append, awhenka.
Appendage, awhong.
Appertenance, tzuga-
hare.
Appetite, obbadit.
Applaud, applaud.
Applauding, applauda.
Applause, bifol, applause
Apple, opple.
Appletree, opplebawm.
Apply, awshprooch, ap-
ply.
Applying, applya.
Application, applica-
tion.
Appoint, appoint.
Appointing, appointa.
Appointment, appoint-
ment.
Appraise, appraise.
Appraisement, appraise-
ment.
Appraising, appraisa.
Appraised, appraised.
Appraiser, appraiser.
Apprentice, prentis.
Approve, approof.
Approving, approofa.

Approval, approofal.
Appropriate, appropri-
ate.
Appropriating, appro-
priata.
Appropriation, appro-
priation.
Approximate,naichera
Approximation, naich-
erung.
April, oppril.
Apron, shartz.
Apt, g'shickt.
Arbitrate, arbitrate.
Arbitration, arbitration.
Arbitrator, arbitrator.
Arbitrating, arbitrata.
Arc, boga.
Arch, g'welb.
Arched, g'welbd.
Architect, bau-maish-
ter, architect.
Architecture, bau-
koonsht.
Ardent, arnshtlich.
Ardor, eifer.
Are, sin, si.
Argue, arga.
Argument, argament.
Aright, tzurecht.
Arise, uf shtæ.
Aristocracy, big-bugeri
Aristocrat, big-bug.
Aristocratic,big-bugish
Arithmetic, rechna.
Arm, awrm.
Arming, arma.
Armory, armory.
Army, ormæ.
Around, rings-rumm.
Arouse, uf wecka.

Arraign, aw klawga.
Arrange, arrange.
Arrangement, arrangement.
Arranging, arranga.
Array, ordnung.
Arrear, rickshtond.
Arrest, arresht.
Arrive, awcooma.
Arrow, pile.
Art, koonsht, awrt.
Artery, oder.
Artful, shicklich.
Article, orticle.
Articulate, ous-sprecha.
Artificial, kinshtlich.
Artillery, artillery.
Artisan, hondwarker.
Artist, kinshtler.
As, os, doh, wann, weil.
Ascend, noof gæ, noof shtiga.
Ascension, uf-shtigung, noof gæ.
Ascertain, ousfinna.
Ascertained, ousg'foona.
Ascribe, tzushriva.
Ascription, tzushrivung.
Ash, esh.
Ashes, esh.
Ashamed, shemt, g'shemt.
Aside, on der side.
Ask, froke.
Asked, g'froked.
Asking, froga.
Asleep, shlofa.
Aspire, ferlonga.
Ass, asle.
Assail, awgrifa.
Assailant, awgrifer.

Assassin, marder.
Assassinate, morda.
Assault, attack, awgriff
Assaulter, awgrifer.
Assemble, fersommel.
Assembling, fersomla.
Assembly, semly.
Assent, agreea.
Assert, bahawpta.
Assertion, bahawptung
Assess, assess.
Assessor, assessor.
Assessed, g'assessed.
Assessing, assessa.
Assessment, sessment.
Assign, assign.
Assignment, assignment.
Assigning, assigna.
Assigned, assigned.
Assignee, assignee.
Assist, helf.
Assistance, hilf.
Assisted, g'hulfa.
Assistant, helfer.
Associate, associate.
Association, association.
Assort, sorta.
Assortment, sortment.
Assume, awnemma.
Assure, fersicher.
Assured, fersichered.
Astonish, ferwooner.
Astray, ferluffa.
At, tzu, aw, by, uf, in, drau.
Atmosphere, looft.
Atone, boosa.
Attach, attach.
Attachment, attachment.
Attached, g'attachcd.
Attaching, attacha.

Attack, awgriff.
Attacking, awgrifa.
Attacked, attacked.
Attain, arraicha.
Attempt, proweer.
Attempting, proweera.
Attempted, proweerd.
Attend, tend.
Attending, tenda.
Attended, g'tend.
Attention, attention.
Attendance, obwartung.
Attest, batzeiga.
Attire, awtzoog.
Attitude, shtellung.
Attorney, lawyer.
Attraction, attraction.
Attracting, attracta.
Attractive, attractif.
Auction, auction, fendu
Auctioneer, fendu-croyer
Audit, audit.
Auditor, auditor.
August, augoosht, au-
    gsht.
Aunt, aunt.

Authority, fulmaucht.
Authorize, fulmechticha.
Autograph, unnershrift.
Autumn, harbsht.
Avail, nootza.
Available, nitzlich.
Avarice, geitz.
Avenge, b'shtrofa.
Average, average.
Avert, obwenda.
Avoid, si lussa, ferheeta
Avow, arclara.
Avowal, arclarung.
Await, awarda.
Awake, wocker.
Award, award.
Aware, wais, wissa.
Away, weck, aweck,
    fordt.
Awe, in engsht.
Awful, shrecklich.
Awhile, tzeit-long.
Awkward, dobbich.
Awl, awl.
Ax, ox.
Axle, oxle.

B.

Babble, bobble.
Babbling, bobbla.
Babe, baby, bubbelly.
Babyish, kintish.
Bachelor, bachelor.
Back, bookle, tzurick.
Backbiter, retcher.
Backbone, rick-knocha
Back-ground, hinner-
    groond.
Back-part, hinner-dale

Backwoods, backwoods
Backward, hinnersich,
    rickwarts.
Bacon, shpeck.
Bad, shlecht.
Bag, sock.
Bags, seck.
Baggage, baggage.
Bail, bail, ous sheppa.
Bailed, g'bailed.
Bailing, baila.

Bait, bait.
Bake, bock.
Baking, bocka.
Baker, becker.
Balance, balance.
Bald, blut.
Baldheaded, blut-kepich.
Ball, bolla.
Ballot, ballot.
Balloting, ballota.
Balm, bolsom.
Ban, ferbut.
Band, band.
Bandage, bond.
Bandbox, bandbox.
Bang, shlawg, shtose.
Bank, bank.
Banker, banker.
Bankrupt, bankrupt.
Banner, banner.
Banter, banter.
Baptism, dawf.
Baptise, dawfa.
Bar, bar.
Barber, bolweerer.
Barberous, barbawrish.
Bare, blose.
Barefaced, unfershamed.
Barefoot, bawrfoos.
Bargain, hondel, barya.
Bark, rin, gowtz.
Barking, gowtza.
Barn, shire.
Barrel, barl.
Barrow, bawr.
Barter, hondla.
Base, mean, falsh, nidder.
Basement, groond-shtuck
Baseness, nidder trech-
    tich.
Bashful, blaid.

Basin, basin, hond-beck
Basket, korb.
Bass, boss.
Bat, briggle, shpeck-
    mouse.
Bathe, bawd,
Bathing, bawda.
Battalion, badolya.
Batter, batter.
Battered, battered.
Battering, battera.
Battery, battery.
Battle, battle.
Bawl, greish.
Bawling, greisha.
Bay, bay.
Be, si, wærra.
Beak, shnovvel.
Beam, bolka.
Bean, bone.
Beans, bona.
Bear, bar, awnemma,
    baitrawg.
Beard, bawrd.
Bearer, traiger.
Beast, deer, shtick-fee.
Beastly, feeish.
Beat, shlawga, kluppa.
Beautiful, shæ.
Beautify, fershenera.
Beauty, shæheit.
Because, wile, dawrum.
Become, awshtæ.
Becoming, awshtælich.
Bed, bet.
Bed-bugs, wonsa.
Bedaub, fershmeera.
Bedding, bet sauch.
Bee, eem.
Beef, beef, rints-flaish.
Beefsteak, beefshtake.

Beer, beer.
Beet, rote-reeb.
Beetle, shleggel.
Before, forhar, fore.
Beforehand, forderhond.
Befriend. g'falla du.
Beg, bettle, bit.
Begging, bettla, bitta.
Beggar, bettlemon.
Begin, awfong.
Began, awg'fonga.
Begone, weck.
Begrudge, begrudge.
Behalf, nootza.
Behave, behafe.
Behaving, behafa,
Behaved, b'hafed.
Behest, bafail.
Behind, hinna.
Behold, aw-sa.
Being, si, is.
Belch, rilpsa.
Belie, baleeg.
Belief, glauwa.
Believe, glawb.
Believer, glauwer.
Bell, bell.
Bellow, greish, brill.
Bellowing, brilla, greisha.
Bellows, blose-bolk.
Belly, bauch, leib.
Belong, g'hara.
Belonged, g'hared.
Beloved, ferleebt.
Below, unna, unner.
Belt, belt.
Bench, bonk.
Bend, boog
Bending, beega.
Benevolent, goothartzich
Benefit, benefit.

Benight, ferdoonkel.
Benighted, ferdoonkeld
Beneficial, beneficial.
Bent, gaboga.
Bequeath, fermaucha.
Bequest, arbshoft.
Bereave, barawb.
Berry, bare.
Berries, bara.
Beseech, bitta.
Beset, basitz.
Beside, besides.
Besmear, fershmeer.
Bespeak, fershprech.
Bespeaking, fershprecha.
Bespit, fershpow.
Best, besht.
Bestow, shenk, geb.
Bestowed, g'shenkd,
  gevva.
Bet, wet.
Betting, wetta.
Betray, ferrote.
Betrayed, ferrota.
Betraying, ferrotung.
Betrayer, ferraiter.
Better, besser.
Between; tzwisha.
Beverage, gatrenk.
Bevy, troop.
Bewail, batrowera.
Beware, sich heeta.
Bewilder, ferwærra.
Bewitch, ferhex.
Bewitching, ferhexa.
Beyond, ivver, weiter.
Bias, neid.
Bibber, drinker.
Bible, beevel.
Bid, gabut, beed.
Bidder, beeder.

Bidding, beeda.
Biding, wohna.
Big, grose.
Bigot, bigot.
Bile, gol.
Bilious, bilious.
Bill, bill, shnovvel.
Bind, binna.
Binding, binna.
Binder, binner.
Bird, fogle.
Birds, feggle.
Birth, gaboort.
Bishop, bishof.
Bit, shtickly, biss.
Bite, bise.
Biting, bisa.
Bitten, g'bissa.
Biter, biser.
Bitch, bitch.
Bitter, bitter.
Blab, bobble.
Black, shwartz.
Blacking, blacking.
Blackberry, black-bare
Blackbird, shtawr.
Blackguard, blackguard.
Blacksmith, blacksbmit.
Bladder, blose.
Blade, kling, holm.
Blame, blame.
Blamed, g'blamed.
Blaming, blama.
Blank, blank.
Blanket, blanket.
Blare, brilla.
Blast, wind shtose, shoos.
Bleed, bloota.
Bleeding, bloota.
Blemish, shondfleck.
Blend, fermixa.

Bless, saiga.
Blessing, saiga.
Blind, blint.
Bliss, salichkeit.
Blissful, salich.
Bloat, ufshwella.
Block, klutz, bluck.
Blood, bloot.
Bloody, blootich.
Blossom, bleea.
Blot, blot, klex.
Blow, blose, shtraich.
Blowing, blosa.
Bludgeon, briggle.
Blue, blo.
Bluff, grub, bluff.
Bluffing, bluffa.
Bluffed, g'bluffd.
Blush, blush.
Blunder, failer.
Blunt, shtoomp.
Blur, flecka.
Bluster, brawla, grose shwetza.
Boar, ever.
Board, board.
Boarding, boarda.
Boarder, boarder.
Boardinghouse, boarding-house.
Boast, boast.
Boasting, brawla, boasta.
Boat, boat.
Body, body.
Boil, g'shweer, koch.
Boiling, kocha.
Boiled, g'kochd.
Boiler, boiler.
Bold, bold.
Bond, bond.
Bone, k'nocha.

Bonnet, bonnet.
Book, booch.
Boor, limmel.
Boot, shtiffle, in barya.
Border, grentz.
Bore, bore.
Boring, bora.
Bored, g'bored.
Borough, boro.
Borrow, borryga.
Borrower, shooldner.
Bosom, broosht.
Boss, boss.
Botch, botch.
Both, bada.
Bottle, buttle.
Bottom, budda.
Bough, nosht.
Bought, kawft.
Bounce, bounce.
Bouncing, bounsa.
Bounced, g'bounced.
Bound, g'bunna.
Bounty, bounty.
Bow, boga, bow.
Bowl, bowl.
Bowels, darm.
Box, box.
Boxing, boxa.
Boxed, g'boxed.
Boxer, boxer.
Boy, bu.
Boys, boova.
Brace, tzomma binna.
Brag, brawla.
Bragging, brawla.
Bragger, brawler.
Brain, gaharn.
Bran, klia.
Branch, branch.
Brand, brond.

Brandy, brandy.
Brass, messing.
Brat, kint.
Brave, brawf.
Bravery, brawfheit.
Brawl, tzonkari.
Brazen, unfershemt.
Breach, brooch.
Bread, brode.
Break, brech, brecht.
Breaking, brecha.
Breakfast, morya-essa.
Breast, broosht.
Breath, odam.
Breathe, shnowfa.
Breed, breed.
Breeding, breeda.
Brethern, breder.
Brew, brow.
Brewing, browa.
Brewery, browerei.
Brewer, brower.
Briar, dorn.
Brick, bocka-shtæ.
Bribe, bribe.
Bribing, briba.
Bribed, g'bribed.
Bride, braut.
Bridge, brick.
Bridle, tzawm.
Bright, hell, clore.
Brimstone, shweffel.
Bring, bring.
Bringing, bringa.
Brisk, brisk.
Bristle, barsht.
Brittle, shwauch.
Brood, braid.
Broader, braider.
Broil, brode.
Broiling, broda.

Brook, runly.
Broom, basa.
Brothel. hoorahouse.
Brother, bruder.
Brotherhood, breder-shoft.
Brotherly, brederlich.
Brought, gabrucht.
Brow, shtarn.
Brown, brown.
Bruise, bruise.
Brush, barsht.
Brute, deer, shtick-fee.
Brutish, feeish.
Buck, buck.
Bucket, amer, kivvel.
Buckle, shnol.
Buggie, buggie.
Bug, keffer.
Bugle, bugle.
Build, bau.
Building, gabi.
Built, gabowd.
Bulky, grose, shaware.
Bull, bull.
Bully, bully.
Bullet, koogle.
Bullock, ux.
Bun, weck.
Bunch, kloompa.
Bundle, boondle.
Bung, shpoonda.

Bungle, bungle.
Bungling, bungla.
Burden, losht.
Burglar, deeb.
Bureau, bureau.
Burial, bagrebniss.
Bury, bagrawb.
Burn, bren.
Burning, brenna.
Burned, ferbrennd.
Burner, brenner, burner.
Burst, burst, fershpring
Bursting, fershpringa.
Bursted, fershproonga.
Bush, gabish.
Bushel, bushel.
Business, bisness.
Busy, fleisich, bissy.
Bustle, larm.
But, awer, os.
Butcher, butcher.
Butt, aw-shtose.
Butter, bootter.
Butter-milk, bootter-millich.
Button, k'nup.
Buy, kawf.
Buying, kawfa.
Buyer, kawfer.
By, by, fun, dorrich, mit, for, uf.
Bye, labe goot.

C.

Cab, cab.
Cabbage, kraut.
Cabin, hit, cabin.
Cabinet, cabinet.
Cackle, goxa.

Cage, kevvich.
Cajole, shmaichla.
Cake, koocha.
Calculate, calculate.
Calculation, calculation.

Calendar, collender.
Calf, colb.
Calico, cordoon.
Call, roof, hais.
Calling, roofa, haisa.
Called, g'roofa.
Calm, shtill, ruich.
Camp, camp.
Campaign, campaign.
Can, con.
Canal, conawl.
Cancer, creps.
Candid, candid.
Candidate, condidawt.
Candlestick, lichter-shtuck.
Candle, licht.
Cane, shtuck.
Canine, hoondish.
Cannon, conone.
Cant, heicheli.
Cap, cop.
Capable, fit, capable.
Capacity, capacity.
Cape, cape.
Caper, shpoocht, caper.
Capers, shpoochta, capers.
Capital, copitawl, capital.
Capitalist, capitalisht.
Captain, captain.
Captive, g'fonganer.
Car, car.
Card, cord.
Care, aucht, foresicht.
Careful, foresichtich.
Careless, nochlessich.
Carpenter, shriner.
Carpet, carpet.
Carriage, carriage.
Carion, ose.
Carry, trawga.

Cart, corrich.
Case, case.
Cash, cash, bawr geld.
Cashier, cashier.
Cask, foss.
Cast, shmisa, geesa.
Casting, casting.
Cat, cots.
Catarrh, shnoopa.
Catch, fonga.
Catcher, fonger.
Catechism, cottakism.
Catholic, cordullish.
Cattle, rintsfee.
Cauldron, kessel.
Cause, ursauch.
Caution, foresicht.
Cave, hailung.
Cease, ufhara.
Cedar, tzader.
Cede, ivver-gevva.
Ceiling, deck.
Celebrate, fira, celebrate.
Celebration, celebration.
Celestial, himlish.
Cell, tzell.
Cellar, keller.
Cemetery, karrich-hof.
Censure, tawdla.
Centre, center, mid.
Central, in der mid.
Century, hoonert-yohr.
Ceremony, ceremony.
Certain, gawiss.
Certainty, for gawiss, for sure.
Certificate, certificate.
Certify, certify.
Certified, g'certified.
Chaff, shprow.
Chain, ket.

Chair, shtool.
Cha'k, gride.
Challenge, challenge.
Chamber, shtoob.
Champion, champion, bully.
Chance, chance.
Change, wexel.
Changeable, ferennerlich.
Changed, ferennered.
Changing, ferennera, ferwexelt.
Chap, chap, bu.
Chapter, chapter, copittle.
Character, corrocter.
Charcoal, hulscoal.
Charge, charge.
Charging, charga.
Charged, g'charged.
Charily, shpawrsom.
Charitable, charitable, frei gevvich.
Charity, charity.
Charming, charma.
Charmed, g'charmed.
Charter, charter.
Chartered, g'chartered.
Chase, chase.
Chased, gachased.
Chasing, chasa.
Chattel, fermaiga.
Chatter, bobble.
Chattering, bobbla.
Chaw, cow.
Chawing, cowa.
Chawed, gacowd.
Cheap, wulfel.
Cheaper, wulfeler.
Cheapest, wulfelsht.
Cheat, b'shise.

Cheated, b'shissa.
Cheating, b'shisa.
Cheater, b'shisser.
Check, check.
Cheerful, goots-moots.
Cheese, kais.
Chemise, weibs-hem.
Cherry, karsh.
Cherries, karsha.
Chestnut, kesht.
Chestnut tree, keshtabawn.
Chest, kisht.
Chew, cow, chaw.
Chewing, cowa.
Chicken, hinkle.
Chief, chief, hawpt.
Child, kint.
Childish, kintish.
Chill, chill.
Chilly, chilly, keel.
Chimney, shornshtæ.
Chin, keen.
Chip, shpone.
Chips, shpane.
Chisel, masle.
Choice, wahl.
Choir, core.
Choke, fershtick, choke
Choking, choka.
Choked, g'choked.
Choose, choose.
Choosing, choosa.
Chosen, g'choosed.
Chop, hock, chop.
Christ, Crishtus.
Christian, crisht.
Christmas, crishdawg.
Church, karrich.
Churn, booterfoss.
Chuckle-head, doomkup.

Cipher, tziffer.
Circuit, rounds.
Circular, rings-rumm,
circular.
Circulation, circulation
umlawf.
Citation, awfeerung.
Cite, awfeera.
Citizen, citizen.
Citizenship, citizenship
City, city, shtadt.
Clad, aw-gadu.
Claim, claim.
Claiming, claima.
Claimed, gaclaimed.
Clapper, clopper.
Clash, gaiga nonner
shlawga.
Clasp, shnolla.
Class, closs.
Classical, classical.
Classification, classifi-
cation.
Clay, groond, ard.
Clean, sauwer.
Cleaned, gabootz'd.
Cleaning, bootza.
Clear, clear, clore.
Clearance, clearance.
Cleared, gacleared.
Clearness, cloreheit.
Clergy, porraleit.
Clerical, porrashriftlich
Clerk, clarrick, clerk.
Clever, clever.
Climb, crottle.
Climbling, crottla.
Climber, crottler.
Clinch, need.
Clinching, needa.
Clinched, ganeed.

Cling, awhenka.
Clipping, shara, clippa,
ous-shnida.
Cloak, cloak.
Clock, uhr, cluck.
Clod, cloompa.
Clog, hinnera.
Cloggy, hinnerlich.
Close, noch, naigsht,
dicht, close.
Closet, shonk, closet.
Cloth, dooch.
Clothe, claida.
Clothes, claider.
Cloud, wulk.
Cloudy, wulkich, treep.
Clover, clæ.
Clown, honswarsht.
Club, briggle, club.
Clubbing, brigla, clubba
Clubbed, g'clubbed.
Cluster, shwarm, cloompa
Clutch, grab, griff.
Coal, coal, coala.
Coarse, grub.
Coarseness, grubheit.
Coat, ruck, coat.
Coating, coating.
Coax, coax.
Coaxing, coaxa.
Coaxed, g'coaxed.
Cobbler, shuflicker.
Cobweb, shpinna-waib.
Cock, hawna.
Cocked, gacocked.
Coffee, coffee.
Coffin, dódalawd.
Cog, tzawn.
Cohabit, tzomma wona
Coin, geld, coin.
Coincide, ivverea shtimma

Cold, kalt.
Colder, kelter.
Collapse, tzomma folla.
Collar, collar.
Collation, kalt-shtick, essa.
Collect, collect.
Collecting, collecta.
Collection, collection.
Collector, collector.
College, college.
Color, forrab.
Coloring, farrava.
Colored, g'farrabd.
Colt, fill, hootchly.
Column, column.
Comb, com.
Combat, g'fecht.
Combination, combination.
Combined, combined.
Combining, combina.
Come, coom.
Comfort, troasht, comfort.
Comic, shpossich.
Coming, cooma.
Comma, comma.
Command, command.
Commanding, commanda
Commander, commander
Commemorate, fira.
Commemorated, g'fired.
Commence, awfong.
Commencement, awfong
Commencing, awfonga
Commenced, awg'fonga.
Commend, lobe.
Commending, lova.
Commerce, hondle.
Commit, commit.

Committing, committa
Common, common.
Commonly, for common.
Commotion, ufroor.
Communicant, communicont.
Communicate, bakont maucha.
Communication, communication.
Communion, nauchtmohl.
Community, community, g'mineshaft.
Compact, ferbinnung.
Companion, comrawd.
Compare, compare, fergleich.
Comparison, comparison.
Compassion, mitlida.
Compel, tzwing.
Compelled, g'tzwoonga
Compelling, tzwinga.
Compensate, balona.
Compete, compete.
Competition, competition.
Competitor, competitor.
Competing, competa.
Competence, competence
Competent, competent
Compile, somla.
Compliment, compliment.
Complain, clawg.
Complaining, clawga.
Complained, g'clawged
Complainant, claiger.
Complete, complete.
Comply, ferwillicha.

Complying, ferwillichung
Complicate, ferwickla.
Compliment, compliment.
Compose, compose.
Composed, composed.
Composer, composer.
Composing, composa.
Composition, composition.
Compositor, typesetzer
Compound, compound
Compounding, com-pounda.
Comprehension, bagriff.
Comprehend, bagrifa.
Compress, tzommadricka
Compromise, compromise.
Compromising, compromisa.
Compromised. g'compromised.
Compute, rechna.
Comrade, comrawd.
Conceal, fershteckle.
Concealing, fershteckla
Concealed, fershteckled
Concede, uf gevva.
Conceit, eibildung.
Conceivable, fershtendlich.
Conceive, bagrifa.
Concentrate, tzommatzeega.
Concerning, batreffung
Concerned, concerned.
Concert, concert.
Concession, arlawbniss
Conclude, b'shleesa, conclude.

Conclusion, conclusion b'shloos.
Conclusive, conclusif.
Concord, tzulawf.
Condemn, condemn.
Condemning, condema
Condense, condense.
Condensing, condensa.
Condition, condition.
Conduct, uffeerung.
Conductor, conductor.
Confectionery, confectionery.
Conference, conference
Confess, confess.
Confessing, confessa.
Confide, fertrowa.
Confine, ei-shparra.
Confined, ei g'shparred
Confirm, confirm.
Confirming, confirma.
Confirmation, confirmation.
Confirmed, confirmed.
Conflagration, fire, ferbrennung.
Conflict, g'fecht.
Confound, confound, ferwærr.
Confounding, ferwærra confounda.
Confounded, ferwærrd. confound.
Confuse, confuse.
Confusing, confusa.
Confusion, confusion.
Congratulate, crotleer.
Congratulating, crotleera
Congregate, fersomla.
Congregation, fersomlung.

Congress, congress.
Conjecture, moot-mose
Conjoin, ferbinna.
Connect, connect.
Connecting, connecta.
Conquer, seecha.
Conquest, seech.
Conscience, g'wissa.
Consent, ferwillicha.
Consider, consider.
Considering, considera.
Considerable, badeident.
Consist, bashtayant.
Consistent, consistent.
Console, troasht.
Consoling, traishta.
Consolidate, consolidate, ferainich.
Conspiring, fershwaira.
Constable, coonshtaweler.
Constant, olsfort.
Constitution, constitution.
Construct, construct.
Constructed, construct.
Constructing, constructa.
Consult, consult.
Consulting, consulta.
Consume, fertzara.
Consumer, consumer.
Contempt, ferauchtung contempt.
Content, g'satisfied.
Contention, shtreit.
Contest, contest.
Contesting, contesta.
Continue, fort-maucha.
Contract, barya, contract.
Contractor, contractor.
Contracting, contracta.

Contradict, contradict.
Contradicting, contradicta.
Contrary, gaiga, tzuwidder.
Contrast, widdershprooch
Contribute, bitrawga, contribute.
Contributing, contributa.
Contribution, contribution.
Contrive, arfinna.
Control, control.
Controling, controla.
Conundrum, raitzel.
Convene, tzommarufa.
Convenience, g'lagenheit.
Convention, convention.
Converse, shwetza.
Conversation, g'shwetz, g'shpraich.
Convert, bakært.
Convey, trawga.
Conveyance, foorwærrick, conveyance.
Conveyancer, shriver.
Convict, convict.
Convince, convince.
Convincing, convinca.
Convulsion, gichter.
Convulsions, gichtra.
Cook, kuch.
Cooking, kucha.
Cooked, g'kuch'd.
Cool, keel.
Cooling, keela.
Coop, coop, hinkleshtall.
Cooper, keefer.

Co-operate, mit-shoffa.
Copious, hifich.
Cooper, cooper.
Copy, copy.
Copying, copya.
Copied, gacopied.
Cord, shnoor, klufter.
Cordial, hartzlich.
Core, krootza.
Cork, corrick.
Corn, grayawg, welsh-korn.
Corner, eck.
Cornered, eckich.
Corporeal, karperlich.
Corpse, doda, leich.
Correct, recht, correct, richtich.
Correcting, correcta.
Correspond, correspond.
Corresponding, corres-ponda.
Corridor, gong.
Corroborate, corrobo-rate, bakrefticha.
Corroborating, corrob-orata.
Corrode, ferrusht.
Corrupt, ferdarwa.
Completed, ferdorwa.
Cost, kushta.
Costive, fershtupt.
Costly, keshtlich, dire.
Cot, hit.
Cotton, bau-wull.
Cough, hooshta.
Council, council.
Counsel, rote.
Counselor, rote-gevver.
Count, tzaila, tzail.
Counter, counter.

Counteract, counteract
Counterfeit, counterfeit
Countermand, counter-mand.
Counterpane, bet-deck,
Country, lond, boosh, gaigend.
County, county.
Couple, pawr.
Courage, currawsh.
Course, gong, coarse, lawf.
Court, court, corriseer.
Courtesy, awganame.
Cousin, cousin.
Covenant, ferbinnung.
Cover, deck.
Covering, deckung.
Covered, gadeckt.
Cow, ku.
Cows, kee.
Coward, coward.
Crab, crebs.
Crabbed, cridlich.
Crack, crack.
Cracking, cracka.
Cracked, g'cracked.
Cracker, cracker.
Cackle, gox.
Cackling, goxa.
Cradle, weeg, reff.
Craft, koonsht.
Cramp, crompf.
Cravat, hols-dooch.
Crave, ferlonga.
Craw, crup.
Crawl, rootsha.
Crazy, narrish.
Cream, rawm.
Crease, roontzel.
Create, arshoffa.

Creation, shepfung, creation.
Creator, Snepfer, Gott.
Creature, deer, credoor.
Credit, creditt.
Creditor, creditor.
Credulous, unglauwich
Creed, creed, glauwa.
Creek, creek.
Creep, rootsh.
Creeping, rootsha.
Crib, crib, shtall.
Crier, croyer.
Criminal, criminal, ferbrecher.
Crime. ferbrecha.
Cripple, cripple.
Critic, critic.
Critical, critish.
Crock, hoffa.
Crooked, kroom.
Crop, arnt, crop.
Cross, kreitz, bais.
Croup, shteck-floos.
Crow, crop. kray.
Crowing, kraya.
Crowd, crowd.
Crowded, gacrowd.
Crowding, crowda.
Crown, crone.
Crude, ro, roheit.
Cruel, grausom.
Crush, quetsh.

Crushing, quetsha.
Crust, croosht.
Crutch, krick.
Cry, kreish.
Crying, kreisha.
Culprit, ferbrecher.
Cultivate, cultivate.
Cultivator, cultivator.
Cultivating, cultivata.
Cup, cuply.
Cupboard, shronk.
Curb, curb.
Cure. cure.
Cured, g'cured.
Curing, cura.
Currency, geld.
Current, lawf, shtrome
Currier, garwer.
Curry, shtriggla.
Curse, flooch.
Cursing, floocha.
Cursed, ferflooched.
Curtail, ferkartza.
Curtain, forehong.
Curve, curve.
Cushion, cushion.
Custom, gabrauch.
Customer, koonda.
Cut, shnide.
Cutting, shnida.
Cylinder, walls.
Cypher, rechen.
Cyphering, rechna.

D.

Dab, clex.
Dabble, clexa.
Daily, daiglich.

Dale, dawl.
Dam, dom.
Damage, shawda, damage

Damaged, gadamaged.
Dame, fraw.
Damn, ferdomma.
Damned, ferdomt.
Damp, feicht.
Damper, damper.
Damsel, maidle.
Dance, dons.
Dancing, donsa.
Danger, g'fore.
Dangerous, g'farelich.
Dare, darf.
Dark, doonkel.
Darkness, doonkleheit.
Darn, shtup.
Darned, g'shtupt.
Darning, shtuppa.
Date, dawtum, date.
Daub, shmeer.
Daubing, shmeera.
Daughter, dochter.
Dawn, demmerung.
Day, dawg.
Daily, daiglich.
Dead, dode.
Deaf, dawb.
Deafness, dawbheit.
Deal, deal, dale.
Dealer, dealer.
Dealing, deala.
Dear, leeb, dire.
Dearest, diarsht, leebsht.
Death, dode.
Debase, ferfelsha.
Debate, debate.
Debating, debata.
Debauch, ferfeera.
Debt, shoold.
Debtor, shooldner.
Decay, ferfolla, fowla.
Decease, shtarwa.

Deceit, batroog.
Deceive, batreega.
Deceiver, batreeger.
Deception, batroog.
Decide, decided, decide
Deciding, decida.
Deck, deck, pock.
Declaration, declaration.
Declaring, declara.
Declare, arclare, declare.
Decline, decline.
Declined, declined.
Declining, declina.
Decoy, lucka.
Decoyed, g'lucked.
Decrease, obnawm.
Decreased, obg'nooma.
Dedicate, eiwei, dedi-
    cate.
Dedication, eiweiung,
    dedication.
Deduct, deduct.
Deducting, deducta.
Deed, deed.
Deep, deef.
Deeper, deefer.
Deface, ferdarwa.
Defaced, ferdorwa.
Defame, ferleshter.
Defamation, ferleshter-
    ung.
Default, default, noch-
    lessich.
Defeat, beat, defeat.
Defeated, gabutta.
Defect, failer, defect.
Defective, defectif.
Defence, defence.
Defend, wair, defend.
Defending, waira, de-
    fenda.

Defended, g'waired, defend.
Defensive, defensif.
Defer, ufsheeva.
Deferred, ufg'shova.
Defile, holewaig.
Define, b'shtimm, define.
Defined, b'shtimmd, defined.
Definate, b'shtimmd.
Defiance, defiance.
Definition, b'shtimmung, definition.
Deform, ung'shtallt.
Defraud, batreega.
Defrauded, batroga.
Defrauder, batreeger.
Defray, betzawla, freihalta.
Defunct, ous g'shtorwa
Defy, defy.
Degenerate, ous-awrta.
Degrade, arnidderich.
Degrading, arnidderichs.
Degree, degree, grawd.
Deject, trauer.
Dejected, traurich.
Delay, uf halta.
Delegate, delegate.
Delegation, delegation.
Delegating, delegata.
Deleterious, shaidlich.
Deliberate, ivverlaiga.
Delicate, tzawrt, delicate.
Delicacy, tzawrtheit, delicacy.
Delicious, awganame.
Delight, plesseer.
Delightful, plesseerlich

Delinquent, shooldner, ferbrecher, delinquent.
Deliver, liffer, deliver.
Delivered, g'liffered, delivered.
Delivering, liffera, delivera.
Delivery, delivery.
Delusion, batroog.
Demagogue, ferfeerer.
Demand, demand.
Demanding, demanda.
Demise, fermaucha.
Democracy, demokratie.
Democrat, demokrawt.
Demolish, umrisa.
Demon, difel.
Demonstrate, bewisa.
Den, den, haleung.
Denial, ferlaignung.
Denominate, benawma
Denomination, benawmung.
Denote, betzeiga.
Denounce, awgevva.
Dense, dicht.
Deny, ferlaigna.
Denying, ferlaigna.
Depart, weck-gæ.
Department, department.
Departure, ob-shtart.
Depend, depend, ferluss.
Depending, dependa, ferlussa.
Depict, b'shriva, obmola.
Deplore, baklawga.
Deponant, tzeiga.
Depose, batzeiga, obsetza.

Deposit, deposit.
Deposition, deposition.
Deprave, ferdarb.
Depraved, ferdorwa.
Depravity, nix-nootz-ichkeit.
Depricate, depricate.
Depress, noonerdricka.
Deprive, barauwa.
Depth, deefung.
Derange, derange.
Deranged, ferrickd, de-ranged,
Derangement, unord-nung.
Deride, shputta.
Derision, shputt.
Derive, harshtomm.
Derogate, ousawrt.
Derogative, shendlich.
Descend, noonergæ, ob-shtiga.
Describe, b'shribe.
Describing, b'shriva.
Description, description, b'shrivung.
Desert, ferdeensht, de-sert.
Deserve, ferdeent.
Design, design.
Desire, ferlong, woonsh
Desirable, desirable.
Despise, ferauchta.
Despoil, plindera.
Despond, fertzawga.
Despondant, fertzawgt.
Destitute, ferlussa.
Destitution, ferlussung
Destroy, destroy, uf usa.
Destructive, destructif.

Detail, ousfeerlich.
Detain, uf halta.
Detect, ufdecka, detect.
Detecting, detecta.
Detention, ufhaltung.
Detest, obshia.
Detestable, obshilich.
Detour, umwaig.
Deuce, tzwæ, difel.
Devastate, ferweesht.
Deviate, obweicha.
Device, arfinnung.
Devil, difel.
Devilish, difelish.
Devolve, tzufalla.
Devotion, devotion.
Devour, uf-fressa, shlooka
Devout, audechtich.
Dew, dow.
Dewy, feicht.
Dial, ura-g'sicht.
Dialect, shproach.
Dialogue, g'shpraich.
Diamond, diamond.
Diaper, windle.
Diarrhœa, dorrich-foll.
Dice, dice.
Dictate, dictate.
Diction, shwetzawrt.
Dictionary, dictionary.
Die, shtarb.
Dier, farwer.
Diet, kusht.
Differ, differ.
Difference, unnersheed difference.
Differing, differa.
Differed, g'differed.
Difficult, difficult.
Difficulty, difficulty.
Diffidence, blaidheit.

Dig, grauwa.
Digest, ferdowa.
Digestion, ferdowung.
Digger, graver.
Dignify, aira.
Dignity, air.
Digress, ob weicha.
Dilapidate, ferloomp.
Diligence, flise.
Diligent, flisich.
Dim, bloss, undeitlich.
Dimension, messung.
Diminish, obnemma.
Dine, middawg-essa.
Dinner, middawg-essa.
Dip, dip, shep.
Dipper, dipper, shep-
per.
Direct, grawd, direct.
Director, director.
Direction, direction.
Directing, directa.
Dirk, dirk-messer.
Dirt, dreck.
Dirty, dreckich.
Disable, disable.
Disadvantage, d i s a d -
vantage.
Disagree, disagree.
Disagreeable,unleidich
Disallow, disarlawb.
Disallowance, d i s a r -
lawung.
Disappear, disappear.
Disappoint, disappoint
Disapprove, disapproof
Disarrange, ferwærra.
Disarrangement, f e r -
wærrung.
Disaster, unglick.
Disastrous, unglicklich

Disavow, laigna.
Disavowal, ferlaignung
Disband, ufbrecha, uf-
gevva.
Disbelieve, net glauwa,
tzweifela.
Disburse, ousbatzawala
Discard, obdonka.
Discharge, gæ-lussa, fri-
gevva, discharge.
Discharged, discharged
Discharging, discharga
Disclose, endecka.
Disconnect, disconnect
Disconsolate, batreebt.
Discontent, untzufridda.
Discontinue, ufhara.
Discord, unainichkeit.
Discount, discount.
Discouraged, obtzoog,
mootlose.
Discover, ous-finna.
Discreet, foresichtich.
Disdain, obshi.
Discuss, discuss, arga.
Discussion, argament,
discussion.
Disease, kronkheit.
Disengage, bafria.
Disgrace, shond.
Disgraceful, shendlich.
Disguise, ferclaida, fer-
shtella.
Disgusted, feraikled.
Dish, shissel.
Dishes, shissla.
Dishonest, unairlich.
Dishonor, shond.
Dishonerable, shend-
lich.
Dismay, shrecka.

Dismiss, dismiss.
Dismount, obshteiga.
Disobey, net fulga.
Disorder, unordnung.
Dispatch, dispatch.
Dispensation, dispensation.
Dispense, daila.
Disperse, fertriva.
Displace, ferricka.
Display, display.
Dispose, dispose.
Disposition, disposition
Dispute, dishbadawt, dispute.
Disputing, dishbadeera disputa.
Disrespect, disreshpect
Dissatisfisd, untzufridda.
Dissimilar, ungleich.
Dissipate, fershwenda, sowfa.
Dissolve, shmels, dissolve.
Dissolving. shmelsa, dissolva.
Distance, distance.
Distasteful, aïklehoft.
Distemper, shtemper.
Distil, brenn.
Distilling, brenna.
Distillery, brennerei.
Distinct, deitlich.
Distinction, distinction
Distinguished, bareemed
Distract, fershtare.
Distraction, fershtarung.
Distress, troovel.
Distribute, ousdala.
Distribution, distribution, ousdailung.

Distributing, distributa
Distrust, mistrowa.
Distrustful, mistrowish
Disturb, fershtare.
Disturbing, fershtara.
Disturbance, fershtarung.
Disunion, trenna.
Ditch, grauwa.
Ditty, g'song.
Dive, dowch.
Diving, dowcha.
Divide, dail, divide.
Division, division.
Dividend, dividend.
Divine, Getlich.
Divinity, Gottheit.
Divorce, shada-breef, divorce.
Do, du, maucha, du'n.
Doctor, duckter.
Doctrine, lehr.
Document, document.
Dodge, dodge.
Dodging, dodga.
Door, deer.
Dog, hoond.
Doing, doots, du.
Doings, hondlung.
Dollar, dawler.
Domestic, hamish, tzawm
Domicil, wohnung.
Domineering, domineera.
Donation, shenkung.
Done, fartich, gedu, gor
Doom, shicksawl.
Dose, dose.
Dot, fleck, clex.
Dotted, ferflecked, ferclexed.

Dotage, kintish.
Double, double.
Doublet, pawr.
Dough, daig.
Dove, dowb.
Dower, dower.
Down, droona, unna, nooner, hee.
Downward, nooner-tzoos.
Doze, shloomera.
Dozy, shlaferich.
Draft, draft, tzoog.
Drag, shlaifa.
Drain, ousdrickla, drain.
Draining, draina.
Drank, g'droonka.
Drake, endrich.
Dram, drom.
Drawer, shooblawd.
Drawing, mola, tzeega.
Dread, bong.
Dreadful, shrecklich.
Dream, drawm.
Dreaming, drawma.
Dreamed, g'drawmed.
Dress, dress.
Dressing, dressa, awdu.
Dressed, g'dressed, aw-gadu.
Drill, drill.
Drilled, g'drilled.
Drilling, drilla.
Drink, drink.
Drinking, drinka.
Dripping, drupsa.
Drive, drive.
Driven, gadrivva.
Driving, driva.
Driver, driver, foormon
Droll, drullich.

Drone, fowlenser.
Drop, druppa.
Dropping, drupsa, droppa
Dropped, g'drupsed, g'-dropped.
Dropsy, wasser-soocht.
Drove, droop, gadrivva
Drover, fee-driver.
Drown, fersowfa.
Drowned, fersuffa.
Drug, meditzeen.
Drug-store, obbadaik.
Druggist, obbadaiker.
Drum, droom.
Drummer, droomer.
Drumming, drooma.
Drunkard, siffer.
Dry, drooka.
Drying, drickla.
Duck, doonk, end.
Due, shooldich, ferfolla
Dull, shtoomp.
Dumb, dumm.
Dunce, dummkup.
Dung, misht.
Durable, dowerhoft.
During, warend.
Dusk, dooshber.
Dust, shtawb.
Dusty, shtaw-wich.
Dutch, deitsh.
Dutchman, Deitsher, Penn. Deitsher.
Duty, duty, shooldich-keit.
Dwarf, tzwærrich.
Dwell, wohna.
Dwelling, wohnhouse.
Dye, farb.
Dying, farwa.
Dysentery, roor.

E.

Each, ya-des.
Eager, eifrich.
Eagle, awdler.
Ear, ohr.
Early, free.
Earn, ferdeen.
Earnings, ferdeensht.
Earning, ferdeena.
Earned, ferdeened.
Earnest, arnsht.
Earnestness, arnshtlich.
Earth, ard.
Ease, ru.
Easy, leicht, ruich.
East, oasht.
Easter, oashter.
Easterly aishtlich.
Eat, ess.
Eaten, g'essa.
Eating, essa.
Eatables, lavas-mittle.
Eccentric, eccentrish.
Echo, echo.
Eclipse, finshterniss.
Economical, shpawrsom.
Economy, shpawrsom-keit.
Edge, shorf-side.
Edged, shorf.
Edifice, gabi.
Edit, edit.
Editing, edita.
Editor, editor.
Editorial, editorial.
Educate, larn.
Education, larnung.
Educating, larna.
Educator, teacher.
Effect, effect.

Effective, effectif.
Efficient, wærksom.
Effort, proweera.
Egg, oy.
Eggs, oyer.
Egotism, eagaleeb.
Egress, obgong.
Eight, aucht.
Eighteen, auchtzæ.
Eighty, auchtzich.
Eighty-eight, aucht-un-auchtzich.
Either, entwedder.
Eject, nous-du.
Elaborate, weitleftich.
Elate, shtuls.
Elbo, elboga.
Elder, der eldsht.
Elderly, eldlich.
Elect, waila, elect.
Election, election.
Element, element.
Elephant, ellefont.
Elevate, elevate.
Elevation, elevation.
Elevating, elevata.
Eleven, elf.
Eleventh, elft.
Elocution, shwetz-kunsht
Elsewhere, o m a n o t-soonsht.
Elude, weck-shlippa.
Emaciated, obgatzared.
Emanate, rousrunna.
Emancipate, bafria.
Embalm, bolsameer.
Embankment, bankment
Embarrass, ferwærra.
Embellish, fershenner.

Embellishment, f e r -
shennerung.
Embers, coala.
Embezzle, embezzle.
Emblem, sinnbild.
Emerge, forecooma.
Emigrant, ouslender.
Emigrate, weck-tzeega.
Eminence, hochshtond
Eminent, hochshten-
dich.
Emission, ousfloos.
Emit, susfleesa.
Emolument, sidelohn.
Emperor, keiser.
Emphasis, eidrook.
Empire, kanichreich.
Employ, dinga, awshtella.
Employment, g'sheft,
arwet.
Empower, fulmechticha.
Empty, lare.
Enable, im shtond si.
Enact, ferordna, enact.
Enactment, enactment
Enacting, enacta.
Encamp, campa.
Encampment, camp-
ment.
Enclose, eifensa.
Enclosure, enclosure.
Encounter, shtreit, g'-
fecht.
Encourage, encourage.
Encouragement, e n -
couragement.
Encouraging, encouraga.
Encumbrance, encum-
brance.
End, end.
Endeavor, proweer.

Endeavoring, proweera.
Endless, unendich.
Endorse, endorse.
Endorser, endorser.
Endow, endow.
Endure, dower.
Enemy, feind.
Energy, fleis, kroft.
Enforce, dorrich-setza,
enforce.
Engage, engage.
Engagement, engage-
ment.
Engaged, engaged.
Engine, engine.
Engineer, engineer.
Engrave, engrave.
Engraver, engraver.
Enhance, tzunawm.
Enhanced, tzu-g'nooma.
Enigma, raitzel.
Enjoy, enjoy.
Enjoyment, enjoyment
Enlarge, fergresser.
Enlarged, fergresserd.
Enlivening, labehoft.
Enormous, shrecklich.
Enough, ganoonk.
Enrage, woot.
Enraged, weetich.
Enroll, enroll.
Ensign, fawna, ensign.
Ensue, nochfulg.
Entangle, ferwickle.
Enter, ni-gæ, ni-fawra.
Entered, ni-gonga.
Entering, entera.
Enterprise, unnernem-
mung.
Enterprising, e n t e r -
prising.

Entertain, unnerhalta.

Entertainment, entertainment.

Enthusiasm, læbheftich.

Entice, awlucka.

Entire, gons, entire.

Entitle, entitle.

Entrails, eigaweida.

Entrance, eigong, entrance.

Entreat, bitta.

Enumerate, tzommatzaila.

Enunciate, declara.

Envelop, envelop.

Envy, neid.

Envious, neidish.

Equal, gleich.

Epualize, gleich-maucha.

Equality, gleichheit, equality.

Equalizing, equalisa.

Equity, rechtmasich.

Era, tzeit poonkt.

Erase, ous-kratza.

Erect, grawd, ufrichta, baua.

Erection, ufrichtung, baua.

Eruption, ousbrooch.

Escape, floocht.

Especial, special.

Esquire, shquire.

Establish, arrichta.

Establishment, estabment.

Established, established.

Estate, estate.

Estimate, shetza, shetzung.

Eternal, eawich.

Eternity, eawichkeit.

Eulogy, lobe-speech.

Evangelical, effongalish.

Evacuate, ferlussa.

Evacuation, ferlussung

Eve, tzufore, owet.

Even, ava, yadoch,

Event, forefol.

Eventful, markwærdich.

Eventual, tzufellich.

Ever, immer, yeamohls

Everlasting, i m m e r - wærend.

Every, yeader, yeades.

Evidence, tzeigniss, evidence.

Evident, awshinelich.

Evil, shlecht, evil.

Exact, exact, genau.

Exactly, exactly.

Examine, unnersooch.

Example, exemple.

Excellent, foretrefflich.

Except, except.

Excepting, excepta.

Exchange, wexla.

Exchanged, ferwexeld, exchanged.

Excite, excite.

Excitement, excitement.

Exclaim, ousroofa.

Excuse, excuse.

Excusing, excusa.

Execute, execute.

Execution, execution.

Executor, executor.

Exempt, ous g'halta.

Exemption, exemption

Exhibit, weisa.

Exhibition, exhibition.

Experience, arfawrung
Expense, expense.
Expensive, expensif.
Expel, expel.
Expelling, expella.
Expend, ousgevva.
Expenditure, ousgawb.
Experiment, experiment
Expert, g'shickt.
Expire, shtarb, enda.
Explain, explain.
Explaining, explaina.
Explanation, explanation.
Explicit, deitlich.
Explode, ferburst.
Explosion, ferburstung
Expose, expose.
Exposing, exposa.
Express, express.
Expressing, expressa.
Extend, fergressera, extend.

Extending, extenda.
Extension, extension.
Extensive, extensif.
Extent, grase.
Exterior, eiserlich.
Exterminate, ousdriva.
External, ouswendich.
Extinct, ousdu, lesha.
Extort, obtzwinga.
Extra, extra.
Extract, extract.
Extracting, extracta.
Extravagance, fershwendung.
Exult, grose g'feel.
Exulting, grose feela.
Eye, awg.
Eye-brow, awga-hore.
Eye-glass, brill.
Eye-lid, awga-deckle.
Eye-sight, g'sicht.
Eye-sore, dorn-im-awg
Eye-witness, awg-tzeiga.

F.

Fable, fawble.
Fabricate, m a u c h a, leega.
Face, g'sicht.
Facing, facing, faca.
Fact, fact.
Fail, fail.
Failing, faila.
Failed, g'failed.
Faint, mot, shwauch.
Fainting, ohnmechtich
Fair, fair, shæ.
Faith, glauwa, tri.
Faithful, gatri.

Fall, foll.
Falling, folla.
Fallen, g'folla.
False, falsh.
Falsehood, falshheit.
Falsify, ferfelsha.
Family, fomelia, family
Famish, hoongera.
Famous, bareemt.
Fancy, fancy.
Far, weit.
Fare, fare.
Farewell, farrywell.
Farm, bauerei.

Farmer, bauer.
Farther, weiter.
Fashion, fashion.
Father, fodder, dawdy.
Fast, fesht, g'shwint.
Fasten, feshticha.
Fat, fet.
Fatty, fettich.
Fault, failer.
Favor, g'folla, favor.
Favored, g'favored.
Favoring, favora.
Fawn, shmeichla.
Fear, ongsht, engsht.
Fearful, farrichterlich.
Feast, essa.
Feat, dawd.
Feather, fedder.
February, Februawr.
Fee, batzawlung.
Feeble, shwauch.
Feed, footer.
Feel, feel.
Feeling, feela.
Feign, fershtella.
Fell, g'falla.
Fellow, karl.
Fellowship, gemineshaft.
Felon, base-ding.
Felonious, gottlose.
Female, weibsmensh.
Fence, fence.
Ferment, yara.
Ferocious, wilt.
Fertile, froochtbawr.
Fervid, eifrich.
Festal, feshtlich.
Festival, fesht.
Fetch, bringa.
Fever, fever.
Feverish, feverish.

Few, wennich.
Fib, leeg.
Fiddle, geig.
Fiddler, geiger.
Fiddling, geiga.
Fidelity, gatri.
Field, feld.
Fiend, feind, difel.
Fiery, firich.
Fifteen, fuftzæ.
Fifteenth, fuftzæt.
Fifth, finft.
Fiftieth, fuftzichsht.
Fifty, fuftzich.
Fight, fecht.
Fighting, fechta.
Figure, figoor.
Fill, fill, filla.
Filthy, shmootzich, dreckich.
Final, tzuletsht.
Find, fin.
Finding, finna.
Finder, finner.
Fine, fine.
Finger, finger.
Finish, finish.
Finished, g'finished.
Fire, fire.
Fireside, firehard.
Firework, firewærk.
Firm, fesht, firm.
Firmament, himmel.
First, arsht.
Fish, fish.
Fishing, fisha.
Fist, fowsht.
Fit, fit, gichter.
Fits, fits, gichtra.
Five, finf.
Fix, fix.

Fixed, g'fixed.
Fixture, fixter.
Flag, flag, fawna.
Flash, flash, blitz.
Flat, flat.
Flat-iron, biggle-isa.
Flatter, flatter.
Flaw, failer.
Flax, flox.
Flea, flo.
Flee, fleega.
Flesh, flaish.
Fleshy, flaishich.
Flinch, ous-backa.
Fling, shmeisa.
Flint, wocka-shtæ.
Flitch, shpeck, sida-shtick.
Float, fleesa.
Flock, troop.
Flog, leddera.
Flood, floos.
Floor, budda, floor.
Flour, male.
Flourish, flourish.
Flourishing, flourisha.
Flow, lawf, shtraima.
Flower, bloom.
Flowers, blooma.
Flowery, bloomich.
Flux, floos.
Fly, mook, fleeg.
Flying, fleega.
Foam, shawm.
Fob, sock.
Foe, feind.
Fold, folta.
Folks, leit.
Follow, fulga.
Follower, fulger.
Folly, norrheit.

Fond, farleebt.
Food, footer.
Fool, norr.
Foolery, norrheit.
Foot, foos.
Footed, feesich.
For, for, noch.
Forbid, forbeed.
Force, force, shtarrick.
Fore, forhar.
Forego, tzugevva.
Foreground, foregroond.
Forehead, shtarn.
Foreigner, ouslender.
Foreign, ouslendish.
Foreman, foremon.
Foremost, feddersht.
Forenoon, formiddawg
Foresight, foresicht.
Forest, boosh.
Forestall, foreshtall.
Forestalling, foreshtalla.
Foretell, foresawg.
Forethought, ivverlaigt.
Forewarned, g'warnd.
Forgetful, fergesslich.
Forgive, fergeb.
Forgiving, tergevva.
Forgiven, fergevva.
Fork, govvel.
Forlorn, ferlora.
Form, form, g'shtolt.
Formal, ragelmasich.
Former, forich.
Fornicate, hoora.
Forsake, ferlussa.
Friday, fridawg.
Friend, freind.
Friendly, freindlich.
Friendship, freindshoft
Fright, fershreck.

Frighten, fershrecka.
Frightened, fershrucka
Frightful, shrecklich.
Frivolous, leichtsinnich.
Frivolity, leichtsinn.
Frock, frock.
Frog, frush.
Frolic, frolic.
From, fun, fum, ous, har.
Front, front, forna.
Frost, frusht.
Froth, shawm.
Forward, farry, forward
Frugal, shpawrsom.
Fruit, oabsht, froocht.
Fry, brod.
Frying, broda.
Fudge, lobberei.
Fuel, huls, coala.
Full, ful, fellich.

Fume, dompf, garooch
Fun, shposs.
Funny, shpossich.
Function, barichtung.
Fund, fund, geld.
Fundament, b u d d a, fundament.
Funeral, leich, bagrebniss.
Funnel, drechter.
Furious, weedich.
Furnace, fornace.
Furnish, fornish, liffera
Furniture, houserote, furniture.
Furrow, forrich.
Further, weiter.
Fury, woot.
Fuss, fuss.
Future, tzukoonft, future.

G.

Gabler, bobbler.
Gable, givvel.
Gain, gawinn.
Gait, gong.
Gale, wind.
Gallon, goll.
Gallows, golga.
Gambling, gamla.
Game, game.
Gap, gap.
Garden, gorda.
Gardening, gartla.
Garlic, g'nuvveloch.
Garret, shpeicher, garret.
Gate, gate, door, darly.

Gather, sommel.
Gathering, sommla.
Geese, gens.
Generation, generation
Gentleman, gentlemon
Generous, goot-hartzich.
German, hoch-deitsh, deitsh.
Get, grick.
Getting, grega.
Ghost, shpook, geisht.
Giddy, dormlich.
Gift, g'shenk.
Gilt, fergilt.
Ginger, ginger.
Ginger-cake, leb-koocha.

Girl, maidle.
Girls, maid.
Give, geb, gevva.
Gives, gebt.
Glad, fro.
Glass, glaws.
Glen, dawl.
Globe, kugle, globe.
Gloom, doonkel.
Glorious, harrlich.
Glory, harrlichkeit.
Gloss, glons.
Glove, hendshing.
Glue, lime.
Glutton, fress-er.
Go, gæ.
Good, goot.
Goose, gons.
Gore, bloot.
Gory, blootich.
Gospel, effongalium.
Gossip, retsha.
Gout, gicht.
Govern, rula.
Government, govern-
    ment, regeerung.
Governor, governeer.
Grab, grab, grobsh.
Grabbing, grabba, grob-
    sha.
Grace, g'nawda.
Grade, grade, grawd.
Grain, froocht.
Grammar, grammar.
Grant, ferwillicha.
Grape, trowb.
Grapes, trowwa.
Grasp, griff.
Grass, graws.
Grassy, grawsich.
Grateful, donkbawr.

Grating, grating.
Gratis, gratis.
Gratuity, g'shenk.
Grave, grawb.
Gravel, gravel.
Gravy, bree.
Grease, shmootz, shmeer.
Greasy, shmootzich.
Great, grose.
Greedy, greedy.
Green, green.
Greet, greesa.
Grey, gro.
Grief, koomer.
Grieve, kimmera.
Grin, grin.
Grind, mawl.
Grinding, (mill,) mawla.
Grinding, (stone) shleifa.
Grindstone, shleifshtæ.
Gripe, griff.
Grit, grit, gritz.
Grocer, grocer.
Grocery, grocery.
Ground, groond.
Groundless, groondlose
Grove, bush.
Grow, wox, woxa.
Growl, groomla.
Growth, g'wex.
Grumble, groomel.
Grunt, grexa.
Guard, guard.
Guardian, guardeen.
Guess, rote.
Guessing, rota.
Guest, gosht.
Guide, guide, feerer.
Guiding, guida.
Guilt, shoold.
Guilty, shooldich.

Gully, grauwa.
Gum, goom.
Gun, flint, conone.
Gust, shtorm.
Gut, dorm.

Guts, darm.
Gutter, gutter.
Guzzle, sowfa.
Guzzler, siffer.

H.

Habit, g'woneheit.
Had, hob, hen, hut, het
Hack, hocka.
Hail, hawgle, kissel.
Hair, hore.
Hairy, horich.
Hale, g'soond.
Half, holb, helft.
Hall, hall.
Halt, halt.
Halter, holfter.
Ham, shoonka.
Hammer, hommer.
Hand, hond.
Handful, hondful.
Handle, handle, shteel.
Handsaw, hondsaig.
Handsome, shæ.
Handwriting, hond-shrift.
Handy, handy, hendich.
Hang, henk.
Hanging, henka.
Hanger, henker.
Happen, happen.
Happening, happena.
Happy, fro.
Hard, hord.
Harden, ferharda.
Hardship, hardship.
Hare, haws.

Harm, shawda, un-recht.
Harmful, shadelich.
Harmless, unshadelich
Harness, g'sharr, har-ness.
Harp, horf.
Harrow, ake.
Harvest, arnt.
Hash, hash.
Haste, eil.
Hasty, eilich.
Hat, hoot.
Hatch, breea.
Hatchet, hatchet.
Hatched, ous gabreet.
Hate, hos, hossa.
Hatred, hos, hossa.
Hatter, hoot-maucher.
Haul, tzeeg, tzoog.
Have, hob, hen, hawa.
Hay, hoy.
He, ar.
Head, hawpt, head, kup.
Headstrong, shtorrkep-pich.
Heal, hale.
Healing, hala.
Healed, g'haled.
Health, g'soondheit.
Healthy, g'soond.

Heap, howfa.
Hear, hare.
Hearing, hara.
Heard, g'hared.
Heart, hartz.
Heat, hitz.
Heathen, hida.
Heathenish, hidish.
Heaven, Himmel.
Heavenly, Himmlish.
Heavy, shware.
Hedge, hecka.
Heed, aucht, foresicht.
Heel, farsh.
Heifer, rind.
Heir, arb.
Heirs, arwa.
Hell, hell.
Help, hilf.
Helper, helfer.
Helpless, hilflose.
Hemp, honf.
Hen, hinkle.
Henceforth, fun now aw.
Her, era.
Herb, kraut.
Herd, meng.
Here, doh.
Hermit, ainsler.
Hero, hero.
Herse, dodakootch.
Herself, se selwer.
Hesitate, hesitate.
Hesitation, hesitation.
Hew, hock.
Hiccough, shlooxa.
Hide, howt, fershteckle
High, hoch.
Higher, haicher.
Hill, barrick.

Hilly, barrickich.
Hilt, heft.
Him, eem, een, 'm.
Himself, een, selwer, ar selwer.
Hind, hinna.
Hinder, hinnera.
Hindermost, hinnersht
Hinge, hawptsotz, bond
Hint, hint.
Hinting, hinta.
Hip, hift.
Hire, lone, ding.
Hireling, gadingta.
Hired, gadingt.
His, si, sina.
History, history.
Hit, shlawg, shtose.
Hitch, awbinna.
Hither, dohar.
Hitherto, bis dohar.
Hoard, foreroat.
Hoarse, haisher.
Hoax, hoax.
Hoe, hock.
Hog, sow.
Hogs, si.
Hoggish, sei-ish.
Hold, halt.
Holding, halta.
Hole, luch.
Holy, heilich.
Hollow, hole.
Home, haimat.
Homely, haimlich.
Honest, airlich.
Honesty, airlichkeit.
Honey, honich.
Honorable, airwardich
Hood, cop.
Hoof, hoof.

Hook, hoka, fonga.
Hooked, g'fonga.
Hoop, raif, hoop.
Hop, hoops.
Hopping, hoopsa.
Hope, huffnung.
Hoping, huffa.
Horn, horn.
Hornet, hornasle.
Horrible, obshilich.
Horror, shrecka.
Horse, gowl.
Horseshoe, hoofeisa.
Horticulture, gardla.
Hose, shtrimp, hose, shtroomp.
Hospital, hospital.
Hot, hais.
Hotel, hotel, wærtshouse.
Hour, shtoond.
Hourly, yady shtoond.
House, house.
Houses, hiser.
Housekeeping, househalta.
How, we
However, demnoch.
Howl, g'heil.

Huckster, huckshter.
Hucksteriug, huckshtera.
Hug, armla, k'noatsha.
Huge, grose.
Hum, brumm.
Humming, brumma.
Human, menshlich.
Humble, dameetich.
Humbug. humbug.
Humor, shposs.
Humorous, shpossich.
Hunch, bookle.
Hundred, hoonert.
Hundredth, hoonersht.
Hunger, hoonger.
Hungry, hoongerich.
Hunt, sooch, yawga.
Hunter, yager.
Hurry, hurry, doomla, eil.
Hurt, wæ du.
Husband, monn.
Hush, shtill, hush.
Hut, hit, did.
Hymn, leed.
Hypocricy, heicheli.
Hypocrite, heichler.
Hysterics, hystericks.

I.

I, ich.
Ice, ice.
Idea, edæ, bragriff.
Identical, gleich, anerlæ.
Idiot, dummkup.
Idle, missich, faul.
If, ob, wann, eb, ub.
Ignorance, unwissend.

Ill, ung'soond, kronk.
Illegal, illegal.
Illiterate, ungalarnd.
Illness, kronkheit.
Illustrating, illustrata.
Image, bild.
Imagine, foreshtellung
Imbecile, shwauch.

Imitate, nochmaucha.
Imitation, imitation.
Immediate, now, grawd
Immigrant, eiwanderer
Impair, ferdarwa.
Impart, mitdaila.
Impartial, unpordei-ish
Impatient, ungadooldich.
Impeach, impeach.
Impede, ferhinnera.
Imperfect, imparfect.
Implement, warktzeich.
Implicate, ferwickla.
Implore, bitta.
Important, wichtich.
Import, import.
Importer, importer.
Importing, importa.
Impose, impose.
Imposing, imposa.
Imposition, imposition
Impossible, unmiglich.
Impossibility, unmig-
lichkeit.
Imposter, imposter, ba-
treeger.
Impression, impression.
Improbable, unwohr-
shinelich.
Improper, unshicklich
Improve, improof.
Improvement, im-
proofment.
Improving, improofa.
Impudent, unfershamed.
In, in, drin, aw, tzu.
Inaccurate, net recht.
Inactive, inactif.
Inattentive, inattentif.
Inauguration, inaugu-
ration.

Inborn, awgabora.
Inception, awfong.
Inch, tzull.
Incident, tzufoll.
Incite, awhetza.
Incline, incline.
Incomprehensible, un-
bagreiflich.
Inconsistent, inconsist-
ent.
Incorporate, incorpar-
ate.
Incorporating, incor-
porata.
Indecent, indecent.
Indeed, wærklich.
Indefinite, unbashtimmt.
Indemnity, indemnity.
Independent, indepen-
dent.
Index, index.
Indian, insh.
Indians, insha.
Indication, indication.
Indicating, indicata.
Indictment, indictment.
Indirect, indirect.
Indiscreet, unbadenkt.
Indisposed, ung'soond.
Indistinct, undeitlich.
Individual, parsone.
Indolence, fowlheit.
Induce, induce.
Inducement, induce-
ment.
Inducing, indusa.
Induct, eifeera.
Industry, fleis.
Inebriate, siffer.
Inexperience, unarfawra
Infamous, shendlich.

Infant, kint, bubbelly.
Infections, awshteckend.
Infirm, krenklich.
Inflamation, inflamation.
Influence, influence.
Ingenious, g'shickt, ingenious.
Ingenuity, ingenuity.
Inhabit, bawohna.
Inhabitant, eiwohner.
Inheritance, arbshoft.
Iniquity, boseheit.
Initiate, initiate.
Injure, shawda, ferletza
Injustice, injustice, unrecht.
Ink, dinda.
Inn, wærıs-house.
Innocent, unshooldich
Inquest, inquest.
Inquire, unnersooch.
Inquiry, unnersoochung.
Insane, insane, narrish
Insinuate, insinuate.
Insinuation, insinuation.
Insinuating, insinuata.
Insight, eisicht.
Insist, insist.
Insolent, unfershamed
Inspect, inshpect.
Inspector, inshpector.
Inspecting, inshpecta.
Institute, institute.
Institution, institution.
Instruct, inshtruct.
Instructor, inshtructor
Insult, insult.
Insulting, insulta.

Insurance, insurance.
Insured, insured.
Insuring, insura.
Intellect, fershtond.
Intelligent, fershtendich.
Intemperate, intemperate, b'suffa.
Intend, intend.
Intention, intention.
Intending, intenda.
Interest, interest.
Interested, intresseerd.
Interfere, interfere.
Interfering, interfera.
Into, in, ni.
Intoxicate, g'suffa.
Introduce, introduce.
Introducing, introdusa
Introduction, introduction.
Invent, arfinna, invent
Invention, arfinnung, invention.
Inventory, inventory.
Invest, invest·
Investigate, investigate
Investigation, investigation.
Investigating, investigata.
Invitation, invitation, eilawdung.
Invite, eilawda.
Involved, ferwickeld.
Involve, ferwickla.
Inwardly, innerlich.
Ire, tzorn.
Iron, isa.
Ironing, bigla.
Irregular, unregular.
Island, insel, island.

Isle, insel.
Issue, issue.
It, es, sell, des.
Itch, kretz.
Item, item.

Iterate, widderhola.
Its, si, des.
Itself, sich, selwer.
Ivory, ivory.

J.

Jacket, jacket.
Jail, jail.
January, yonuawr.
Jar, boomps.
Jaw, keenbocka.
Jealous, jealous.
Jelly, jelly.
Jest, shposs.
Jew, yood.
Jesus, Yasus.
Jewel, jewel.
Jig, jig, dons.
Jingle, clingle.
Job, job.
Jobber, jobber.
Jog, shtose.
Join, join.
Joining, joina.
Joint, joint.
Joke, joke.
Jolly, looshtich.
Journal, dawga booch, journal.

Journey, rais.
Joy, fraida.
Joyous, frailich.
Jubilee, yubelee.
Judge, judge.
Judgment, judgment.
Jug, kroog.
Juice, sawft.
July, july, yooly.
Jump, joomp.
Jumping, joompa.
June, june, yoony.
Juror, jurymon.
Jury, jury.
Just, yoosht, nooma, recht.
Justice, recht, yooshtas
Justify, justify.
Justification, justification.
Juvenile, yingler.
Juxtaposition, mitawshtellung.

K.

Kalendar, collender.
Keen, shorf.
Keep, b'holta.
Keeper, keeper.
Keg, fessly.

Kettle, kessel.
Key, shlissel.
Kick, kick.
Kicking, kicka.
Kicked, g'kicked.

Kidney, neer.
Kill, dote maucha.
Kiln, uffa.
Kin, freindshaft.
Kind, awrt, goot.
Kindle, awshtecka.
Kindness, freindlichkeit.
Kiss, koos.
Kitchen, kich.
Kite, kite.
Kitten, yungv cots.
Knave, shelm.

Knee, k'nee.
Knife, messer.
Knit, shtricka.
Knitting, shtricka
Knock, shlawg.
Knocking, shlawga.
Knocker, knocker.
Knot, k'nup.
Know, wais.
Knowing, wissa.
Knuckle, knuckle.

L.

Labor, arwet, shoffa.
Laborer, dawglaner, shofmon.
Lad, bu.
Ladder, lader.
Ladle, leffel.
Lady, lady.
Lamb, lom.
Lame, lawm.
Lamp, lomp.
Lance, lonce.
Land, lond.
Landing, landing.
Landlord, wært.
Landlady, wærtsfraw.
Lane, lane.
Language, sproach.
Lantern, loddarn, lootzer.
Lap, lap, shose.
Lapping, lappa.
Lard, shmaltz.
Large, grose.
Larger, gresser.
Largest, graisht.
Lark, larrich.

Lash, lash.
Lass, maidle.
Last, letsht.
Latch, latch.
Late, shpoat.
Lately, kartzlich.
Later, shpaiter.
Latest, shpaitsht.
Lath, lod, lodda.
Latin, lodinish.
Latitude, latitude.
Latter, letsht.
Laud, lohwa.
Laugh, lauch.
Laughable, lecherlich.
Laughing, laucha.
Laughter, g'lechter.
Launch, launch.
Lavish, fershwenda.
Law, law.
Lawful, lawful.
Lawsuit, lawsuit.
Lawyer, lawyer.
Lay, laig, laiga, ligga.
Laziness, fowlheit.

Lead, bli, feer, lead.
Leading, feera, leada.
Leader, leader.
Leaf, blot.
Leak, rin.
Leaking, rinna.
Lean, mawger.
Leap, shpring.
Leaping, shpringa.
Learn, larn.
Learning, larna.
Learned, g'larnd.
Least, wennichsht.
Leather, ledder.
Leave, luss, lussa.
Leaves, bletter.
Lecture, lecture.
Left, linx.
Leg, bane, bæ.
Legal, legal.
Legged, banich.
Legislation, legislation.
Legislating, legislata.
Legislature, legislature.
Lend, lain.
Lender, lainer.
Length, leng.
Lengthen, ferlenger.
Less, wennicher.
Lest, dos.
Let, luss, lussa.
Letter, breef, bushtawb.
Level, level.
Leveling, levla.
Lever, lever.
Lexicon, wardta-booch.
Liable, liable.
Liar, ligner.
Libel, libel.
Liberal, liberal.
Liberty, freiheit.

Library, library.
Lick, shleck.
Licked, g'shlecked.
Licking, shlecka.
Lid, deckel.
Lie, leeg.
Life, lava.
Lift, lift, ufhava.
Light, licht.
Lighten, ferleichta, leicht.
Lightening, blitz.
Like, gleich.
Likely, woreshinelich.
Likeness, awganame, likeness.
Liking, g'folla.
Limb, gleed.
Limber, loomerich.
Lime, collich.
Limit, limit, grentz.
Limitation, limitation.
Limp, hickle.
Limping, hickla.
Line, line.
Linen, leinich.
Linguist, shproach-maishter.
Lining, footer, lining.
Lion, laib.
Lip, lip, lefts.
Liquid, liquid.
Liqidation, liquidation
Liquor, gatrenk.
List, lisht.
Literal, wærdlich.
Literature, literature.
Litigation, law, shtreit.
Little, klæ, klanes.
Live, levendich, lava, wona.

Lively, lively, looshtich
Liver, levver.
Living, living.
Load, load.
Loaf, laib, loafa.
Loafer, loafer.
Loan, loan.
Loaning, laina.
Loathe, obshia.
Local, artlich.
Location, location.
Lock, shluss.
Locket, locket.
Locomotive, locomotif.
Locust, locus.
Lodge, lodge.
Lodging, lodging.
Loft, uvva noof.
Log, bluck.
Logic, logic.
Lone, allæ.
Lonesome, lonesom.
Long, long.
Longways, leng noch.
Look, gook.
Looking, gooka.
Looked, gagookd.
Looking glass, shpiggle

Loop, shloop.
Loose, lose.
Loosen, lose maucha.
Lord, Hærr.
Lordship, Hærrshaft.
Lose, ferleera, lose.
Loss, ferloosht.
Lot, lut.
Lottery, lutteree.
Loud, loud.
Louse, louse.
Love, leeb.
Low, nidder.
Lower, nidderer.
Lowest, niddersht.
Luck, glick.
Lucky, glicklich.
Lumber, bau-huls.
Lump, lump, kloompa.
Lunatic, narrisher.
Lunch, kalt shtick.
Lung, loong.
Lust, g'loosht.
Lusty, g'looshtich.
Lustre, glontz.
Lutheran, Luderish.
Luxury, im hoch lava.
Lying, leega.

M.

Machine, masheen.
Mad, baise, weetich.
Magistrate, shquire.
Magnify, fergressera.
Maid, mawd.
Maiden, yung maidle.
Mail, mail.
Main, main, hawpt.
Mainly, hawptsechlich.

Maintain, arhalta.
Maintenance, unnerbalt.
Majority, m a r e h e i t,
    majority.
Make, mauch, du.
Maker, maucher.
Male, mon, male.
Malice, boseheit.
Malt, maltz.

Man, mon.
Manage, manage.
Managed, g'managed.
Manager, manager.
Managing, managa.
Management, manage-
ment.
Mane, mane.
Manful, menlich.
Mankind, mensha-g'-
shlecht.
Manner, monneer.
Mannerly, m o n n e e r-
lich.
Mansion, wonehouse.
Manslaughter, dote-
shlawg.
Mantle, montle.
Manufacture, manu-
facture.
Manure, misht.
Manuscript, hondshrift
Many, feel.
Map, map.
Marble, marwel.
March, martz, march.
Marched, g'marched.
Marching, marcha.
Mare, mærr.
Mark, marrick.
Market, morrickt.
Marriage, hirawt.
Married, g'hired.
Marry, hira.
Marrow, mork.
Marshal, marshal.
Marvel, woonera.
Mash, mesh.
Mason, maurer, mason
Mast, mosht.
Master, maishter.

Match, match.
Mate, mate.
Matrimony, hireshtond
Matter, sauch.
Mattress, mottrotz.
Maxim, grundsotz.
May, moy, mawg, con.
Mayor, mayor.
Me, mich, ich, meer,
mer.
Meadow, wiss.
Meal, male.
Mean, mean, mane.
Meaning, manung.
Measles, measles.
Measure, mose, mess.
Measuring, messa.
Meat, flaish.
Mechanic, hondwarker
Meddle, meddle.
Meddling, meddla.
Mediator, middler.
Medicine, meditzeen.
Meditate, denka.
Meek, sonft.
Meet, somla, meeta.
Meeting, meeting.
Melody, melodee.
Melon, melone.
Melt, shmels.
Melting, shmelsa.
Memory, gadechtniss.
Men, menner.
Mend, flick, bessera.
Mended, g'flicked.
Mending, flicka.
Mendicant, bettler.
Mention, mention.
Mentioning, mentiona.
Merchandise, shtore-
sauch.

Merchant, shtore-keeper.
Mercy, bormhartzich.
Meredian, middawg.
Merit, ferdeent.
Merry, looshtich.
Mess, ess-shtick.
Message, message.
Messenger, messenger.
Messiah, Messias.
Messuage, groond-shtick.
Metal, metal.
Method, wæg.
Methodist, meddadisht
Mice, mice.
Mid, mid.
Middle, mid.
Middling, middlemasich.
Midway, holbwæg.
Might, maucht, gawalt
Mighty, mechtich.
Migrate, travella.
Mild, mild.
Militia, millitz.
Milk, millich.
Mill, meel.
Mill-dam, meel-dom.
Miller, miller.
Milliner, milliner.
Mind, gameet, geisht,
  sinn, mind.
Mine, mine.
Miner, miner.
Mineral, mineral.
Minister, porra.
Minor, minor.
Minority, minderheit,
  minority.
Minstrel, senger.
Minute, minoot.
Mirror, shpiggle.
Misbehave, misbehafe.

Mischief, mischief.
Miser, geitzhals.
Misfortune, unglick.
Mishap, unfol.
Mislay, ferlaiga.
Mislaid; ferlaiged.
Misprint, drookfailer.
Misrule, unordnung.
Mission, mission.
Missionary, missionary
Mist, nevvel.
Mistake, mistake, failer
Mistaking, mistaka.
Mistaken, mistaken.
Mistrust, mistrow.
Misunderstand, unfer-
  shtonna.
Mix, mix, misha.
Mixing, mixa.
Mob, mob.
Mock, shput.
Mocking, shputta.
Mocker, shpetter.
Mode, awrt.
Modest, modest.
Modify, modify.
Moist, feicht.
Molten, g'shmulsa.
Moment, awgablick.
Momentous, wichtich.
Mónday, moondawg.
Money, geld.
Monopoly, monopoly.
Monstrous, ungahire.
Month, moonot.
Monthly, moonotlich.
Monument, monument.
Moon, mohnd.
Mop, weshloompa.
Moral, m o r a w l i s h,
  moral.

More, mai, maner.
Morn, morya.
Morrow, morya.
Mortal, shtarblich.
Mortgage, mortgage.
Mosquito, mushkitter.
Moss, mose.
Most,. mensht, marsht.
Mostly, marshtens.
Mother, mootter.
Motion, motion
Motive, motif.
Mould, mould, shimmel.
Moulder, f e r f o w l a,
    moulder.
Mouldy, shimlich.
Mount, gabarrig, uf-
    shteiga.
Mountain, barrig.
Mountainous, barrick-
    igich.
Mourn, trowra.
Mouse, mouse.
Mouth, mowl.
Mouthful, mowlful.
Move, moof.
Movement, moofment.

Mow, may.
Mowing, maya.
Much, feel.
Mud, dreck, marrosht.
Muddy, dreckich.
Mug, groog.
Mule, mule, asle.
Multiply, multiply.
Multitude, mengmensha.
Murder, mord,
Murdering, morda.
Murderer, marder.
Murmur, groomla.
Museum, mussaum.
Music, moosick.
Musical, mussicawlish.
Muslin, musleen.
Muss, muss.
Must, moos.
Mute, shtoom.
Mutiny, ufroor.
Mutter, groomla.
Mutton, shofe-flaish.
My, my, mine.
Myself, ich selwer.
Mystery, gahameniss,
    mystery.

N.

Nail, noggle.
Nails, neggle.
Naked, nockich.
Name, nawma, haisa,
    hais.
Namely, namelich.
Namesake, namesake.
Nap, shloomera.
Narrative, shtory.
Narrow, eng, shmall.

Nasty, weesht.
National, national.
Native, natif.
Natural, noddeerlich.
Nature, noddoor.
Naturalize, naturalize.
Naughty, unawrtich.
Navel, nauvel.
Navigate, navigate.
Navigation, navigation

Navigating, navigata.
Near, noch, naigsht.
Nearly, sheer.
Neat, net, shæ.
Necessary, noatwendich.
Necessity, noatwend-
 ichkeit.
Neck, hols.
Need, mongle.
Needle, nodle.
Needy, in der noat.
Negative, negatif.
Neglect, nochlessicha.
Negociate, negociate.
Negociating, negociata.
Negro, nager.
Neighbor, nochber.
Neighborhood, noch-
 bershoft.
Nephew, nephew.
Nerve, narf.
Nest, nesht.
Net, netz.
Netting, netzwarrick.
Never, nimmy, nemohl
Nevermore, nimmer-
 mæ.
New, ni.
New year, ni yohr.
News, niichkeit, news.
Newspaper, Tzeitung.
Next, naigsht.
Nice, shai.
Nickname, nicknawma.
Night, naucht.
Nightly, nechtlich.
Nine, nine.
Nineteen, ninetzæ.
Ninety, ninetzich.
Nineteenth, ninetzainsht
Ninth, nine't.

No, nay, kæ, ken.
Nobody, nemond.
Nod, nook.
Noise, larm.
Noisy, larmich.
Nominate, nominate.
Nominating, nominata
None, kens, ken, kenner.
Nonsense, unsinn.
Nonsensical, unsinnich
Nook, eck.
Noon, middawg.
Nor, noch, aw, net.
North, nord.
Northward, nardlich.
Nose, naws.
Not, net.
Note, note.
Noted, bakonnt.
Nothing, nix.
Notice, notice.
Notified, g'notified.
Notify, notify.
Notifying, notifya.
Notion, notion, eifol.
Notorious, bereemt.
Nourish, nawra.
Nourishment, nawrung.
November, nuffember.
Now, now, yetz.
Nowhere, narryats.
Nude, nockich.
Nuisance, nuisance.
Null, fernicht.
Number, noomer.
Numbering, noomera.
Numeration, tzailung.
Numerous, tzawlreich.
Numskull, doomkup.
Nurse, nurse.
Nursing, nursa.

Nursery, nursery.
Nut, nuss.
Nuts, niss.

Nutmeg, muskawta-
nuss.
Nutriment, nawrung.

O.

Oak, aicha.
Oar, rooder.
Oats, haw-wer.
Obedient, gahoresom.
Obey, fulg.
Obeying, fulga.
Object, object.
Objection, objection.
Objecting, objecta.
Oblige, oblige.
Obscene, shendlich.
Obscure, ferdoonkel.
Observation, observation
Observe, obsarf.
Observer, obsarfer.
Observing, obsarfa.
Obstinate, shtuvverich.
Obtain, grick.
Obtained, grickd.
Obtaining, greega.
Occasion, galagenheit.
Occupant, b'sitzer.
Odd, ungleich,
Odds, unnersheed.
Odious, ferhosst.
Of, fun, ous, ob, weck.
Off, fun, aweck, nous,
ob.
Offence, argerniss, of-
fense.
Offender, offender.
Office, omt, office.
Officer, officer.
Offer, offer.

Offering, offera.
Official, official.
Offset, offset.
Offspring, nochcoomer
Often, uft.
Oh, auch, oh.
Oil, ail.
Old, olt, olter.
Older, elter.
Oldest, eldsht.
On, aw, uf, tzu, mit.
Once, eamohl.
One, anes, ane.
Only, ainsich.
Onward, forwarts.
Open, uf, effentlich.
Opening, effnung, uf
maucha.
Operate, operate.
Operation, operation.
Operating, operata.
Opinion, opinion, main-
ung.
Opponant, gaigner.
Oppose, oppose.
Opposing, opposa.
Opposition, opposition.
Opportunity, galagen-
heit.
Opposite, dergaga, gaga.
Option, wahl.
Or, odder.
Orator, shwetzer.
Oration, oration.

Orchard, bawm-gorda.
Order, order, ordnung.
Ore, artz.
Organ, orrigle.
Organist, orrigle shpeeler.
Organizing, organiza.
Organize, organize.
Organization, organi-
zation.
Origin, uhrshprung.
Original, original.
Ornamenting, ornamenta
Ornament, ornament.
Ostler, hosler.
Other, onner.
Ought, set, setsht.
Ounce, ounce.
Our, unser.
Out, nous, drous.
Outlive, ous-lava.
Outlandish, ouslendish
Outward, eiserlich.

Oven, uffa.
Over, nivver, ivver,
drivva.
Overcoat, ivver-ruck.
Overcharge, ivver-charge
Overcome, ivver-coom.
Overdo, ivver du.
Overlook, ivvergook.
Overrule, ivverule.
Oversee, ivver sa.
Overseer, ivver sare.
Overtake, ivvernemma
Overtaken, ivvernooma.
Overture, umshtartza.
Owe, shooldich.
Owing, shooldich si.
Own, aigna.
Owner, aigner.
Ox, ux.
Oxen, uxa.
Oyster, oyshter.

P.

Pace, shritt.
Pack, pock.
Packing, pocka.
Page, page.
Paid, batzawlt.
Pail, aimer.
Pain, shmartz.
Painful, shmartzlich.
Paint, forb, paint.
Painter, painter.
Painted, gapaint.
Painting, painta.
Pair, pawr.
Pale, bloss.
Pan, pon.
Pane, fenshtershibe.

Pantaloons, hussa.
Pap, bri, dad.
Papa, pap, dad.
Parade, parade.
Pardon, pardon.
Pardoning, pardona.
Pardoned, g'pardoned.
Pare, shala.
Parents, eltra.
Parlor, parlor.
Parrot, bobbagoy.
Parson, porra.
Part, dale, awdale.
Partake, dale nemma.
Partner, partner.
Party, party, portei.

Pass, ga, gong.
Passage, passage.
Passenger, passenger.
Passing, passa.
Passion, tzorn.
Past, ferbei, fergonga.
Paste, paste.
Passtime, tzeit-fertreib, pass-time.
Pastor, porra.
Pasture, waid.
Patch, patch, shtick.
Pate, kup.
Path, pawd.
Patience, gadoold.
Patient, kronka.
Patriot, potriut.
Pattern, mooshter.
Paper, bobbeer.
Pauper, ormer.
Pavement, pafement.
Pay, batzawl.
Payable, tzawlbawr.
Paying, batzawla.
Payment, batzawlung.
Paid, batzawlt.
Peace, freeda.
Peacable, freedlich.
Peach, parshing.
Pear, beer.
Pears, beera.
Peas, arbsa.
Peanuts, groondniss.
Peacock, pohawna.
Peddler, peddler.
Peddling, pedla.
Peel, shaila.
Pealings, shawla.
Peck, beck.
Peep, gook.
Peeping, gooka, peepa.

Pen, fedder, shtall.
Pencil, pencil.
Penny, bens.
People, fulk, lite.
Pepper, peffer.
Perfect, parfect.
Perform, perform.
Performer, performer.
Performing, performa.
Perhaps, ferleicht.
Peril, g'fore.
Period, poonkt.
Perish, umcooma.
Perjure, falsh shwaira.
Permit, arlawb.
Permitted, arlawb'd.
Permitting, arlauwa.
Person, parsone.
Personal, parsanelich.
Pest, pesht.
Pester, ploga.
Pet, pet.
Petted, gapet.
Petting, petta.
Petition, petition.
Petitioning, petitiona.
Petticoat, unnerruck.
Petty, garing.
Pew, pew.
Pewter, tzinn.
Phrase, shwetz-awrt.
Pick, pick.
Picking, picka.
Picked, g'picked.
Pickle, pickle.
Pie, pie.
Piece, shtick.
Pierce, shtech.
Piercing, shtecha.
Piety, frummichkeit.
Pig, sily.

Pigeon, dowb.
Pile, howfa.
Pilfering, shtala.
Pill, pill.
Pills, pilla.
Pillow, kissa.
Pin, shpell.
Pincer, bise-tzong.
Pinch, pinch, petz.
Pinching, petza.
Pint, pint.
Pious, frumm.
Pipe. rohr, pife.
Piper, pifer.
Pistol, pishtole.
Pit, groob.
Pitch, pitch.
Pitching, pitcha.
Pitcher, kroog.
Pitiful, yemmerlich.
 pity, dauer.
Pitying, dauera.
Place, plotz.
Plain, plain, deitlich.
Plaintiff, plaintiff.
Plan, plawn.
Plane, huvvell.
Plank, plonk.
Plant, plontz.
Planting, plontza.
Planted, gaplontzed.
Plantation, plontawsh.
Plaster, ploshter
Plasterer, pleshterer.
Plastering, pleshtera.
Plate, deller.
Platform, platform.
Play, shpeel.
Playing, shpeela.
Played, g'shpeeld.
Plea, plea.

Pleasant, plesseerlich.
Pleasure, plesseer.
Please, please, g'falla.
Pleasing, pleasa.
Pledging, pledga.
Pledge, pledge.
Pledged, gapledged.
Plenty, plenty.
Plot, plot.
Plow, ploog.
Pluck, moot.
Plum, plowm.
Plump, ploomp.
Plunder, rawb.
Plundered, g'rauwbd.
Plundering, rauwa.
Pocket, sock.
Pocketing, in sock du.
Poetry, poetry.
Point, poonkt, point, shpitza.
Polish, polish.
Polishing, polisha.
Pointing, weisa, shpitza pointa.
Poke, poke.
Pole, pole.
Police, police.
Policy, policy.
Polish, polish.
Polishing, polisha.
Polished, gapolished.
Polite, polite.
Poll, poll.
Pond, deich, dom.
Pony, pony.
Poor, awram.
Poorly, armlich.
Poplar, popla.
Popular, popular.
Population, bafelkerung.

Pork, si-flaish.
Portrait, portrait.
Positive, positeef.
Possess, b'sitz.
Possession, b'sitzung.
Possible, miglich.
Post, pusht.
Postage, postage.
Postpone, uf-sheeb.
Postponed, uf-g'shova.
Postponement, uf-shoob.
Pot, hoffa.
Pots, heffa.
Potato, krumbeer.
Potter, heffner.
Pound, poont.
Pour, gees, ousshenka.
Poverty, ormoot.
Power, gawalt.
Powerful, g a w e l t i c h,
powerful.
Powder, pulfer.
Practice, practice.
Praise, lobe.
Praising, lova.
Praised, galobed.
Pray, baita.
Prayer, gabait.
Preacher, preddicher.
Preach, preddich.
Preaching, preddicha.
Preached, gapreddich'd.
Prefer, foretzeega.
Preference, foretzoog.
Prejudice, prejudice.
Premature, untzeitich.
Premium, premium.
Prepare, prepare.
Preparing, prepara.
Present, derbi, doh, g'-
shenk.

Presented, g'shenkt.
Presenting, presenta,
shenka.
Preserving, presarfa.
Presume, fermoot.
Pretend, pretend.
Prevented, ferhinnert.
Prevent, ferhinner.
Preventing, ferhinnera
Price, wært, price, lone
Prick, shtecha.
Pride, shtultz.
Principal, principal.
Principle, grundsotz,
principle.
Print, drook.
Printer, drooker.
Printing office, drookerei
Prison, g'fengniss, pressen
Prisoner, g ' f o n g n e r,
prisoner.
Private, private.
Privy, ob-dritt.
Prize, preis.
Probable, worshinelich
Proeeeding, proceeda.
Proceedings, proceed-
ings.
Procession, procession.
Proclaim, ousrufa.
Proclamation, procla-
mation.
Proclaiming, proclaima.
Procure, aw-shoffa.
Produce, produce.
Producing, produsa.
Production, production.
Profess, bakenna.
Professing, professa.
Profession, profession.
Profit, proffit.

Profitable, prufitlich.
Progress, fortshritt.
Prolong, ferlengera.
Prominent, prominent.
Promise, fershprech.
Promising, fershprecha.
Promised, fershprucha
Promote, promote.
Promoting, promota.
Prompt, shnell, grawd.
Proof, proof, baweis.
Prop, shteiber.
Proping, shteibera.
Proper, richtich.
Property, property, fermaiga.
Prophet, prophait.
Proportion, proportion
Proposing, proposa.
Proposal, foreshlawg, proposal.
Proposition, proposition.
Proscription, proscription.
Prosecute, prosecute.
Prosecuting, prosecuta
Prosecution, prosecution.
Prosecutor, prosecutor
Prospect, prospect, oussicht.
Prosper, glick.
Protector, protector.
Protection, protection.
Protect, protect, shitza.
Protecting, protecta.
Protest, protest.
Protesting, protesta.
Protestant, proteshtond.
Proud, shtultz, hochmoot.

Prove, proof, beweis.
Proving, proofa.
Proven, gaproofed.
Proverb, shprichwardt.
Provide, provide, fershaffa.
Providing, provida.
Provision, provision, foresicht.
Provoking, provoka.
Prudent, foresichtich.
Publish, publish.
Published, gapublished
Publishing, publisha.
Publisher, publisher.
Public, public.
Pudding, levverwarsht, pudding.
Puff, puff.
Puffing, puffa.
Puking, kutza.
Puked, gakutzed.
Pull, tzweg.
Pulling, tzeega.
Pulled, g'tzoga.
Pulpit, konsel.
Pulse, poolse.
Pump, boomp.
Punch, punch.
Punctual, pinklich.
Punctuate, punctuate.
Punctuating, punctuata.
Pupil, shooler.
Puppy, yoonger hoond.
Purchase, kawf.
Purchaser, kawfer.
Purchased, g'kawft.
Purchasing, kaufa.
Pure, pure, sauwer.
Purge, loxecr.
Purging, loxeera.

Purged, g'loxeerd.
Purpose, porpas.
Purse, geld-sock.
Pursue, fulga.
Pursuit, noch ga.
Push, push, g'shova.

Pushed, g'pushed.
Pushing, pusha, sheeva
Put, aw, draw, du.
Puzzle, puzzle.
Puzzling, puzzla.
Puzzled, gapuzzled.

Q.

Quack, quack.
Quadruped, credoor, feer-feesich.
Quail, botreesel.
Quake, tzitter.
Quaking, tzittera.
Quality, quality.
Quantity, quantity.
Quarrel, shtreit.
Quarreling, shtreita.
Quarreled, g'shtritta.
Quarry, shtæ-brooch.
Quart, quart.
Quarter, fartle.
Queen, queen.

Queer, coryose.
Question, froke.
Quick, g'shwint.
Quicker, g'shwinter.
Quickest, g'shwintsht.
Quiet, shtill.
Quill, fedder.
Quilt, quilt.
Quince, quit.
Quinces, quitta.
Quit, uf-hara, uf-gevva.
Quite, gons.
Quote, quote.
Quoting, quota.
Quotation, quotation.

R.

Rabbit, haws.
Rabbits, hawsa.
Race, race.
Racing, rasa.
Rack, reff, rack.
Radical, radical.
Raddish, reddich.
Raffle, raffle.
Raffled, g'raffled.
Raffling, raffla.
Raft, raft.
Rag, loompa.

Ragged, ferloompt.
Rage, woot.
Rail, riggle.
Railing, railing.
Railroad, railroad.
Raiment, claidung.
Rain, raiga.
Rained, garaigert.
Raining, raigna.
Rain-bow, raiga-boga.
Rain-water, raiga-wasser
Raise, raise.

Raised, g'raised.
Raising, raisa.
Raisin, raseen.
Rake, recha.
Rally, rally.
Ram. shofe-buck.
Ramrod, lawd-shtecka.
Range, range.
Rank, rank, roy.
Rap, rap, shlawga.
Rape, rape.
Rapid, shnell.
Rare, rawr, ro.
Rascal, rascal.
Rasp, roshpel.
Rate, rate, price.
Rather, leever, rather.
Ratifying, ratifya.
Ratify, ratify.
Ratified, g'ratified.
Rattle, ropple.
Rattling, roppla.
Raw, ro.
Ray, shtrawl.
Reach, long, raich.
Reaching, longa, raicha
Read, laisa, galaisa.
Ready, ready,
Real, rale.
Realize, bagreifa.
Ream, ream.
Reap, arnta.
Rear, hinna, letsht.
Reason, fershtond, ur-
sauch.
Receipt, risseet.
Receive, bacooma.
Receiver, receiver.
Recent, kartzlich.
Reception, reception.
Recite, widder-hola.

Reciting, recite, recita.
Reckon, rechna.
Reckoning, rechnung.
Recollect, b'sinn.
Recollecting, b'sinna.
Recollected, b'soona.
Recommend, recommend
Recommending, re-
commenda
Recommendation, re-
commendation.
Recompense, beloh-
nung.
Reconciling, reconcila.
Reconcile, reconcile.
Reconciled, reconciled.
Record, record.
Recorder, recorder.
Recording, recorda.
Recover, recover.
Recovered, recovered.
Recovering, recovera.
Rectify, rectify.
Rectified, rectified.
Rectifying, rectifya.
Red, road.
Redeem, redeem.
Redeemed, redeemed.
Redeeming, redeema.
Redeemer, Arlaiser.
Reduce, reduce.
Reduced, reduced.
Reducing, redusa.
Refer, refer.
Referred, referred.
Referee, referee.
Refering, refera.
Reflect, reflect.
Reflecting, reflecta.
Reform, reform.
Reformed, reformeerd.

Reformer, reformer.
Refrain, tzurick-halta.
Refuge, t'zufloocht.
Refugee, refugee.
Refund, t'zurick-t'zawla.
Region, gaigend.
Register, register.
Regret, laid.
Regular, regular
Regulate, regulate.
Regulating, regulata.
Regulated, g'regulate.
Regulator, regulater.
Rehearse, widderhola.
Rein, line.
Reject, ferwærfa.
Relate, fertzaila.
Relation, freindshaft.
Relative, ferwonta.
Released, released.
Release, release.
Releasing, releasa.
Relent, noch-gevva.
Reliance, fertrowa.
Relieve, l o s e-l u s s a,
  helfa.
Rely, ferluss.
Reliance, ferlussung.
Relying, ferlussa.
Remain, bleiva.
Remark, bemarkung.
Remarking, bamarka.
Remedy, mittle.
Remember, b' s i n n a,
  arinnera.
Remind, arinner.
Reminding, arinnera.
Reminded, arinnered.
Remit, gevva, shenka.
Remove, weck du, moof
Removing, moofa.

Removed, g'moofed.
Renewing, renewa.
Renew, renew.
Renewed, renewed.
Rent, rent.
Renting, renta.
Repeal, repeal.
Repealed, repealed.
Repealing, repeala.
Repeat, widderhola.
Repent, boosa-du.
Reply, ontwarta.
Report, report.
Reporting, reporta.
Request, awshprooch.
Require, ferlonga.
Rescue, safa.
Resemblance, ainlich-
  keit.
Reside, wohn.
Residence, wohn-plotz.
Resident, wohnhaft.
Residing wohna.
Resigned, resigned.
Resign, resign.
Resigning, resigna.
Resist, widdershtay.
Resistance, w i d d e r-
  shtond.
Resolute, resolute.
Resolution, resolution.
Resolved, b'sh l u s s a,
  b'shloos.
Resolving, resolva.
Resource, mittle.
Respecting, reshpecta.
Respect, reshpect.
Respectable, reshpect-
  able.
Response, ontwart.
Rest, ru.

Resting, rua.
Restore, widder har-shtella.
Resume, widder awfonga.
Retailed, retailed.
Retail, retail.
Retailing, retaila.
Retain, tzurick-halta.
Retire, tzurick gæ.
Retrace, noch gevva.
Retract, widder-rufa.
Retreat, retreat.
Retreating, retreata.
Revenge, revenge.
Revenue, ei-cooma.
Revise, dorrich-sæ.
Revival, revival.
Revive, widderhola.
Revoke, widder-rufa.
Reward, reward.
Rewarding, rewarda.
Rheumatism, roomatis
Rhyme, rhyme.
Rhyming, rhyma.
Rib, rib.
Ribs, ribba.
Rich, reich.
Riches, reichtoom.
Rid, lose.
Ride ride.
Riding, rida.
Rifle, bix.
Rig, rig.
Right, recht.
Righteous, garecht.
Rigerous, shtreng.
Rim, rond.
Ring, ring.
Riot, ufroor, riot.
Rip, rip.
Ripping, rippa.

Ripe, tzeitich.
Rise, uf shtæ, uf gæ.
Risked, risked.
Risk, risk.
Risking, riska.
River, revver.
Road, waig.
Roar, brooma.
Roast, roasht.
Rob, rawb.
Robber, raw-wer.
Robbed, g'rawbd.
Rock, felsa, shuckle.
Rocking, shuckla.
Rockingchair, shuckle-shtool.
Roll, rull.
Roller, wols, roller.
Roof, dauch.
Root, wortzel.
Rope, shtrick.
Rose, rose.
Rot, fowl.
Rotten, ferfowld.
Rotting, fowla.
Rough, grupp, rau.
Round, droom, roond, room.
Row, larm.
Rue, ga-ria.
Ruin, ruineer.
Rule, rule, tzull-shtuck
Ruler, ruler.
Rum, rum.
Rumor, shtory, rumor.
Run, shpringa, run.
Rupture, brooch.
Rush, rush.
Rusk, rusk, weck.
Rust, rusht.
Rye, korn.

S.

Sabbath, soondawg.
Sack, sock.
Sacrament, n a u c h t-
mohl.
Sacred, heilich.
Sad, trowrich.
Saddle, soddle.
Saddler, soddler.
Safe, safe, sicher.
Safety, sicherheit.
Sake, ursauch.
Sail, sail, saila.
Sallad, sullawd.
Salary, salary, lohn.
Sale, ferkawf.
Saloon, saloon.
Salt, sols.
Salty, solsich.
Salute, groos, salute.
Salutation, salutation.
Salvation, salichkeit.
Same, namelich, same.
Sameness, anerlai.
Sand, sond.
Sandy, sondich.
Sane, fershtendich.
Sap, soft.
Sash, sash.
Satan, difel.
Satisfaction, satisfac-
tion.
Satisfy, satisfy.
Satisfying, satisfya.
Satisfied, g'satisfied.
Saturday, somshdawg.
Sausage, brode-warsht.
Save, safe, shpawr.
Saving, safa, shpawra.

Saved, g'safed, g'shpawrd.
Savior, Heilond.
Saw, g'sa, saig.
Say, sawg.
Saying, sawga.
Said, g'sawt.
Scab, kretz.
Scald, bree.
Scalding, breea.
Scalded, g'breed.
Scale, woag.
Scandal, shond.
Scandalous, shendlich.
Scant, k'nop.
Scare, aungsht, engsht.
Scared, fergelshtered.
Scenery, scenery.
Scheme, shkeem.
Scholar, shooler.
School, shool.
Schoolmaster, s h o o l-
maishter.
Science, science.
Scissors, shair.
Scoff, shputt.
Scold, t'zonk.
Scolding, t'zonka.
Scolded, g'tzonked.
Scour, shire.
Scouring, shira.
Scoured, g'shired.
Scramble, shkramble.
Scrape, shkrape.
Scratch, krotz.
Scrawl, kritzel.
Scrawling, kritzla.
Screw, shrowb.
Screwing, shrowwa.

Screwd, g'shrowbd.
Scripture, shrift.
Scrub, shkrub.
Scum, shawm.
Sea, sæ.
Seal, siggle.
Seam, noad.
Search, sooch.
Searched, g'soocht.
Searching, soocha.
Season, season, yohr-t'zeit.
Seat, sitz.
Seating, sitza.
Seated, g'setzt.
Second, second, tzwett, seccoont.
Secondly, tzwettens.
Section, section.
Secular, weltlich.
Secure, sicher, secure.
Seduce, ferfeera.
See, sæ, sana.
Seed, soma.
Seek, sooch.
Seeking, soocha.
Seems, sheint.
Seen, g'sæ, g'sana.
Seldom, selden.
Select, ouslaisa, select.
Selecting, selecta.
Self, selwer.
Sell, ferkawf.
Selling, ferkawfa.
Seller, ferkawfer.
Seminary, seminary.
Senate, senawt.
Senator, senator.
Send, shick.
Sending, shicka.
Sent, g'shickd.

Senior, eldsht.
Sense, fershtond.
Sensible, fershtendich.
Sentence, sentence.
Sentiment, sentiment.
Separate, separate.
Separating, separata.
Separated, g'separate.
Serious, arnsht.
Seriously, arnshtlich.
Sermon, preddich.
Serpent, shlong.
Serve, deen.
Serving, deena.
Served, g'deened.
Set, set, sitz.
Settee, settee.
Setting, setza, sitza.
Settle, settle.
Settlement, settlement.
Settling, settla.
Settled, g'settled.
Sever, trenna.
Several, etlich.
Severe, shtreng, severe
Sew, nai.
Sewing, naia.
Shabby, loompich.
Shade, shodda.
Shadow, shodda.
Shaft, shoft.
Shake, shittle.
Shaking, shittla.
Shall, sull, moos.
Sham, sham.
Shame, shond.
Shameful, shendlich.
Shape, shape.
Share, share.
Sharp, shorf.
Sharpen, sharfa.

Shave, bolweer, shafe.
Shaving, bolweera, shafa.
Shawl, shawl.
She, se.
Shear, shair.
Shed, shuppa.
Sheep, shofe.
Sheet, bed-dooch, boga
Shelf, shelf.
Shell, shawl.
Shelter, shootz.
Shepherd, shafer, hært.
Sheriff, sheriff, shreef.
Shield, shild.
Shift, ferwexla, shift.
Shifting, shifta.
Shin, shin.
Shingle, shindle.
Ship, shiff.
Shirt, hem.
Shock, shock.
Shoe, shoe.
Shoot, shees.
Shooting, sheesa.
Shot, shoos, g'shussa.
Shop, shop.
Short, kortz.
Shorten, kartza.
Shouldered, g'shoolderd.
Shoulder, shoolder.
Shouldering, shooldera
Shout, greish.
Shouting, greisha.
Shove, sheeb.
Shovel, showfel.
Show, show, weis.
Shower, shower.
Shrink, ei-gai.
Shroud, dodaclaid.
Shrub, shrub.

Shutter, lawda.
Shy, shy.
Sick, kronk.
Sickness, kronkheit.
Side, side.
Sift, seeva.
Sight, sicht.
Sign, sign.
Signal, signal.
Signing, signa.
Silence, shtill.
Silk, seida.
Silly, aifeltich.
Silver, silver.
Simple, simple.
Sin, sind.
Sincere, ufrichtich.
Sing, sing.
Singing, singa.
Single. leddich, anesel.
Sink, sink.
Sinking, sinka.
Sister, shweshter.
Sit, sitz, setz, huck.
Sitting, setza, hucka.
Six, sex.
Sixteen, sechtzain.
Size, grais.
Skill, g'shickt si.
Skilful, shicklich.
Skin, howt.
Skinning, obtzeega.
Skip, shkip.
Skirt, skirt, ruck.
Skunk, biscotz.
Sky, himmel.
Slack, slack, nochlussa
Slander, baleega.
Slanderer, ligner.
Slap, shlawg, shlap.
Slate, shlate.

Slating, shlata.
Slaughter, shlauchta.
Slave, shklawf.
Slay, dode shlawga.
Sled, bluck-shlidda.
Sledge, shleggle.
Sleek, shlick.
Sleep, shlofe.
Sleeping, shlofa.
Slept, g'shlofa.
Sleepy, shlefferich.
Sleeve, armel.
Sleigh, shlitta.
Slice, shnitt.
Slide, shlide.
Sliding, shlida.
Slight, klæ.
Slime, shlime.
Slip, shlip.
Slipping, shlippa.
Slipped, g'shlipped.
Slippery, shlipperich.
Slobber, shlovver.
Slop, shlop.
Slope, shlope.
Slow, longsom.
Sluggard, fowlenser.
Slumber, shloomer.
Sly, shly.
Smack, shmack.
Small, klæ.
Smart, shmart.
Smell, reech.
Smelling, reecha.
Smelled, garucha.
Smith, shmit.
Smoke, shmoke.
Smoked, g'shmoked.
Smoking, shmoka.
Smoothe, aiva, glot.
Smother, fershtick.

Smothering, fershticka
Smut, shmootz.
Snail, shneck.
Snake, shlong.
Snap, shnap.
Snarl, ferwickla.
Sneak, shneek.
Sneaking, shneeka.
Sneer, shputta.
Sneeze, shnees.
Sneezing, shneesa.
Snore, shnorrix.
Snoring, shnorrixa.
Snored, g'shnorrixed.
Short, kortz.
Snotnose, rutznaws.
Snow, shnai.
Snuff, shnuff.
Snug, shnug.
So, so.
Soak, soak.
Soaking, soaka.
Soaked, g'soaked.
Soap, saif.
Sober, sober.
Social, social.
Society, society.
Sod, wawsam.
Sofa, sofa.
Soft, waich.
Soil, lond.
Soldier, suldawt.
Sole, sole.
Solicit, fuddera, solicit.
Soliciting, solicita.
Solid, solid.
Solvent, solvent.
Some, ennich, an, dale,
    derfu.
Sometimes, ebmohls.
Son, sohn.

Song, song.
Soon, bol.
Sore, woond, waias.
Sorrow, trower.
Sorry, trowrich.
South, seed.
Soul, sæl, soul.
Sound, sound.
Soup, soup.
Sour, sour.
Southern, seedlich.
Sow, lose.
Spade, shpawd.
Span, shponn.
Spank, pletch.
Spanking, pletcha.
Spare, shpare.
Spark, foonka.
Spasm, kromp.
Speak, shwetz.
Speaker, shwetzer.
Speaking, shwetza.
Spear, shpees.
Special, special.
Specie, specie.
Specify, specify.
Specimen, specimen.
Speculate, shpeculate.
Speculating, shpeculata.
Speculator, shpeculator.
Speech, speetch.
Speed, g'shwint.
Spell, shpell.
Spelling, shpella.
Spelled, g'shpelled.
Spend, shpend.
Spending, shpenda.
Spent, g'shpent.
Spew, kutz.
Spewing, kutza.
Spewed, gakutzed.

Spider, shpin.
Spike, shpike.
Spill, fershitt.
Spilling, fershitta.
Spin, shpin.
Spire, torm.
Spirit, geisht.
Spit, shpau.
Spite, shpite, neid.
Spittoon, shpit-box.
Splash, spritza.
Splice, shplice.
Splinter, shliffer.
Split, shplit, shpolt.
Spoil, ferdarwa.
Spoke, g'shwetzt.
Sponge, shwamm.
Spool, shpool.
Spoon, leffle.
Sport, shport.
Sportsman, shports-
    man, yaiger.
Spot, flecka, shpot.
Spout, shpout.
Spread, shprai, shpread
Spring, shpring.
Sprinkle, shpritz.
Sprinkling, shpritza.
Spunk, shpunk.
Spur, shpora.
Squabble, shtreit.
Squall, shtose-wind.
Square, shquare, feer-
    eckich.
Squat, huck.
Squatting, hucka.
Squeeze, dricka.
Squirrel, shquarl.
Stab, shtech.
Stabbed, g'shtucha.
Stabbing, shtecha.

Stable, shtoll.
Stack, shtuck.
Stage, stage.
Stagger, dorrygle.
Staggering, dorrygla.
Stain, flecka.
Stair, shtoof, shtaig.
Stake, shtake.
Stalk, shtongle.
Stall, shtall.
Stammer, shtutter.
Stammering, shtuttera.
Stamp, shtamp.
Stand, shtond, shtand.
Standing, shtæ, shtand.
Star, shtarn.
Starch, shtarrick.
Stare, shtawr.
Start, shtart.
Starve, ferhoongera.
State, shtawt, shtate.
Steady, shtudy
Studying, shtudya.
Station, station.
Stay, bleib, ward.
Staying, bleiva, warda.
Steadfast, shtondhoft.
Steady, shteady.
Steak, shteak.
Steal, shtale.
Stealing, shtala.
Steam, shteam.
Steel, shtawl.
Steeple, torm.
Steer, ux.
Stem, shtom.
Stench, g'shtenk.
Step, shtep, shritt.
Step-father, shteef-dawdy
Step-mother, s h t e e f-
  mommy.

Steward, steward.
Stick, shtecka.
Stiff, shteif.
Still, shtill.
Sting, shtich.
Stink, shtink.
Stinking, shtinka.
Stir, bawaiga.
Stitch, shtich.
Stock, shtock.
Stocking, shtroomp.
Stockings, shtrimp.
Stomach, mawga.
Stone, shtane.
Stone-quarry, s h t æ -
  brooch.
Stony, shtanich.
Stool, shtool,
Stoop, bick.
Stooping, bicka.
Stop, shtup.
Stopping, shtuppa.
Stopped, g'shtupped.
Stopper, shtupper.
Store, shtore.
Storm, shtorm.
Stormy, shtarmich.
Story, shtory, shtuck.
Stout, shtout.
Stove, uffa.
Stoves, effa,
Straight, grawd.
Straighten, g r a w d-
  maucha.
Strained, g'shtrained.
Strain, shtrain,
Shtraining, shtraina.
Strange, frem.
Stranger, fremmer.
Strangle, fershticka.
Straw, shtro.

Stray, ferlora, ferluffa.
Streak, shtreak.
Stream, shtrome.
Street, shtrose.
Strength, shtarrick.
Strengthen, fershtar-
ricka.
Stretch, shtreck.
Stretching, shtrecka.
Stretched, g'shtrecked.
Strict, shtrict.
Strike, shlawg.
Striking, shlawga.
Stricken, g'shlawga.
String, shnoor.
Strings, shneer.
Strip, shtrip.
Striped, shtraifich.
Stripe, shtraifa.
Stroke, shtraich.
Strong, shtorrick.
Struggle, g'fecht.
Strumpet, hoor.
Stubborn, shtuvverich.
Stud, hengsht.
Student, shtudent.
Study, shtudeera.
Stuff, shtuff.
Stuffing, filsel.
Stumble, shtulver.
Stump, shtoompa.
Stupid, shtupeed.
Sty, si-shtall.
Style, shtyle.
Subject, subjeet.
Submit, uf gevva.
Subscribe, subscribe.
Subscribing, subscriba.
Subscriber, subscriber.
Subscribed, subscribed.
Substantial, substantial

Substitute, substitute.
Subtract, subtract.
Subtracting, subtracta.
Succeed, succeed.
Succeeding, succeeda.
Successful, successful.
Suck, sookle.
Sucking, sookla.
Such, so, suddich.
Sudden, pletzlich.
Sue, shue.
Suffer, leid, suffer.
Suffering, suffera.
Suffered, g'suffered.
Sufficient, g'noonk.
Suffocate, fershticka.
Sugar, tzooker.
Suit, suit.
Sulpher, shweffel.
Sum, soom.
Summer, soomer.
Summon, soomon.
Sun, soon.
Sunnay, soondawg.
Superintend, superintend
Superintending, super-
intenda.
Supervise, supervise.
Supervising, supervisa.
Supper, naucht-essa.
Support, unnershtitz.
Supporting, unnershtitza
Supply, awshaffa.
Supposition, supposition
Suppose, suppose.
Supposing, supposa.
Sure, sure, gawiss.
Surname, tzu-nawma.
Surpass, ivvertreffa.
Surpassing, foretrefflich.
Surplus, ivverfloos.

Surprise, ferwoonera.
Surround, surround, umring.
Surrounding, umringa.
Surveyor, lond-messer.
Survive, ivverlaiva.
Suspicion, suspicion.
Suspect, suspect.
Suspecting, suspecta.
Suspend, suspend.
Suspending, suspenda.
Suspicion, ferdaucht, suspicion.
Sustain, unnershtitza.
Swallow, shlook.
Swallowed, g'shlooked.
Swallowing, shlooka.
Swamp, shwammi.
Swap, shwap.
Swapping, shwappa.
Swarm, shwarm.

Swear, shwear, flooch.
Swearing, shweara, floocha.
Sweat, shwitz.
Sweating, shwitza.
Sweep, kara.
Sweet, sees.
Sweeter, seeser.
Swell, g'shwill.
Swelling, g'shwilla.
Swift, shwift.
Swim, shwim.
Swimming, shwimma.
Swindle, shwindle.
Swindling, shwindla.
Swing, gowntsch, shwing.
Swinging, s h w i n g a, gowntsh a.
Switch, wiply.
Sword, daiga.
System, system.

T.

Table, dish.
Tablespoon, ess-leffle.
Table-cloth, dish-dooch
Tactics, tactics.
Tail, shwantz.
Tailor, shneider.
Take, nem, nemma.
Tale, shtory.
Talent, tollent.
Talk, blaudera, shwetza
Tall, grose, long.
Tallow, inshlich.
Tame, t'zawm.
Tan, lo.
Tangle, ferhootlc.
Tanner, garwer.

Tap, shlawg.
Tape, tape.
Tar, dorr.
Taste, fersooch.
Tattle, tattle.
Tavern, wærtshouse.
Tax, tox.
Tea, tæ.
Tea-spoon, tæ-leffle.
Teach, larn.
Teacher, teacher.
Team, foor.
Teamster, foormonn.
Tear, train, ferrisa.
Tears. traina.
Teat, titz.

Teeth, t'zæn.
Temper, temper, geisht
Temperance, temperance.
Temptation, temptation.
Ten, tzain.
Tend, tend.
Tent, tent.
Term, tarm.
Test, proof, test.
Testament, teshtament.
Testify, batzeiga.
Testimony, testimony, tzeigniss.
Than, os, ols.
Thank, donk.
Thankful, donkbawr.
That, sell, seller, selly.
The, de, des, es.
Theft, shtailung.
Their, eera.
Them, eena, selly.
Themselves, se selwer.
Then, don, d'no.
Theory, theory.
There, hee, dort, onna.
These, de.
They, se.
Thick, dick.
Thicker, dicker.
Thickest, dicksht.
Thief, deeb.
Thievery, shtaileri.
Thigh, shenkle.
Thimble, fingerhoot.
Thin, din.
Thinner, dinner.
Thinnest, dinsht.
Thine, di, deer.
Thing, ding.

Think, denk.
Thinking, denka.
Third, dritt.
Thirst, dorsht.
Thirsty, dorshtich.
Thirteen, dreitzain.
Thirty, dreisich.
This, des.
Thistle, dishtle.
Thorn, dorn.
Thorny, dornich.
Through, dorrich-ous.
Those, selly.
Thought, gadenkt, gadonka.
Thoughtless, nochlessich.
Thousand, daussend.
Thrash, dresh.
Thrashing, dresha.
Thrashing-floor, shire den.
Thread, naitz.
Threat, droh.
Threatening, droha.
Three, dri.
Thrifty, shpawrsom.
Thrive, tzunemma.
Throat, hols.
Throne, trone.
Through, dorrich.
Throw, shmeis.
Throwing, shmeisa.
Thrown, g'shmissa.
Thumb, dowma.
Thump, shtose.
Thunder, dooner.
Thunder-gust, doonerwetter.
Thursday, doonershdawg.

Thus, so, den-waig.
Thy, di.
Tie, binna, band.
Tight, tight, fesht.
Timber, bauhuls.
Time, tzeit.
Timid, fertzawgt.
Tipple, tipple.
Tired, meed.
Title, tittle.
To, um, tzu, aw.
Tobacco, duwack.
Toe, t·zaya.
Toll, toll.
To-morrow, morya.
Tongue, tzoong.
To-night, de naucht.
Too, t'zu, aw.
Tool, g'sharr.
Tooth, t'zaw.
Top, top.
Torch, torch.
Toss, toss.
Touch, awreera, feela.
Tough, t'zay, tough.
Tow, wærrick.
Towell, hond-dooch.
Town, shtadt, town.
Township, township.
Toy, shpeel-sauch.
Trace, marrick.
Tract, shtick, tract.
Trade, hondle.
Train, train.
Traitor, traitor.
Tramp, lond-lafer.
Transfer, transfer.
Translate, ivversetz.
Translating, ivversetza.
Transport, transport.
Trap, foll.

Trash, trash.
Travel, travel.
Traveling, travela.
Traveled, g'traveled.
Tread, tritt.
Treasury, treasury.
Treat, treat.
Treating, treata.
Tree, bawm.
Trees, bame.
Trembling, tzittera.
Trick, trick.
Trifle, klanichkeit, trifle.
Trim, trim.
Trimming, trimma.
Trip, trip.
Troop, troop.
Trouble, troovel.
Trout, ferella.
Truck, truck.
True, wohr.
Trump, troomp.
Trumpet, trumpait.
Trunk, trunk.
Trust, trow.
Trustee, trustee.
Trusting, trowa.
Truth, wohret.
Try, proweer.
Trying, proweera.
Tried, proweered,
Tub, foss, tzoover.
Tubs, fesser.
Tumble, shtartza.
Tune, tune.
Turkey, welsh-hinkle.
Turn, dra.
Turning, drai.
Turned, gadraid.
Turnip, reeb.

Turnips, reeva.
Twins, t'zwilling.
Twine, twine.
Twist, twist.
Two, tzwæ.

Tye, bina.
Tied, g'bunna.
Tying, binna.
Type, type.
Tyrant, tyronn.

U.

Ulcer, g'shweer.
Umbrella, umbrell.
Unaware, unfersane.
Unbecoming, unawsh-
tendich.
Unbelief, unglawa.
Unborn, Ungebora.
Uncle, uncle.
Uncommon, uncommon.
Unconcerned, gleich
giltich.
Unconverted, unbakairt.
Uncover, uf-decka.
Under, unner.
Undertake, unnernem.
Undertaking, unner-
nemma.
Undermining, unner-
mina.
Undiscovered, unendeckt
Undisputed, unbesh-
tritta.
Undivided, unferdaild.
Undoubted, unfertzwei-
felt.
Uneasy, unrooich.
Unequal, unaiva.
Unfailing, unfailbawr.
Unfair, unfair.
Unfaithful, untrei.
Unfasten, lose binna.

United, ferainicht, unite.
Unfit, net fit.
Unfriendly, unfriendlich.
Ungrateful, undonkbawr.
Unguarded, unforesich-
tich.
Unhandy, unhandy.
Unhurt, unferletzt.
Uniform, uniform.
Unite, unite.
Unjust, ungarecht.
Unkind, unfreindlich.
Unlikely, unwarshein-
lich.
Unload, ob-lawda.
Unlock, uf-shleesa.
Unlucky, unglicklich.
Unmarried, leddich.
Unmerited, unferdeent
Unmixed, unfermixed.
Unmoved, unbawaigd.
Unnatural, unnoddeer-
lich.
Unpaid, net betzawlt.
Unprotected, unfer-
sichert.
Unprovided, unfersane.
Unreasonable, unfer-
ninftich.
Unripe, un tzeitich.
Unroof, ob decka.

Unsettle, unsettle.
Unsound, un g'sund.
Unto, tzu, aw, bis.
Untried, unproweert.
Untrue, unwohr.
Unwilling, net willens.
Unwise, unweislich.
Up, uf, noof, ruf.
Uphill, barrick noof.
Upon, uf, druf, aw.
Upper, uvva.

Upright, ufrichtich.
Uproar, ufroor.
Upwards, noof tzoos.
Urge, driva, dringa.
Us, uns.
Use, brauch, use.
Useful, nitzlich.
Used, g,used.
Useless, unnaitich.
Usual, for common.
Utter, sawga.

V.

Vacant, vacant.
Vacancy, vacancy.
Vacate, vacate.
Vacation, vacation.
Vaccinate, vaccinate.
Vagrant, lond-lafer.
Vain, aklehoft.
Vanity, aklehoft.
Vale, dawl.
Valediction, obsheed.
Valid, recht.
Valley, dawl, valley.
Valor, brawf.
Valuable, feel wært.
Value, wært.
Valve, valve.
Vanish, fershwinna.
Vanquish, beeta, uf-usa
Vantage, fordle.
Vapor, vapor.
Vaporate, fergæ.
Variable, ferennerlich.
Variance, widdershprooch
Variation, ferennerung
Varied, fersheedlich.
Varnish, varnish.

Vary, ferennei.
Varying, ferennera.
Vast, grose, ungahire.
Vault, g'welb.
Vaunt, prawl.
Vaunter, prawler.
Vaunting, prawla.
Veal, kalb-flaish.
Vegetable, vegitable, gamees.
Veil, veil.
Vein, oder.
Velocity, shnellichkeit.
Velvet, velvet.
Vend, terkawfa.
Vender, ferkawfer.
Veneer, veneer.
Venerable, airwardich.
Venerate, ferara.
Venom, gift.
Venamous, giftich.
Ventilate, ous lifta.
Ventilation, ous liftung
Venture, venter, riska.
Veracity, wohrhoft.
Verb, t'zeit wardt.

Verbal, wærdlich.
Verbatum, wardt for wardt.
Verdict, verdict.
Verge, grentz.
Verify, bewora.
Verily, wohrlich.
Verity, wohret.
Verse, farsh.
Versed, g'larnd.
Version, de manung.
Very, orrick, wærklich.
Vessel, g'fess, shiff.
Vest, vest, jacket.
Veteran, olter suldawt.
Vex, quala, boddera.
Vexation, bodderation.
Vial, glaws.
Viand, ess-sauch.
Vibrate, shwinga.
Vice, shrowb-shtuck, shendlich.
Vicious, shendlich.
Victim, victim.
Victory, seech.
Victorious, seech-reich
Victual, lavasmittle.
View, ous-sight, blick.
Vigilant, wauchsom.
Vigilance, wachsom-keit.
Vigor, shtarrick.
Vigorous, shtorrick, kreftich.
Vile, niddertrechtich.
Villify, abusa.
Village, shteddle.
Villain, shpitzbu.
Villainous, n i d d e r - trechtich.
Vindicate, rechtshtella

Vindication, rechshtel-lung.
Vindicator, rechtshtel-ler.
Vindictive, shpiteful.
Vine, vine, ronk.
Vinegar, essich.
Vineyard, wine-barrick
Violate, ferletza,violate
Violation, ferletzung, violation.
Violating, ferletza, vio-lata.
Violence, force, gawalt.
Violin, geig.
Virgin, yoong fraw.
Virtual, kreftich.
Virtue, wært.
Virtuous, airlich, sau-wer.
Visible, sicht-bawr.
Vision, arshinung.
Vision, eibildung, vision
Vital, lavendich.
Vitiate, fernichta.
Vivid, labehaft.
Vivify, balava.
Vocabulary, w æ r t a - booch.
Vocal, sing-music.
Vocation, g'sheft.
Voice, shtimm.
Void, giltnix, void.
Violence, mit force.
Volume, volume.
Voluminous, weitleftich.
Voluntary, friwillich.
Volunteer, volunteer.
Volunteering, volunteera
Volunteered, g'volun-teerd.

Vomit, kutz.
Vomiting, kutza.
Vomited, g'kutzd.
Vote, shtimm, vote.
Voting, shtimma, vota.
Voted, g'shtimmed, g'-
vote.
Vouch, tzeigniss.

Voucher, tzeiga, voucher.
Vow, fershprechung.
Vowel, vowel.
Voyage, rais.
Voyaging, raisa.
Vulgar, weesht, dreckich.
Vulgarity, weeshtchkeit.

W.

Wabble, wanka.
Wad, shtupper.
Wadding, wadding.
Wade, bawd.
Wading, bawda.
Wag, shposs maucher.
Waggery, shposs.
Wages, lohn.
Wagon, wauga.
Wagoner, foor mon.
Wail, klawg.
Wailing, klawga.
Wait, ward.
Waiting, warda.
Waited, g'ward.
Waiter, deener, waiter.
Waive, uf gevvung.
Wake, wocker.
Waked, g'wecked.
Waking, wecka.
Waking up, uf wecka.
Walk, lawf.
Walking, lawfa.
Walked, g'luffa.
Walker, lawfer.
Wall, mauer.
Wallow, weela.
Waltz, waltz.
Wander, wander.

Wandering, r u m m -
lawfa.
Want, note, natich.
Wanting, noat, mongle
War, greek.
Ward, ward.
Warden, warden.
Wardrobe, claidershonk.
Ware, wawr, ware.
Warehouse, warehouse
shtorehouse.
Warfare, greek.
Warm, warm.
Warn, warn, warna.
Warning, warnung.
Warned, g'warned.
Warp, fertzeeg.
Warped, fertzoga.
Warrant, warrant.
Warrior, suldawt.
Wart, wartz.
Was, war.
Wash, wesh.
Washing, wesha.
Washed, g'wesha.
Washerwoman, wesh-
fraw.
Wasp, weshp.
Waste, ferdarb.

Wasting, ferdarwa.
Watch, watch.
Watching, watcha.
Watched, g'watched.
Water, wasser.
Watering, wessera.
Waterish, wesserich.
Wave, walla, well.
Waver, nooch-gevva.
Wavering, om noch gevva.
Wax, wox.
Way, waig.
Way-lay, laura.
We, meer, mer.
Weak, shwach.
Weaken, fèrshwecha.
Weakly, shwechlich.
Weakness, shwachheit.
Wealth, reichtoom.
Wealthy, reich.
Wean, ob g'waina.
Weapon, g'wair.
Wear, wear.
Wearing, weara.
Weary, meed.
Weather, wedder.
Weave, waib.
Weaving, waiva.
Weaver, waiver.
Web, waib.
Wed, hira.
Wedge, keitle.
Wednesday, mitwuch.
Weed, unkraut.
Week, wuch.
Weekly, wechlich.
Weep, heil.
Weeping, heila.
Weigh, weeg.
Weighing, weega.

Weighed, g'woga.
Weight, gewicht.
Weighty, shwair, wich-tich.
Welcome, wilcom.
Welfare, wohlshtond.
Welkin, himmel.
Well, well, goot, broona.
West, wesht.
Westward, weshtlich.
Wet, nos.
Wether, hommel.
Whale, wol-fish.
Wharf, wharf.
What, wass, well, weller
Wheat, waitza.
Wheel, um draia, rawd
When, wann, os, dos.
Whence, wohar.
Where, wo, doh.
Whet, wetza, sharfa.
Whether, ub, wann.
Which, well, wellas, weller, wær, wass.
While, wile, tzeitlong.
Whine, klawga.
Whip, wip.
Whisker, wisker.
Whiskey, wiskey.
Whisper, pishper.
Whispering pishpera.
Whispered, g'pishperd.
Whistle, peif.
Whistling, peifa.
Whistled, gapiffa.
Whit, klanichkeit.
Whittle, shnitzle.
Whittling, shnitzla.
White, weis.
Whitewash, weisla.
Who, wær, ar, des, dar.

Whole, gons.
Wholesale, wholesale.
Wholesome, g'soond.
Whom, weller, sellam, well.
Why, warum.
Wick, ducht.
Wicked, bais, gottlose.
Wide, braid, wide.
Widen, arweider.
Widow, widfraw.
Widower, widmon.
Width, braidung.
Wife, fraw.
Wild, wilt.
Wilderness, wiltness.
Wilful, wilful.
Will, will, willa.
Willed, g'willed.
Willing, willens.
Willow, weida.
Wily, shlau.
Win, g'win.
Winning, g'winna.
Wind, wind.
Windy, windich.
Wind. wickle.
Winding, wickla.
Windlass, winn.
Windle, shpindle.
Window, fenshter.
Wine, wine.
Wing, fliggle.
Wink, wink.
Winking, winka.
Winter, winter.
Wipe, wish.
Wiping, wisha.
Wiped, g'wishd.
Wire, drote.
Wisdom, weisheit.

Wise, g'shite, erfawra.
Wish, woonsh.
Wishing, winsha.
Wished, g'winshed.
Wit, witz.
Witch, hex.
Witchcraft, hexerei.
With, mit.
Withdraw, tzurick gæ, derfu-gæ.
Wither, ferwelka.
Withhold, tzurick halta
Within, innerlich.
Witness, tzeiga.
Witted, witzich.
Witty, witzich.
Woe, troovel.
Woful, traurich.
Wolf, wulf.
Woman, weibsmenth, fraw.
Womb, leib, womb.
Wonder, wooner.
Wonderful, woonerlich
Wondering, woonera.
Wondered, g'woondered.
Wood, huls.
Woods, boosh.
Wooden, hulsich.
Wool, wull.
Woolen, wullich.
Word, wardt.
Wording, wærdung.
Work, shauf, arwet.
Working, shauffa.
Worker, shauffer.
Worked, g'shaufd.
Workingday, shauf-dawg
Workshop, shop.
World, ard, welt.
Worldy, weltlich.

Worm, warram.
Wormy, wærmich.
Worry, quaila.
Worse, shlechter.
Worship, gott-deena.
Worshiping, g o t t e s -
 deensht.
Worst, shlechtsht, ar-
 ricksht.
Worth, wært.
Worthless, nix wært.
Worthy, wærdich.
Would, wært, wet, dait,
 daita.
Wound, wound.
Wrangle, tzonka.
Wrangler, wrangler.
Wrapper, wrapper.

Wrath, tzorn.
Wrathy, tzornich.
Wreck, smash-up.
Wrench, f e r t w i s t a,
 draya.
Wrestle, pocka.
Wretch, nix nootzicher
Wretched, nix noot-
 sich.
Wring, dray.
Wringing, draya.
Wrinkle, roontzel.
Writ, writ.
Write, shreib.
Writing, shreiva.
Written, g'shrivva.
Writer, shreiver.
Wrong, letz.

Y.

Yard, yard, hofe.
Yarn, gawrn.
Ye, eer, eich.
Yea, yaw.
Year, yohr.
Yearly, yarelich.
Yearling, yareling.
Yell, greisha, hila.
Yellow, gail.
Yeoman, londmon.
Yes, yaw.
Yesterday, geshter.

Yet, doch, noch, sogawr
Yield, nochlussa.
Yoke, yuch.
Yolk, dudder.
You, du, eer.
Young, yoong.
Youngster, yingling.
Your, di, eier, eer, du.
Yours, di, eier, eer, du.
Yourself, dich selwer.
Youth, yunger bu.

Z.

Zeal, eifer.
Zealous, eifrich.
Zero, nool.
Zealot, eiferer.

Zink, tzink.
Zone, umfong.
Zounds, sopperlut.

Deitsh-Englishe Ivversetzung fun Wardta.

Dutch–English Translation
of Words.

ABLE.

Able, able.
Abordich, particularly.
About, about.
Abuse, abuse.
Abusa, abusing.
Abusif, abusive.
Abused, abused.
Accept, accept.
Accepta, accepting.
Accommodata, accommodating.
Accomplisha, accomplishing.
Accounta, accounting.
According, according.
Accordingly, accordingly.
Accusa, accusing.
Acknowledge, acknowledge.
Acknowledga, acknowledging.
Acknowledgment, acknowledgment.

ADMINISTERA.

Acknowledged, acknowledged.
Act, act.
Acta, acting.
Acter, actor.
Action, action.
Actif, active.
Add, add.
Adda, adding.
Address, address.
Addressa, addressing.
Addressed, addressed.
Addjourna, adjourning
Adopta, adopting.
Adferdise, advertise.
Adferdisement, advertisement.
Adferdised, advertised.
Adferdisa, advertising.
Admit, admit.
Admission, admission.
Admitta, admitting.
Administera, administering.

Administrator, administrator.
Administration, administration.
Advansa, advancing.
Advantage, advantage.
Advisa, advising.
Advocata, advocating.
Affarm, affirm.
Affarma, affirming.
Affarmed, affirmed.
Affronta, affronting.
Afford, afford.
Afforda, affording.
Agent, agent.
Agitata, agitating.
Agree, agree.
Agreea, agreeing.
Agreed, agreed.
Aicha, oak.
Aichel, acorn.
Aifeltich, silly.
Aigna, to own.
Aigner, owner.
Aig, harrow.
Aiga, harrowing.
Aiklehoft, disgusting.
Ail, oil.
Ail-con, oil can.
Ail-dooch, oil-cloth.
Ains, once.
Ainlich, resemble.
Ainsich, only.
Ainlichkeit, resemblance.
Air, honor.
Airlich, honest.
Airlichkeit, honesty.
Airwærdich, honorable
Aishtlich, easterly.
Aiva, even, smooth.

Allæ, alive.
Allænich, alone.
Alley, alley.
Allowance, allowance.
Allmechtich, Almighty
Alter, age.
Also, also.
Amend, amend.
Amenda, amending.
Amendment, amendment.
Amer, bucket.
Amohl, once.
Amounta, amounting.
Amusement, amusement.
Amusa, amusing.
An, an, a.
Anecdote, story, anecdote.
Annexa, annexing.
Anonner, another.
Announsa, announcing.
Announcement, announcement.
Anyhow, anyhow.
Appeala, appealing.
Appealed, appealed.
Appeara, appearing.
Appearance, appearance.
Applauda, applauding.
Application, application.
Appoint, appoint.
Appointa, appointing.
Appointment, appointment.
Appraisa, appraising.
Appraised, appraised.

Appraisement, appraise-
ment.
Approof, approve.
Approofa, approving.
Approofed, approved.
Appropriata, appropri-
ating.
Appropriation, appro-
priation.
Ar, he.
Arb, heir.
Arbshoft, inheritance.
Arba, heirs.
Arbitrate, arbitrate.
Arbitrata, arbitrating.
Arbitration, arbitration
Arbitrator, arbitrator.
Ard, earth, clay.
Arbsa, peas.
Arclara, avowing.
Arclarung, avowal.
Arfinna, invent.
Arfinnung, invention.
Arfawrung, experience
Arhalta, maintaining.
Arhaltung, mainte-
nance.
Arga, argue.
Argament, argument.
Argera, torment, pro-
voke.
Argerlich, provoking.
Arinner, remind.
Arinnera, reminding.
Arinnered, reminded.
Arkenna, recognize.
Arkennt, recognized.
Arlaiser, Redeemer.
Arlawbniss, concession
Arlawb, allowance.
Arlawbed, allowed.

Arlaw-wa, allowing.
Arma, arming.
Armel, sleeve.
Armlich, poorly.
Arnire, renew.
Arniddericha, degrad-
ing.
Arnsht, earnest.
Arnshtlich, earnest-
ness.
Arnt, harvest.
Arnta, harvesting.
Arraicha, attain.
Arranga, arranging.
Arresht, arrest.
Arricht, dispose.
Arrichta, disposing.
Arricksht, worst.
Arshina, appearing.
Arsht, first.
Arshtens, firstly.
Arshoffa, created.
Arwa, to inherit, heirs.
Arwaild, elect.
Arwarda, awaiting.
Arwet, work, employ-
ment.
Asle, ass, mule.
Assess, assess.
Assessa, assessing.
Assessed, assessed.
Assessor, assessor.
Assign, assign.
Assigna, assigning.
Assigned, assigned.
Assignee, assignee.
Assignment, assign-
ment.
Association, associa-
tion.
Associata, associating.

At, drau.
Attach, attach.
Attacha, attaching.
Attached, attached.
Attachment, attach-
ment.
Attack, attack.
Attecka, attacking.
Attacked, attacked.
Attracta, attracting.
Attractif, attractive.
Attraction, attraction.
Attenda, attending.
Attentif, attentive.
Auch, alas! oh!
Aucht, care, eight.
Auchtzæ, eighteen.
Auchtzich, eighty.
Aucht-un-auchtzich,—
eighty-eight.
Auchtzaint, eighteenth
Auchtzichsht, eightieth
Aucht-gevva, taking
care.
Audit, audit.
Auditor, auditor.
Audita, auditing,
Augoosht, august.
Aunghsht, fear.
Aunt, aunt.
Author, author.
Authority, authority.
Authorize, authorize.
Average, average.
Aw, too, also.
Awdale, part.
Awdler, eagle.
Awbinna, hitching, ty-
ing.
Awdu, dressing.
Awdechtlich, devotion.

Awcooma, arrived.
Awclava, cleave.
Aweck, away.
Awer, but.
Awfong, begin.
Awfonga, beginning.
Awg'fonga, begun.
Awg, eye.
Awga, eyes.
Awga-deckle, eye-lid.
Awga-hore, eyebrows.
Awgablick, instant.
Awgabora, inborn.
Awgadu, dressed.
Awganame, agreeable.
Awganooma, accepted,
adopted.
Awgevva, to make com-
plaint.
Awgevver, complain-
ant.
Awg'fonga, commenced.
Awgriff, attack.
Awgrifa, attacking.
Awgagriffa, attacked.
Awgarota, counseled.
Awklawg, complaint.
Awhenka, append.
Awhong, appendage.
Awhetza, to incite.
Awmice, ants.
Awnawm, acceptance.
Awnemma, accepting,
adopting.
Awg'nooma, accepted.
Awl, awl.
Awlucka, allure.
Awpossa, to fit.
Awram, poor.
Awreera, to touch.
Awrm, arm.

Awrt, art, mode.
Awsana, behold.
Awsicht, aspèct.
Awshtæ, become.
Awshtælich, becoming.
Awshinelich, evident.
Awshoffa, to procure.
Awshpreoch, request.
Awshtose, adjoin, abut
Awshtosung, abutment

Awshtond, decorum.
Awshtecka, to kindle.
Awshteckich, infectious.
Awshtella, installing, feigning.
Awtriva, carrying on.
Awtzeega, attract.
Awtzoog, attire.
Awwenda, investing.

B.

Baboon, baboon.
Bacooma, becoming.
Bachelor, bachelor.
Badeenta, servant.
Badeident, considerable.
Badolya, batalion.
Bæ, leg.
Bafail, behest.
Bafria, emancipate.
Baggage, baggage.
Bagrawb, bury.
Bagrawa, burying.
Bagrebniss, burial.
Bagrifa, to comprehend.
Bagriff, comprehension
Bahawpt, contend.
Bahawpta, contending.
Baid, pray.
Baida, praying, both.
Bail, bail.
Baila, bailing.
Bailed, bailed.
Bait, pray.
Baita, praying.
Bakare, convert.

Bakared, converted.
Bakenna, concede, profess
Bakont, acquaint.
Bakonta, acquaintance
Baklawgd, accused.
Baklawga, accusing.
Baklawger. accuser.
Bakrefticha, corroberating.
Balance, balance.
Balansa, balancing.
Baleeg, belie.
Baloga, belied.
Balone, to compensate.
Balonung, compensation.
Ballot, ballot.
Ballota, balloting.
Band, band.
Band-box, band-box.
Bank, bank.
Banker, banker.
Bankrupt, bankrupt.
Bankment, embankment.
Banner, banner.

Bar, bar.
Bara, berries.
Barawb, to rob.
Barbawrish, barberous.
Bare, berry.
Bareemt, famous.
Barl, barrel.
Barrig, mountain, hill.
Barrigich, mountainous, hilly.
Barriga, mountains, hills
Barrya, bargain.
Barsht, brush, bristle.
Barshta, brushes, bristles.
Basa broom.
Basa-shteel, broom-stick.
Base, angry, cross.
Bashful, bashful.
Basits, beset.
Basitzer, occupant.
Batreebt, sad.
Batreega, cheating.
Batroog, fraud.
Batroga, defrauded.
Batrowra, bewail.
Batter, batter.
Battered, battered.
Battery, battery.
Battle, battle.
Batzawl, pay.
Batzawlt, paid.
Batzawla, paying.
Batzawlung, payment.
Batzeiga, to testify.
Bau, build.
Baua, to build.
Baua, farming.
Bauer, farmer.
Bauerei, farm.

Bau-huls, lumber.
Bau-koonsht, architecture.
Bau-maishter, architect.
Bauch, belly.
Bau-wull, cotton.
Ba-waiga, agitate.
Ba-weis, proof.
Bawd, bathe.
Bawda, bathing, wading.
Bawm, tree.
Bawm-gorda, orchard.
Bawr, bare, barren.
Bawrd, beard.
Bawr-feesich, barefooted.
Bawohn, inhabit.
Beat, beat.
Beata, beating.
Becker, baker.
Beed, bid.
Beeda, bidding.
Beef, beef.
Beef-shtake, beef- steak.
Beeg, bend.
Beega, bending.
Beera, pears.
Beevel, bible.
Behafe, behave.
Behafung, behavior.
Beitrawg, contribution.
Beitrawga, contribute.
Bell, bell.
Belt, belt.
Bemarkung, remark.
Benefit, benefit.
Beneficial, beneficial.
Bendle, string.
Bens, penny.
Besht, best.

Besser, better.
Beshriva, describing.
Beshrivung, description.
Bet, bed.
Bet-dooch, bed-sheet.
Bet-dedk, bed-cover.
Betlawd, bedstead.
Bedsauch, bedding.
Bettla, begging.
Bettle, beg.
Bettlar, beggar.
Bifol, applause.
Big, stoop.
Bigga, stooping.
Bigbug, aristocrat.
Bigbugish, aristocratic.
Bigbugeri, aristocracy.
Biggla, ironing.
Biggleisa, flat-iron.
Bild, picture.
Bilder, pictures.
Bill, bill.
Billiards, billiards.
Bin, tie.
Binna, tying, binding.
Binner, binder.
Bise, bite.
Bisa, biting.
Bisetzong, pincers.
Bit, beg.
Bitch, bitch.
Bit, entreat, beg, pray.
Bitta, praying, entreating.
Bitter, bitter.
Bishof, bishop.
Bissle, little.
Bix, rifle.
Black, black.
Blacka, blacking.

Black-bara, black-berries.
Blackguard, blackguard.
Black-shmit, blacksmith.
Blaid, bashful.
Blaidheit, bashfulness.
Blame, blame.
Blama, blaming.
Blank, blank.
Blanket, blanket.
Blaudera, talking.
Blee, blossom.
Bleea, blossoming.
Blech, tin.
Bleib, stay.
Bleiva, staying.
Bletter, leaves.
Bli, lead.
Bli-pencil, lead pencil.
Blint, blind.
Blick, view.
Blitz, lightning.
Blo, blue
Bloat, bloat.
Bloom, flower.
Blooma, flowers.
Bloomich, flowery.
Bloot, blood.
Bloota, bleeding.
Blootich, bloody.
Blot, blot.
Blose, bare.
Blose, bladder.
Blose, blow.
Blosa, blowing.
Blosebolk, bellows.
Bloss, pale.
Bluck, block, log.
Bluff, bluff.
Bluffa, bluffing.

Blut, bald.
Blut-keppish, bald-headed.
Blush, blush.
Board, board.
Boarda, boarding.
Boast, boast.
Bobbeer, paper.
Bobbagoy, parrot.
Bobbla, babbling.
Bobbler, babbler.
Bobblemaul, gabbler.
Body, body.
Bodderation, bother-ation.
Bo, beau.
Boga, bow.
Bocka, bake.
Bocka, cheek, baking.
Bockshtae, brick.
Bock-uffa, bake-oven.
Bock-moold, dough-trough.
Boiler, boiler.
Bol, soon.
Bolweer, shave.
Bolweera, shaving.
Bolweer-messer, razor.
Bolka, beam.
Bold, bold.
Bolsom, balm.
Bolsomeera, embalm.
Bone, bean.
Bona, beans.
Bond, bond, bandage.
Bond, hinge.
Bong, fear.
Bonk, bench.
Bonnet, bonnet.
Bore, bore.
Bora, auger, boring.

Borrick, trust.
Borrya, borrowing.
Bormhartzich, mercy-ful.
Boshta, husking.
Boss, boss.
Boseheit, malice.
Boshknawda, parsnips.
Botch, botch.
Botreesle, partridge.
Bounce, bounce.
Bounsa, bouncing.
Bounty, bounty.
Bowl, bowl.
Box, box.
Boxer, boxer.
Boxa, boxing.
Booch, book.
Booch-waitza, buckwheat
Bookle, back.
Boomp, pump.
Boomps, jar.
Boondle, bundle.
Boosh, woods.
Bootter, butter.
Bootterfos, churn.
Boottermillich, butter-milk.
Braid, broad.
Braider, broader.
Braidsht, broadest.
Braidung, width.
Branch, branch.
Brandy, brandy.
Brauch, use.
Braucha, using.
Brawf, brave.
Brawfheit, bravery.
Brawl, boast.
Brawler, boaster.
Brech, break.

Brecha, breaking.
Breechshtong, crowbar.
Breder, brethren.
Brederlich, brotherly.
Bredershoft, brother-
hood.
Bree, gravy, juice.
Bree, scald, hatch.
Breea, scalding, hatch-
ing.
Breed, breed.
Breeda, breeding.
Breef, letter.
Breef-shriva, letter-
writing.
Bren, burn.
Brenna, burning.
Brenna, distilling.
Bri, pap.
Brick, bridge.
Bribe, bribe.
Briggle, bludgeon, bat.
Briggla, clubbing.
Bring, bring.
Bringa, bringing.
Brill, spectacles.
Brill, bellow.
Brilla, bellowing.
Brisk, brisk.
Brond, brand.
Brode, bread.
Broda,, frying.
Brode-warsht, sausage.
Brode-pon, frying-pan.
Broud, baide.
Brow, brew.
Browa, brewing.
Brower, brewing.
Broweri, brewery.
Brown, brown.
Brooch, breach, rupture.

Broosht, bosom, breast.
Broom, hum.
Brooma, roaring.
Broona, well.
Bruder, brother.
Bruise, bruise.
Brush, brush.
Bu, boy.
Budda, bottom.
Buwa, boys.
Bubbelly, baby.
Buck, buck.
Bucket, bucket.
Bugle, bugle.
Buggie, buggie.
Bull, bull.
Bully, bully.
Bungle, bungle.
Bureau, bureau.
Butcher, butcher.
Butchera, butchering.
Buttle, bottle.
Bisness, business.
Bushel, bushel.
Bushtawb, letter.
Bushtaweer, spell.
Bushtaweera, spelling.
B'holta, keep.
B'shisa, cheating.
B'shissa, cheated.
B'shtimm, define.
B'shtimma, bespeak.
B'shtrofed, punished.
B'shleesa, conclude.
B'shloos, conclusion.
B'shlussa, conclude.
B'sin, recollect.
B'soona, recollected.
B'sinna, recollecting.
By, by.
Bywona, abide.

C.

Cabinet, cabinet.
Calculata, calculating.
Calculation, calculation.
Camp, camp.
Campaign, campaign.
Campa, encamp.
Campment, encamp-
　ment.
Candid, candid.
Candy, candy.
Canvass, canvass.
Canvassa,.canvassing.
Canvasser, canvasser.
Captain, captain.
Capacity, capacity.
Cape, cape.
Caper, caper.
Car, car.
Carpet, carpet.
Carpet-loompa, carpet
　rags.
Case, case.
Casting, casting.
Cash, cash.
Cashier, cashier.
Celebrate, celebrate.
Celebrata, celebrating.
Celebration, celebra-
　tion.
Cent, cent.
Certificate, certificate.
Challenge, challenge.
Challenga, challenging
Champion, champion.
Chance, chance.
Chawa, chewing.
Chaw, chew.
Charma, charming.

Charge, charge.
Charga, charging.
Charter, charter.
Chartera, chartering.
Chasa, chasing.
Check, check.
Checka, checking.
Chilla, chilling.
Choose, choose.
Choosa, choosing.
Choke, choke.
Choka, choking.
Cider, cider.
Circus, circus.
City, city.
Citizen, citizen.
Circular, circular.
Clæ, clover.
Clæ-soma, cloverseed.
Claider, clothes.
Claidung, clothing.
Claida, clothe.
Claider shonk, w a r d -
　robe.
Claiger, complainant.
Claim, claim.
Claima, claiming.
Clarrick, clerk.
Clawg, complaint.
Clawga, complaining.
Clear, clear.
Cleara, clearing.
Clearanca, clearance.
Clever, clever.
Clex, blot.
Clexa, blotting.
Clingle, jingle.
Clip, clip.

Clippa, clipping.
Cloak, cloak.
Clopper, clapper.
Clore, clear.
Cloreheit, clearness.
Clora, clearing.
Closs, class.
Clook, hen.
Cloompa, clod.
Club, club.
Clubba, clubbing.
Coach, coach.
Coala, coal.
Coax, coax.
Coaxa, coaxing.
Cocked, cocked.
Coffee, coffee.
Coffee-meel, coffee mill
Cohoogla, political chi-
  canery.
Colb, calf.
Colb-flaish, veal.
Collar, collar.
Collateral, collateral.
Collect, collect.
Collecta, collecting.
Collector, collector.
Collection, collection.
Collender, almanac.
College, college.
Collich, lime.
Com, comb.
Combine, combine.
Combina, combining.
Combination, combi-
  nation.
Comfort, comfort.
Comforta, comforting.
Comfortable, comfort-
  able.
Comfoogler, bummer.

Comma, comma.
Command, command.
Commanda, command-
  ing.
Commander, commander
Commit, commit.
Committa, committing
Commission, commis-
  sion.
Commissioner, c o m -
  missioner.
Common, common.
Communicont, c o m -
  municant.
Compare, compare.
Comparison, compari-
  son.
Compara, comparing.
Competa, competing.
Compete, compete.
Complya, complying.
Completa, completing.
Complete, complete.
Compliment, compli-
  ment.
Complimenta, compli-
  menting.
Composa, composing.
Compose, compose.
Composition, composi-
  tion.
Compound, compound
Compounda, c o m -
  pounding.
Compromise, compro-
  mise.
Compromisa, compro-
  mising.
Comrawd, camrade.
Con, can.
Conawl, canal.

Concert, concert.
Conclusif, conclusive.
Condense, condense.
Condensa, condensing.
Condem, condemn.
Condema, condemning
Condidawt, candidate.
Condition, condition.
Conductor, conductor.
Confess, confess.
Confessa, confessing.
Confession, confession.
Confessed, confessed.
Confer, confer.
Confera, confering.
Conference, conference
Confectionery, confectionery.
Confident, confident.
Confidence, confidence
Confirm, confirm.
Confirma, confirming.
Confirmation, confirmation.
Confine, confine.
Confina, confining.
Confined, confined.
Confound, confound.
Confounda, confounding,
Congress, congress.
Connect, connect.
Counecta, connecting.
Connection, connection.
Conone, cannon.
Consel, pulpit.
Consider, consider.
Considera, considering
Consistent, consistent.
Constitution, constitution.

Constrau-wa, currents.
Constructa, constructing.
Construction, construction.
Consulta, consulting.
Consolidata, consolidating.
Contradict, contradict.
Contradicta, contradicting.
Contradiction, contradiction.
Contest, contest.
Contesta, contesting.
Contract, contract.
Contracta, contracting.
Contributa, contributing.
Continua, continuing.
Continent, continent.
Convince, convince.
Convinsa, convincing.
Convict, convict.
Convicta, convicting.
Conviction, conviction.
Cop, cap.
Copittle, capital.
Copy, copy.
Copya, copying.
Coodle-fleck, tripe.
Coom, come.
Cooma, coming.
Coomd, coming.
Coonshtaweller, constable.
Cooper, copper.
Cord, card.
Cordullish, Catholic.
Cordoon, calico.
Core, choir.
Correcta, correcting.

Corresponda, corresponding.
Corrich, cart.
Corrick, cork.
Corrisseera, courting.
Corrocter, character.
Corryose, curious.
Cotz, cat.
Cotza, cats.
Cotzakraut, catnip.
Cow, chew.
Cowa, chewing.
Coward, coward.
Court, court.
County, county.
Cousin, cousin.
Council, council.
Counterfeit, counterfeit.
Countermand, countermand.
Counter, counter.
Crack, crack.
Cracka, cracking.
Cracker, cracker.
Crape, crape.
Crebs, cancer.
Creditt, credit.
Creditor, creditor.
Creddoor, animal.

Creps, crab.
Creek, creek.
Crib, crib.
Critish, critical.
Crittlich, crabbed.
Cripple, cripple.
Crisht, christian.
Crishtus, Christ.
Crishdawg, Christmas.
Croosht, crust.
Cromp, cramp.
Crottle, climb.
Crottla, climbing.
Crottler, climber.
Crottlera, congratulating.
Crotza, scratching.
Crup, craw.
Crowd, crowd.
Croyer, auctioneer.
Curbshtæ, curbstone.
Cure, cure.
Cura, curing.
Cultivata, cultivating.
Cuply, cup.
Currawsh, courage.
Currawshich, courageous
Curve, curve.
Cushion, cushion.
Cute, accute.

D.

Daig, dough.
Dait, would.
Daiya, sword.
Daiglich, daily.
Daig-maucha, dough-kneeding.
Dail, divide.

Daila, dividing.
Darly, small gate.
Daitzember, december
Darf, dare.
Darm, bowels.
Darnoch, after.
Dasha, dashing.

Dauch, roof.
Dauer, pity.
Dauera, pitying.
Dawb, deaf.
Dawdy, father.
Dawf, baptism.
Dawfa, baptising.
Dawfel, slate.
Dawg, day.
Dawga, days.
Dawglaner, day laborer
Dawl, dale.
Dawler, dollar.
Daurum, because.
Dawtam, date.
De, the, they.
Deal, deal.
Dealer, dealer.
Deala, dealing.
Debate, debate.
Deducta, deducting.
Deck, ceiling, bed cover
Deckel, lid.
Decide, decide.
Decida, deciding.
Declara, declaring.
Declaration, · declaration.
Declina, declining.
Deed, deed.
Deer, beast, door.
Deen, serving.
Deef, deep.
Deefer, deeper.
Deefsht, deepest.
Deefung, depth.
Deener, waiter.
Defeat, defeat.
Defense, defense.
Defensif, defensive.
Defenda, defending.

Defendant, defendant.
Defectif, defective.
Define, define.
Defina, defining.
Defya, defying.
Defy, defy.
Degree, degree.
Deitsh, dutch, german.
Deitlich, distinct.
Delegate, delegate.
Delegation, delegation.
Delicate, delicate.
Delivera, delivering.
Deller, plate.
Demand, demand.
Demanda, demanding.
Demnoch, therefore.
Demokrawt, democrat.
Demokrawtie, democracy.
Demmerung, dawn.
Den, this, den.
Den-wæg, this way.
Denk, think.
Denka, thinking.
Department, department.
Deputy, deputy.
Derbi, along with, among.
Derfu, from.
Dergaiga, against.
Derhame, at home.
Design, design.
Detarmina, determining.
Di, your.
Diagram, diagram.
Diamond, diamond.
Dictionary, dictionary.
Dick, thick,
Dicker, thicker.

Dicksht, thickest.
Difle, devil.
Differ, differ.
Differa, differing.
Difficulty, difficulty.
Din, thin.
Dinner, thinner.
Dinsht, thinest.
Dinda, ink.
Dinda-fos, inkstand.
Ding, thing.
Dinger, things.
Dinshdawg, tuesday.
Dire, dear.
Direr, dearer.
Diresht, dearest.
Direct, direct.
Directa, directing.
Disagree, disagree.
Disagreea, disagreeing.
Disadvantage, disadvantage.
Disappointa, disappointing.
Disappeara, disappearing.
Dispatch, dispatch.
Discharge, discharge.
Discharga, discharging
Discussion, discussion.
Discussa, discussing.
Discount, discount.
Discounta, discounting.
Dissecta, dissecting.
Dismiss, dismiss.
Dismissa, dismissing.
Dismissed, dismissed.
Displaya, displaying.
Disband, disbanding.
Distance, distance.

Disposed, disposed.
Disposa, disposing.
Dishbadawt, dispute.
Dishbadeera, disputing.
Distribution, distribution.
Distributa, distributing
Dissolve, dissolve.
Dissolva, dissolving.
Disreshpect, disrespect.
Disreshpectful, disrespectful.
District, district.
Dish, table.
Dish-dooch, table cloth.
Divida, dividing.
D'no, then, thereupon.
Dobbich, awkward.
Dode, dead.
Doda-claid, shroud.
Doda-lawd, coffin
Dode-shlawga, to slay.
Dodge, dodge.
Dodga, dodging.
Doch, yet, though.
Document, document.
Doh, here.
Dohar, hither.
Dohr, large gate.
Dom, dam.
Domineer, domineer.
Domineera, domineering.
Donk, thank.
Donkbawr, thankful.
Donka, thanking.
Dons, dance.
Donsa, dancing.
Dooch, cloth.
Doom, dumb.
Doomel, hurry.

Doomla, hurrying.
Dooner, thunder.
Doonera, thundering.
Doonershdawg, thurs-
day.
Doonka, immersing.
Doonkel, dark.
Doonker, Baptist.
Dooshper, dusk.
Dorr, tar.
Dorm, gut.
Dorn, thorn.
Dorrygla, staggering.
Dorrygle, stagger
Dorrich, through.
Dorrich gæ, abscond.
Dorrich-fol,diarrhoe.
Dorsht, thirst.
Dorshtich, thirsty.
Dort, there.
Dose, dose.
Double, double
Double-g'sichtich, doub-
le-faced.
Dow, dew.
Dowb, dove.
Dower, pity, enure.d
Dowera, pitying, en-
during.
Dowerhoft, durable.
Dowch, dive.
Dowcha, diving.
Dowma, thumb.
Drai, turn.
Draia, turning,
Draft, draft.
Drau, to, at, into.
Drawer, drawer.
Drawm, dream.
Drawma, dreaming.
Drechter. funnel.

Dreck, dirt.
Dreckich, dirty.
Dreckluch, mudhole.
Dresh, thresh.
Dresha, threshing.
Dresh-machine, thresh-
ing machine.
Dress, dress.
Dressa, dressing.
Dri, three.
Dritzain, thirteen.
Drisich, thirty.
Dritt, third.
Drisichsht, thirtieth.
Drick, squeeze.
Drickla, drying.
Drink, drink.
Dainka, drinking.
Drill, drill.
Drilla, drilling.
Drive, drive.
Driva, driving.
Drivva, over, across.
Droh, threat.
Droha, threatening.
Drom, dram.
Droof, on, upon.
Drook, print.
Drooka, printing, dry.
Drookeri, printing office.
Droom, drum, about it.
Drooma, drumming.
Droona, down, below.
Droop, flock, drove.
Drote, wire.
Drous, out.
Drover, drover.
Drullich, droll.
Druvva, up, above.
Du, do, you.
Du'n, do, doing.

Dudder, yolk.
Duckter, doctor.
Ducktera, doetoring.

Du.'t, does. doing.
Duty, duty
Duwock, tobacco.

E.

Eb, if, before, rather.
Ebmohls, sometimes.
Eaga, self.
Eaga-leeb, egotism.
Eamohl, one time.
Eawich, eternal.
Eawichkeit, eternity.
Eb, if, whether.
Ebber, some one.
Ebmohls, sometimes.
Eck, corner.
Eckich, cornered.
Eem, bee, him, his.
Eema, bees.
Een, him, himself.
Ena, them.
Era, hers.
Edita, editing.
Effa, stoves.
Effecta, effecting.
Effectif, effective.
Effentlich, public.
Effnung, opening.
Effongalish, evangelical.
Effongalium, gospel.
Eibild, vision.
Eibildung, visionary.
Eich, you.
Eidrook, impression.
Eifer, zeal.
Eiferich, zealous.
Eifeera, inducting.
Eifensa, fencing in.

Eifol, notion.
Eifloos, influence.
Eigæ, shrink.
Eig'shparrd, confined.
Eigalawda, invited.
Eigaweit, dedicate.
Eigaweida, entrails.
Eil, hurry.
Eila, hurrying.
Eilawda, invite.
Eigalawda, invited.
Eilawdung, invitation.
Eir, your.
Eiserlich, outward.
Eishparra, confining.
Eisicht, insight.
Eiwanderer, immigrant.
Eiwia, dedicating.
Eiwendung, objection.
Elboga, elbow.
Elder, older, senior.
Eldlich, elderly.
Eldsht, oldest.
Election, election.
Element, element.
Elevate, elevate.
Elevata, elevating.
Elf, eleven.
Elft, eleventh.
Ellefont, elephant.
Elt, age.
Eltra, parents.
Enaucht, care, caution
End, end, duck.

Enda, ending, ducks.
Endrich, drake.
Endecka, to discover, disclose.
Endorse, endorse.
Endorsa, endorsing.
Endorser, endorser.
Encourage, encourage.
Encouraga, encouraging.
Encouragement, encouragement.
Enforsa, enforcing.
Engaga, engaging.
Engaged, engaged.
Engagement, engagement.
Engine, engine.
Engineer, engineer.
Engineera, engineering.
Engrava, engraving.
Engle, angel.
Engsht, fear.
Engshtlich, fear, anxiety.
Enjoya, enjoying.
Enjoyment, enjoyment
Ennich, any.
Enrolla, enrolling.
Entera, entering.
Entertaina, entertaining.
Entertainment, entertainment.
Entitled, entitled.
Entwedder. either.
Epple, apples.
Equaliza, equalizing.
Etlich, several.
Era, her, hers, their.

Es, it, that, the.
Ess, eat.
Essa, eating.
Esser, eater.
Ess-leffel, tablespoon.
Ess-shtick, lunch.
Essich, vinegar.
Esh, ashes.
Exact, exact.
Exactly, exactly.
Examina, examining.
Excuse, excuse.
Excusa, excusing.
Excused, excused.
Exhibita, exhibiting.
Excepta, excepting.
Executa, executing.
Executor, executor.
Executif, executive.
Execution, execution.
Exercise, exercise.
Exemple, example.
Expensif, expensive.
Expense, expense.
Expenda,. expending.
Expella, expelling.
Explain, explain.
Explaina, explaining.
Explanation, explanation.
Exploda, exploding.
Exposa, exposing.
Experimenta, experimenting.
Express, express.
Expressa, expressing.
Extra, extra.
Extracta, extracting.
Extenda. extending.
Extensif, extensive.
Ever, boar.

Evada, evading.
Evasion, evasion.
Evil. evil.

Evidence, evidence.
Evva, but, though.

F.

Fact, fact.
Facing, facing.
Fært, fourth.
Færtens, fourthly.
Færtzain, fourteen.
Færtzich, forty.
Fail, fail.
Faila, failing.
Fail'd, failing.
Failer, fault.
Failerhoft, faulty.
Failure, failure.
Fair, fair.
Falsh, false.
Falshheit, falsehood.
Family, family.
Fan, fan.
Fanna, fanning.
Fancy, fancy.
Fare, fare.
Farrich, fear.
Farrichta, fearing.
Farrichterlich, fearful.
Farrava, coloring.
Farraver, dier.
Farry, forwards.
Farrywell, farewell.
Farsh, heel, verse.
Farsha, heels.
Farsich, forwards.
Færtle, quarter.
Færtle-dawler, quarter-dollar.
Færtle-yarich, quarterly.

Færtich, finished.
Fasa, facing.
Fashion, fashion.
Fawble, fable.
Fawda, thread.
Fawna, flag.
Fawr, ride, haul, drive.
Fawra, driving, hauling.
Favor, favor.
Favora, favoring.
Februawr, february.
Fecht, fight.
Fechta, fighting.
Fedder, pen, quill.
Feddera, feathers.
Feddersht, foremost.
Fee, cattle, fee.
Feeish, beastly.
Feel, much, many, feel
Feela, feeling.
Feer, four.
Feer-eckich, four cornered.
Feer-feesich, four footed.
Fees, feet.
Feggle, birds.
Feind, enemy.
Feicht, damp, moist.
Feld, field.
Felder, fields.
Fellich, fully.
Felsa, rock.
Felsich, rocky.

Fence, fence.
Fensariggle, fence-rail.
Fendu, vendu.
Fendu croyer, vendu-
cryer.
Fenshter, window.
Fenshter-shibe, window-
pane.
Ferainich, unite.
Ferainicha, uniting.
Feraira, honoring.
Ferainsla, consorting.
Feraikled, disgusted.
Ferawlussa, to infer.
Ferauchta, despising.
Ferbeed, forbid.
Ferbei, past.
Ferbessera, bettering.
Ferbessered, bettered,
improved.
Ferbin, bind.
Ferbinna, binding.
Ferbinnung, covenant.
Ferbrech, break.
Ferbrecha, breaking.
Ferbrucha, broken.
Ferbrecher, criminal.
Ferbrend, burned.
Ferbutta, forbidden.
Ferburst, explode.
Ferbursta, exploding.
Ferclex, to blot.
Ferclexed, blotted.
Ferdarb, spoil.
Ferdarwa, spoiling.
Ferdail, divide.
Ferdaila, dividing.
Ferdailung, division.
Ferdeen, earn.
Ferdeened, earned.
Ferdeena, earning.

Ferdeensht, earnings.
Ferdomt, damned.
Ferdomma, to damn.
Ferdorwa, spoiled.
Ferdow, digest.
Ferdowa, digesting.
Ferdowung, digestion.
Ferdoonkel, darken.
Ferdoonkelt, benighted
Ferdroos, affront.
Ferella, trout.
Ferenner, alter, change
Ferennera, changing,
altering.
Ferennered, changed,
altered.
Ferennerung, altera-
tion.
Ferennerlich, changa-
ble.
Ferfalsh, debase.
Ferfeer, seduce, mis-
lead.
Ferfeera, seduction.
Ferfelsh, falsify, adul-
terate.
Ferfelsha, falsifying,
adulterating.
Ferfelshung, adultera-
tion, falsification.
Ferfleck, blot.
Ferflecked, bloted, dotted
Ferflooch, accurse.
Ferfloocha, accursing.
Ferflooched, accursed.
Ferfolla, due.
Ferfowl, rot.
Ferfowla, rotting.
Ferfowled, rotten.
Fergæ, evaporate.
Fergeb, forgive.

Fergonga, past, gone.
Fergess, forget.
Fergessa, forgotten. foretting.
Fergleich, compare.
Fergleicha, comparing, contrasting.
Fergresser, magnify, enlarge.
Fergressera, magnifying, enlarging.
Fergressered, enlarged, magnified.
Ferheeta, avoiding.
Ferhex, bewitch.
Ferhexa, bewitching.
Ferhinner, hinder.
Ferhinnera, hindering.
Ferhinnerd, hindered.
Ferhofta, apprehending.
Ferhoftung, apprehension.
Ferhoongera, starving.
Ferhoongert, starved.
Ferhootled, tangled.
Ferhootla, tangling.
Ferkawf, sale, sell.
Ferkawfa, selling.
Ferkawfd, sold.
Ferkartza, shortening, curtailed.
Ferclaid, disguised.
Ferlaigna, denying.
Ferlaiga, mislaying.
Ferlaig'd, mislaid.
Ferleebt, fond, amerous.
Ferleera, losing.
Ferlora, lost.
Ferlenger, lengthen.

Ferlengera, lengthening.
Ferlengered, lengthened.
Ferletz, injure.
Ferletza, injuring.
Ferleicht, perhaps.
Ferleshter, defame.
Ferleshtera, defaming.
Ferleichta, lighten.
Ferlong, desire, crave.
Ferlonga, craving, desiring.
Ferloomp'd, ragged.
Ferloompa, delapidating.
Ferloosht, loss.
Ferlora, astray, lost.
Ferluffa, astray.
Ferluss, rely, forsake, depend.
Ferlussa, relying, forsaking, depending.
Fermaiga, property.
Fermara, augment, increase.
Fermaucha, bequeath.
Fermoota, presuming.
Fermixa, blend, mix.
Fermichta, annulling.
Fernochlussa, neglecting.
Ferordna, enacting,
Ferposst, overlooked, neglected.
Ferraiter, betrayer.
Ferricht, accomplished
Ferricked, deranged.
Ferricka, deranging.
Ferrisa, tearing.
Ferrissa, torn.
Ferroontzelt, wrinkled.
Ferrote, betray.

Ferrota, betraying.
Ferrusht, corrode, rust
Fersicher, assure.
Fershenner, beautify.
Fershennera, beautify-
ing.
Fersheedlich, varied.
Fersheia, abhor.
Fershmeer, besmear.
Fershmeera, besmear-
ing.
Fershoffa, providing.
Fershtendich, sensible.
Fershtond, sense.
Fershtella, disguising,
feigning.
Fershtick, smother,
choke.
Fershticka, smothering
Fershtara, disturbing.
Fershtared, disturbed.
Fershtorwena, deceased.
Fershitt, spill.
Fershitta, spilling.
Fershpowa, bespiting.
Fershpow, bespit.
Fershprech, promise.
Fershprecha, promis-
ing.
Fershprucha, promised.
Fershpritzed, bespat-
tered.
Fershpring, burst.
Fershpringa, bursting.
Fershproonga, bursted
Fershreck, fright.
Fershrecka, frighten.
Fershrucka, frightened
Fershtarrick, strengthen
Fershtaricka, strength-
ening.

Fershteckle, hide, con-
ceal.
Fershteckla, hiding,
concealing.
Fershteckled, hidden,
concealed.
Fershtup'd, costive.
Fershtond, sense.
Fershtendich, sensible.
Fershwara, conspiring,
conjuring.
Fershwenda, dissipat-
ing, spending.
Fershwinna, vanishing
Fershwecha, weaken-
ing
Fershwoppa, swapped.
Fersichered, assured.
Fersommel, assemble.
Fersomla, assembling.
Fersomlung, assembly.
Fersooch, taste.
Fersoocha, tasting.
Fersowfa, drowning.
Fersuffa, drowned.
Fertrowa, entrusting.
Fertzaira, to consume.
Fertzaila, relating, tell-
ing.
Fertzailed, related, told
Fertzoga, warped.
Fertzeega, warping.
Fertzawgt, timid, afraid
Ferunglicked, failure.
Feruresauch'd, caused.
Ferwass, why
Ferwært, deranged.
Faewærra, confound-
ing.
Ferwarfa, reject.
Ferwelka, wither.

Ferwexeld, exchanged.
Ferwexlung, alteration
Ferwcesht, devastate.
Ferwickle, involve.
Ferwickla, involving.
Ferwillich, consent.
Ferwillicha, consenting.
Ferwooner, astonish.
Ferwoonera, astonishing.
Ferwoonered, astonished.
Ferwonta, relative.
Fesser, tubs.
Fessly, keg.
Fesht, fast, tight, festival.
Feshticha, fastening.
Fet, fat.
Fettich, fatty.
Fever, fever.
Figoor, figure.
Fill, fill, colt.
Filla, filling.
File, file.
Fila, filing.
Filsel, stuffing.
Fin, find.
Finna, finding.
Fine, fine.
Finey, fine.
Finger, finger.
Finger-hoot, thimble.
Finf, five.
Finft, fifth.
Finish, finish.
Finisha, finishing.
Finner, finder.
Finshter, dark.
Finshterniss, eclipse.

Fira, firing, celebrating
Fire, fire.
Fire-dawg, holliday.
Fire-warrick, fireworks
Fire-hard, fire hearth.
Firemon, fireman.
Fish, fish.
Fisha, fishing.
Fish-gad, fishing rod.
Fish-line, fish-line.
Fish-hoka, fish-hook.
Fit, fit.
Fix, fix.
Fixa, fixing.
Fixter, fixture.
Flaish, meat.
Flaishich, fleshy.
Flatter, flatter.
Flauch, flat.
Fleck, spot.
Flecka, spot, blur.
Fleega, flying.
Fleesa, floating.
Fleis, industry.
Fleisich, industrious.
Flick, mend.
Flicka, mending.
Fliggle, wing.
Flint, gun.
Flooch, curse.
Floocha, cursing.
Floos, flood, flux.
Floocht, escape.
Flo, flea.
Flourish, flourish.
Flox, flax.
Fodder, father.
Fogle, bird.
Fol, fall, trap, case.
Folla, falling.
Folta, fold.

Folter, bars.
Fomelia, family.
Fonga, catch.
Fooftzain, fifteen.
Fooftzaint, fifteenth.
Fooftzich, fifty.
Fooftzichsht, fiftieth.
Foonka, spark.
Foor, team.
Foor-gaishel, cart whip
Foormon, teamster.
Foor-warrick, vehicle.
Foos, foot.
Foos-bawd, foot-bath.
Footer, food, fodder.
Foox, fox.
For, for.
Forb, paint, color.
Forbeed, forbid.
Forbeeda, forbidding.
Fordt, away.
Forderhond, before-
hand.
Fordle, advantage.
Fore, appears, seems,
fore.
Forebringa, bring forth
Forecooma, emerge.
Fore-eltra, ancestors.
Fore-fol, event.
Foregroond, foreground.
Forehong, curtain.
Foremon, foreman.
Fore-ous, advance.
Fore-roat, hoard.
Foresawga, foretell.
Foresicht, foresight.
Foresichtich, discrete.
Foreshmeisa, casting
it up.
Fore-shtoob, ante room

Foreshtellung, imagi-
nation.
Foretrefflich, excellent
surpassing.
Foretzeega, prefering.
Foretzoog, preference.
Forfit, forfeit.
Forge, forge.
Forhar, before.
Forma, forming.
Formiddawg, forenoon
Forna, front, afore.
Forness, furnace.
Fornish, furnish.
Fornisha, furnishing.
Forrich, furrow.
Fortshritt, progress.
Fortmaucha, continue.
Fortune, fortune.
Forwarts, forward.
Foss, tub, cask.
Fowl, rot, lazy.
Fowla, rotting.
Fowlenser, drone, slug-
gard.
Fowlheit, laziness.
Fowsht, fist.
Fracture, fracture.
Fraida, joy.
Frama, framing.
Frame, frame.
Fraw, wife.
Free, early.
Freedlich, peacable.
Freer, freeze.
Freera, freezing.
Fremmer, stranger.
Fressdeer, glutton.
Freiheit, freedom.
Friend, friend.
Freindlich, friendly.

Freindshoft, relative, relation.
Fri-gevva, discharged.
Fri, free.
Fridawg, friday.
Friction, friction.
Frish, fresh.
Fro, glad.
Frock, frock.
Froke, ask, question.
Froka, asking.
Frolic, frolic.
Froocht, grain.
Froochtbawr, fruitful.
Frusht, frost.
Frush, frog.
Frumm, pious.

Fudder, demand, ask.
Fuddera, demanding, asking.
Fuftzain, fifteen.
Fuftzich, fifty.
Fun, if, from.
Fundament, fundament.
Fund, fund.
Fum, off, from.
Ful, full.
Fullens, in full.
Fulga, follow.
Fulgende, following.
Fulmaucht, authority.
Fulk, people.

G,

Gæ, go.
Gæd, going.
Gæ-lussa, let go.
Gabailed, bailed.
Gabaid, prayer.
Gabi, building.
Gabiss, bit.
Gabish, bush.
Gablamed, blamed.
Gablivva, remained.
Gabloot, bled.
Gaboga, bent.
Gabored, bored.
Gabootzt, cleansed.
Gaboort, birth.
Gabowt, built.
Gabounced, bounced.
Gaboxed, boxed.
Gabreed, scalded, hatched
Gabribed, bribed.

Gabrauch, accustom.
Gabroomel, low murmuring.
Gabrucht, brought.
Gabut, bid.
Gabutta, beaten.
Gaboona, bound.
Gacharged, charged.
Gachartered, chartered
Gachoked, choked.
Gachoosed, chosen.
Gacured, cured.
Gaelaimed, claimed.
Gacleared, cleared.
Gacoaxed, coaxed.
Gacowd, chewed.
Gacracked, cracked.
Gadecked, covered.
Gadechtniss, memory.
Gadeened, served.

Gadingta, hireling.
Gadonka, thoughts.
Gadonked, thanked.
Gadoold, patience.
Gadraid, turned.
Gadrawmed, dreamed.
Gadroonka, drank.
Gafolla, fallen.
Gaglicha, liked.
Gagrish, loud cry.
Gagooked, looked.
Gahaled, healed.
Gahame, mysterious.
Gahameniss, mystery.
Gaharn, brain.
Gahared, heard.
Gahired, married.
Gahile, howl.
Gahoresom, obedient.
Gahulfa, helped.
Gaiga, against.
Gaigner, adversary.
Gaigend, neighborhood
Gail, yellow.
Gakawft, bought.
Gakicked, kicked.
Gakuchd, cooked.
Gakutzed, puked.
Galaisa, read.
Galarnd, learned.
Galagenheit, opportu-
nity.
Galauched, laughed.
Galechter, laughter.
Galobe'd, praised.
Galuck'd, decoyed.
Galuffa, walked.
Game, game.
Gamawla, ground, (in
mill.)
Gamla, gambling.

Gamler, gambler.
Gamees, vegetables.
Gameet, mood.
Gameinshoft, commu-
nity.
Gamooft, moved.
Ganeed, clinched.
Ganoonk, enough.
Ganooma, took, taken.
Gap, gap.
Gapaint, painted.
Gapardoned, pardoned
Gapeddled, peddled.
Gapitched, pitched.
Gapicked, picked.
Gapiffa, whistled.
Gapishpered, whispered.
Gaplonsed, planted.
Gapledged, pledged.
Gapolished, polished.
Gapreddichd, preached
Gaprooft, proven.
Gapublished, published
Gapushed, pushed.
Gapuzzled, puzzled.
Garaiched, reached.
Garaigert, rained.
Garaised, raised.
Garawbd, robbed.
Gardla, gardening.
Garia, rue.
Garisht, prepared.
Garecht, righteous.
Garegulate, regulated.
Gareid, rued.
Garent, rented.
Garing, petty trifling.
Garooch, oder, smell.
Garoofa, called.
Garver, tanner.
Garret, garret.

Gas, gas.
Gashenk, present.
Gashwetz, conversation
Gasing, sing.
Gatend, attended.
Gatraveled, traveled.
Gatrenk, beverage.
Gatri, faithful.
Gatzoga, moved, pulled
Gatzonk'd, scolded.
Gatzwoonga, compelled.
Gawalt, power.
Gawared, defended.
Gawaned, addicted.
Gaweltich, powerful.
Gawiss, certain.
Gawissa, conscience.
Gawrn, yarn.
Gawoga, weighed.
Gawohnt, resided, accustomed.
Gawohnheit, custom.
Gawora, worn.
Gaventered, ventured.
Gavote, voted.
G'act, acted.
G'answered, answered.
G'certified, certified.
G'failed, failed.
G'fairlich, dangerous.
G'farrabd, colored.
G'favored, favored.
G'fecht, combat.
G'fengniss, prison.
G'fired, commemorated.
G'fixed, fixed.
G'flicked, mended.
G'folla, favor, pleased.
G'fonga, caught.
G'fongner, prisoner.
G'foona, found.

G'fore, danger.
G'foona, found.
G'froked, asked.
G'fulkd, obeyed.
G'hulfa, assisted.
G'hara, belong.
G'hared, belonged.
G'hot, had.
G'loosht, lust.
G'looshtich, lusty.
G'loxeerd, purged.
G'managed, managed.
G'marched, marched.
G'raffled, raffled.
G'sawt, said.
G'safed, saved.
G'satisfied, satisfied.
G'sentenced, sentenced
G'setz, statue.
G'setzed, seated.
G'settled, settled.
G'shafed, shaved.
G'shared, shared.
G'sharr, tools.
G'sheft, vocation.
G'shenk, present.
G'shenked, presented.
G'shickd, sent, ingenious.
G'shired, scoured.
G'shleckd, licked.
G'shliffa, ground (stone
G'shlipt, slipped.
G'shlawga, struck.
G'shlofa, slept.
G'shlookd, swallowed.
G'shlussa, locked.
G'shmeerd, greased.
G'shmoked, smoked.
G'shmulsa, melted.
G'shnitzled, whittled.

G'shnorrixd, snored.
G'shnowfd, breathed.
G'shoolderd, shouldered.
G'showfeld, shoveled.
G'shoffd, worked.
G'shpawrd, saved.
G'shpeeld, played.
G'shpelld, spelled.
G'shpend, spent.
G'shpiked, spiked.
G'shpliced, spliced.
G'shplit, split.
G'shpraich, dialogue.
G'shpraid, spread.
G'shribe, writing.
G'shrivva, written.
G'shrowbd, screwed.
G'shtæ, acknowledge.
G'shtenk, stench.
G'shtrecked, stretched.
G'shtrained, strained.
G'shtritta, quarreled.
G'shtolt, form.
G'shtola, stolen.
G'shtonna, confessed.
G'shtoompt, bluffed.
G'shtucha, stabbed.
G'shtuddeert, studied.
G'shtupt, stopped, darned
G'shussa, shot.
G'shweer, boil.
G'shwetzd, conversed.
G'shwint, quick.
G'shwinter, quicker.
G'shwindsht, quickest.
G'shwindichkeit, celerity.
G'shwill, swell.
G'shwilla, swelling.
G'shwindled, swindled.
G'sicht, face, sight.

G'signed, signed.
G'soaked, soaked.
G'soond, healthy.
G'soondheit, health.
G'soocht, searched.
G'sookled, sucked.
G'soonga, sung.
G'suffa, drunk.
G'suffered, suffered.
G'used, used.
G'ward, waited.
G'ware, weapon.
G'warnd, warned.
G warrickd, choked.
G'watched, watched.
G'welb, vault, arch.
G'welbd, arched.
G'wesha, washed.
G'weckd, waked.
G'wex, tumor, growth.
G'winna, winning.
G'winshd, wished.
G'wisht, wiped.
G'wissa, shown, exhibited, conscience.
G'woonert, wondered.
G'wora, worn.
G'woxa, grown.
G'woxner, adult.
G'woona, won.
Geb, give.
Gebt, gives.
Gedonka, thought.
Gedu, done.
Gees, pour, cast.
Geesa, casting.
Gees-con, watering can
Geig, violin, fiddle.
Geiga, fiddling.
Geiger, fiddler.
Geisht, spirit.

Geishtlich, spiritual.
Geitz, avarice.
Geitz-hols, miser.
Geld, money.
Gelta, admitting.
Gemeinshoft, fellow-ship.
Gens, geese.
Geography, geography
Geshter, yesterday.
Gessa, guessing.
Gettlich, divine.
Getrei, faithful.
Gevva, giving, given.
Gewicht, weight.
Gicht, gout.
Gichtra, fits.
Givvel, gable.
Glawb, believe.
Glauwa, belief, faith.
Glaws, glass.
Gleed, limb.
Gleich, alike, equal.
Gleichheit, equality.
Gleichgiltich, uncon-cerned.
Glensich, brilliant.
Gli, immediately.
Glick, luck.
Glicklich, lucky.
Glons, brilliant.
Glot, smoothe.
Goll, gallon.
Golga, gallows.
Gol, bile.
Gons, goose, entire, whole.
Gong, passage, going.
Gonga, went, gone.
Gooka, looking.
Goot, good.

Goot-hartzich, benevo-lent, good-hearted.
Gor, done, entire.
Gorda, garden.
Gorn, yarn.
Gott, God.
Gottesdeensht, worship
Gottheit, divinity.
Gottlose, depraved.
Govvel, fork.
Gox, cackle.
Goxa, cackling.
Gowl, horse.
Gowntsh, swing.
Gowtz, bark.
Gowtza, barking.
Grab, grab.
Grabba, grabbing.
Grais, size.
Graiser, larger.
Graisht, largest.
Grammar, grammar.
Grauwa, gutter, ditch, digging.
Grausom, cruel.
Gravel, gravel.
Graver, digger.
Grawb, grave.
Grawd, straight, grade.
Graws, grass.
Graws-holm, grass-blade
Grawsich, grassy.
Gray-awg, corn.
Greega, getting.
Greeg, war.
Greesa, greeting.
Greish, bellow, shout, bawl.
Greisha, shouting.
Greislich, horrible.
Grens, border.

Gresser, larger.
Grexa, grunting.
Gride, chalk.
Griff, grasp.
Grick, grasp.
Grick, get.
Grickd, obtained, gotten.
Gro, grey.
Grobsh, grab.
Grobsha, grabbing.
Grose, large, great.
Groog, mug, pitcher.

Groomla, grumbling.
Groond, ground.
Groond-niss, groundnuts.
Groondlose, groundless
Groondshtick, messuage.
Groos, salute.
Groove, groove.
Grub, rough.
Grubheit, coarseness.
Guld, gold.
Guardeen, guardian.

H.

Hærr, lord.
Hærrshoft, lordship.
Haich, height.
Haicher, higher.
Haigsht, highest.
Haim, home.
Haimat, home.
Haimwai, homesick.
Hais, hot.
Haist, named, called.
Haisher, hoarse.
Hale, heal, hollow.
Hala, healing.
Halung, hollow, cave.
Hall, hall.
Halt, hold, halt.
Handla, handling.
Handle, handle.
Handy, handy.
Har, here.
Hara, hearing.
Hare, hear.
Hared, hears.
Harbsht, autumn.

Hardship, hardship.
Harrlich, happy.
Harrlichkelt, happiness.
Harrshtom, ancestry.
Hartz, heart.
Hartzlich, hearty.
Hatchet, hatchet.
Hawwer, oats.
Hawa, have.
Hawgle, hail.
Haws, rabbit.
Hawsa, rabbits.
Hawna, cock.
Hawpt, principal.
Hawptsechlich, mainly
Hecka, brushwood.
Hee, down, hence, there.
Heeta, watching.
Heffa, crocks.
Heft, hilt.
Heichler, hypocrite.
Heichelei, hypocricy.

Heida, heathen.
Heidish, heathenish.
Heifla, heaping up.
Heil, weep.
Heila, weeping.
Heilich, sacred.
Heilond, Savior.
Helf, help.
Helfa, helping.
Helfer, helper.
Helft, half.
Hell, bright, hell.
Hem, shirt.
Hen, hob.
Hend, hands.
Hendich, handy.
Hendshing, gloves.
Hengsht, stallion.
Henk, hang.
Henka, hanging.
Henker, hangman.
Hesitata, hesitating.
Hesslich, hateful.
Hevvel, club.
Hex, witch.
Hexeri, witchcraft.
Hickle, limp.
Hickla, limping.
Heifich, copious.
Hift, hip.
Hilf, help.
Hilflose, helpless.
Himmel, Heaven.
Himmelish, heavenly.
Hinna, back, behind.
Hinner, behind.
Hinnera, hinder.
Hinkle, hen.
Hinkle-nesht, hen nest
Hinnerlich, backward.
Hinnersht, hindmost.

Hitz, heat.
Hira, marry.
Hirawt, marriage.
Heiser, houses.
History, history.
Hit, cot.
Hoax, hoax.
Hoaxa, hoaxing.
Hoch, high.
Hoch-deitsh, german.
Hoch-moot, pride.
Hoch-meetich, proud.
Hoch-shtond, eminence.
Hoch-shtendich, emi-
    nent.
Hob, had, have.
Hock, hoe, chop.
Hocka, hoing, chop-
    ping.
Hoffa, crock, pot.
Hofe, yard.
Hoka, hook.
Holb, half.
Holb-waig, half way.
Hole, hollow.
Holewaig, defile.
Holfter, halter.
Hols, throat, neck.
Holsdooch, cravat.
Holwer, half.
Holwer-dawler, h a l f-
    dollar.
Hommer, hammer.
Hommel, wether.
Hond, hand.
Hond-dooch, towel.
Hond ful, hand-full.
Hondle, trade.
Hondlung, doings, bus-
    iness.
Hond-beck, basin.

Hond-saig, hand-saw.
Hondwærk, trade.
Hond-wærklich, mechanism.
Hondwærksmon, mechanic.
Honswarsht, clown.
Hoof, hoof.
Hoofeisa, horseshoe.
Hoomel, bumble-bee.
Hoonnert, hundred.
Hoonnerdsht, hundredth
Hoond, dog.
Hoondly, pup.
Hoondish, dogish.
Hoonger, hunger.
Hoongera, hungering.
Hoongerich, hungry.
Hoops, hop.
Hoopsa, hopping.
Hooshta, coughing, cough.
Hootchelly, colt.
Hoot, hat.
Hootzela, dried peaches.
Hord, hard.
Hore, hair.
Horich, hairy.
Horf, harp.
Horn, horn.
Hornasle, hornet.
Horning, february.
Hos, hate.
Hossa, hating.
Hosler, ostler.
Hoshpittle, hospital.

House, house.
Houseuhr, house clock
House-rote, furniture.
House-deer, front door
House-shtire, wedding present.
Howfa, heap, pile.
Howt, skin.
Hoxet, hogshead.
Hoy, hay.
Hoy-govvel, hay fork.
Hoy-maucha, haymaking.
Huchtzich, wedding.
Huck, sit, squat.
Hucka, sitting, squatting.
Huckshter, huckster.
Huckshtera, huckstering.
Huff, hope.
Huffa, hoping.
Huffnung, hope.
Hulderbara, elderberries.
Huls, wood.
Hulsich, wooden.
Huls-coala, charcoal.
Huls-saig, wood-saw.
Hurry, hurry.
Hurrya, hurrying.
Hussa, pants.
Huvvel, plane.
Huvvel-bonk, workbench.
Huvvel-isa, plane-bit.

I.

Ich, I. | Ice, ice.

Ifer, ardor.
Illegal, illegal.
Imitata, imitating.
Immer, always, evermore.
Impression, impression
Impressa, impressing.
Impose, impose.
Imposa, imposing.
Improof, improve.
Improofa, improving.
Improofment, improvement.
Import, import.
Importa, importing.
In, in.
Inactif, inactive.
Inauguration, inauguration.
Incorporation, incorporation.
Inconsistent, inconsistent.
Include, include.
Indecent, indecent.
Independent, independent.
Indirect, indirect.
Index, index.
Initiate, initiate.
Initiata, initiating.
Initiation, initiation.
Innerlich, inward.
Inflata, inflating.
Influence, influence.
Influensa, influencing.
Influential, influential.
Inflama, inflaming,
Inflamation, inflamation.
Ingenuity, ingenuity.

Intention, intention.
Intend, intend.
Intenda, intending.
Interfere, interfere.
Interfera, interfering.
Interest, interest.
Intresseerd, interested.
Introdusa, introducing.
Insel, island.
Insist, insist.
Insista, insisting.
Insinuate, insinuate.
Insinuata, insinuating.
Insh, indian.
Insha, indians.
Inshlich, tallow.
Inshlich-licht, tallow-candle.
Inshpect, inspect.
Inshpecta, inspecting.
Inshpector, inspector.
Inshtrument, instrument.
Inshtruct, instruct.
Inshtructor, instructor
Institute, institute.
Insure, insure.
Insura, insuring.
Insurance, insurance.
Insult, insult.
Insulta, insulting.
Invent, invent.
Inventa, inventing.
Invention, invention.
Inventory, inventory.
Invesht, invest.
Inveshta, investing.
Investigate, investigate
Investigata, investigating.
Isa, iron.

Isa-hoffa, cooking pot.
Isa-wærk, iron works.
Isa-artz, iron ore.
Issue, issue.
Itemiza, itemizing.
Ivver, over, above.
Ivver-charge, overcharge
Ivver-cooma, overcome.
Ivver-du, overdue.
Ivver-floos, abound.
Ivver-gooka, overlook-
ing.
Ivverich, over.
Ivverlaiga, delibera-
ting.
Ivverlaigt, considered.
Ivverlaiva, outliving.
Ivverlussa, abandon.

Ivvernooma, overtak-
ing.
Ivvernumma, overtaken.
Ivver-ruck, overcoat.
Ivver-rula, over ruling.
Ivver-sæ, over see.
Ivver-sær, overseer.
Ivversetz, translate.
Ivversetza, translating.
Ivversetzer, translator.
Ivversetzed, translated.
Ivversetzung, transla-
tion.
Ivvertreffa, surpassing.
Ivvertzwærrich, cross-
ways.
Ivverwelma, overwhelm.

J.

Jail, jail.
Jealous, jealous.
Jig, jig.
Jigger, dram.
Jobba, jobbing.
Jobber, jobber.
Joina, joining.
Jointa, jointing.
Joke, joke.
Joka, joking.

Joomp, jump.
Joompa, jumping.
Journal, journal.
Judge, judge.
Judgment, judgment.
Jury, jury.
Jurymon, juror.
Justice, justice.
Justify, justify.

K.

Kæ, no, none.
Kais, cheese.
Kalt, cold.
Kalt-shtick, lunch,
Kara, sweeping.

Kare, sweep.
Karich-blech, dusting-
pan.
Karl, fellow.
Karbs, pumpkin.

Karbsa-pie, pumpkin-pie
Karper, body.
Karrich, church.
Karsh, cherry.
Karsha, cherries.
Karsha-pie, cherry pie.
Kartza, shorten.
Kartzlich, lately, shortly.
Kawf, buy.
Kawfa, buying.
Kawfer, purchaser.
Kee, cows.
Keefer, cooper.
Keel, cool.
Keeler, cooler.
Keela, cooling.
Keen, chin.
Keenbocka, jaw.
Keeper, keeper.
Keffer, bug.
Keller, cellar.
Keller-deer, cellar door.
Kelter, colder.
Keitle, wedge.
Ken, none.
Kenn, know.
Kenna, can.
Kenner, none.
Kent, could.
Kesht, chestnut.
Keshta, chestnuts.
Keshta-baum, chestnut tree.
Keshtlich, costly.
Kessel, kettle.
Ket, chain.
Ketta chains.
Kevvich, cage.
Kich, kitchen.
Kicha-dish, kitchen-table.

Kicka, kicking.
Kimmera, grieving.
Kinner, children.
Kint, child.
Kintish, childish, babyish.
Kinshtler, artist.
Kinshtlich, ingenious, artificial.
Kisht, chest.
Kissa, pillow.
Kivvel, bucket.
Klæ, small.
Klænes, little one.
Klænichkeit, trifle.
Kling, blade.
Klia, bran.
Klufter, cord.
Klufter-huls, cord wood.
Klup, knock.
Kluppa, hammering.
Klutz, log, block.
K'nechel, ancle.
K'nee, knee.
K'nep, buttons.
K'noatcha, to fondle.
K'nop, scant.
K'nucha, bone.
K'nup, button.
Knuvveloch, garlic.
Kommer, bed chamber
Koocha, cake.
Koogle, bullet.
Koonda, customer.
Koondshoft, custom.
Koonsht, craft, art.
Koos, kiss.
Korb, basket.
Korbful, basket full.
Korn, rye.
Kortz, short.

Kraut, cabbage.
Kreftich, vigorous.
Kreish, cry.
Kreisha, crying.
Kreiter, herbs.
Kreitz, cross.
Kreitzich, crucify.
Kretz, itch.
Krenklich, sickly.
Krick, crutch.
Kritzel, scrawl.
Kritzla, scrawling.
Kronk, sick.
Kronka, patients.
Kronkheit, sickness.
Kroom, crooked.
Kroog, jug.

Krootza, cob, core.
Krut, toad.
Ku, cow.
Ku-shtall, cow stable.
Kuch, cook, boil.
Kucha, cooking, boiling.
Kuch-uffa, cooking-stove.
Kup, head.
Kup-wai, headache.
Kusht, cost.
Kushta, costing.
Kusht, boarding, diet.
Kusht-genger, boarder.
Kutz, vomit.
Kutza, vomiting.

L.

Labe, live.
Labe'd, lives.
Labehoft, enlivening.
Lader, ladder.
Lady, lady.
Laib, lion.
Laid, regret.
Laiga, laying.
Laigna, denying.
Lain, loan, borrow.
Lainer, lender.
Lais, read.
Laisa, reading.
Lane, lane.
Landing, landing.
Lappa, lapping.
Lare, empty.
Larram, alarm.
Larmich, noisy.
Larn, learn.

Larna, to learn.
Larnung, learning.
Larrich, lark.
Lash, lash.
Lasha, lashing.
Latch, latch.
Lauch, laugh.
Laucha, laughing.
Laug, lye.
Launch, launch.
Lauera, watching, to waylay.
Lava, living.
Lavas-mittle, eatables.
Law, law.
Lawda, loading, shutter.
Lawd-shtecka, ramrod.
Lawf, walk.
Lawfa, walking, flowing.

Lawfer, walker.
Lawful, lawful,
La-wendich, alive.
Lawm, lame.
Lawsuit, lawsuit.
Lawyer, lawyer.
Lead, lead.
Leada, leading.
Leader, leader.
Leb-koocha, ginger cake.
Lecherlich, laughable.
Lecture, lecture.
Ledder, leather, flog.
Leddera, flogging.
Leddich, unmarried.
Leeb, dear, love.
Leebsht, dearest.
Leed, hymn.
Leeder, hymns.
Leeg, lie.
Leega, lying.
Leever, rather.
Leffle, spoon.
Legal, legal.
Legislata, legislating.
Lehr, doctrine.
Leib, belly, abdomen.
Leich, corpse.
Leicht, light, easy.
Leichtsinn, frivolous.
Leid, suffer.
Leida, suffering.
Leinich, linen.
Leit, people, folks.
Leshtera, abusing.
Lesha, extinguish.
Lesson, lesson.
Letsht, last.
Letz, wrong.
Level, level.
Levela, leveling.

Levendich, alive.
Le-ver, rather.
Levvich, alive.
Levver, liver.
Levver-warsht, pudding
Liable, liable.
Liability, liability.
Liberal, liberal.
Library, library.
Lice, lice.
Licht, candle, light.
Lichter, candles.
Lichter-shtuck, candle-
    stick.
License, license.
Lidderlich, indolent.
Liffer, deliver.
Liffera, delivering.
Lift, lift.
Lifta, lifting.
Lifta, ventilating.
Ligga, lying down.
Ligner, liar.
Likeness, likeness.
Lime, glue.
Limit, limit.
Limitation, limitation.
Line, line.
Lining, lining.
Lip, lip.
Lisht, list.
Literature, literature.
Living, living.
Lively, lively.
Lo, tan.
Load, load.
Loafer, loafer.
Loan, loan.
Lobe, praise.
Lobberei, nonsense.
Lobbich, silly.

Locus, locust.
Locata, locating.
Location, location.
Locomotif, locomotive.
Loddarn, lantern.
Lodge, lodge.
Lodga, to lodge.
Lodging, lodging.
Lodger, lodger.
Lodinish, latin.
Lodwærrick, applebutter.
Logic, logic.
Lohn, wages.
Lom, lamb.
Lomp, lamp.
Lommel, boor.
Lond. soil, land.
Lond-laifer, tramp.
Lond-messer, surveyor
Lonesome, lonesome.
Long, long.
Longa, reaching, handing.
Longsom, slow.
Looft, air, atmosphere.
Looftich, airy.
Loomerich, limber.

Loompa, rags.
Loompa-carpet, rag-carpet.
Loompich, ragged.
Loosht, humor.
Looshtich, jolly.
Lootzer, lantern.
Lose, sow.
Lose, loose, rid.
Losht, burden.
Lotta, lathes.
Loud, loud
Louse, louse.
Lova, praising.
Loxeer, purge.
Loxeera, purging.
Loxeerd, purged.
Luch, hole.
Luck, call, decoy.
Lucka, decoying.
Ludderish, lutheran.
Luff, love.
Luff-letters, love letters
Luss, let.
Lussa, letting.
Lust, lets.
Lut, lot.
Lutteree, lottery.

M.

Mærr, mare.
Machine, machine.
Magazine, magazine.
Male, flour, meal.
Maltz, malt.
Mai, more.
Maid, girls.
Maidle, girl, damsel.
Mail, mail.

Mainer, more.
Maintain, maintain.
Maintaina, maintaining.
Maishter, master.
Majority, majority.
Manage, manage.
Managa, managing.
Manager, manager.

Mane, mean.
Mana, meaning.
Manung, meaning.
Map, map.
March, march.
Marcha, marching.
Marder, murderer.
Marshtens, mostly.
Mareheit, majority.
Markwærdich, remarkable.
Martz, march.
Marrick, mark.
Marrosht, mud, slush.
Marshal, marshal.
Masle, chisel.
Match, match.
Matcha, matching.
Mauch, make.
Maucha, making.
Maucher, maker.
Mawd, maid.
Mawg, may.
Mawga, stomach.
Mawger, lean.
Mawl, grind.
Mawla, grinding.
May, mow.
Maya, mowing.
Mayor, mayor.
Mean, mean.
Measle, measle.
Mechtich, mighty.
Medadisht, methodist.
Meddla, meddling.
Meditzeen, medicine.
Meed, tired.
Meeldom, mill dam.
Meer, we.
Mer, we, us.
Meet, meet.

Meeting, meeting.
Melodee, melody.
Melone, melon.
Meng, multitude, herd.
Menlich, manful.
Menner, men.
Mensh, hnman being.
Mensha, people.
Mensht, most.
Mention, mention.
Mentiona, mentioning.
Mess, measure.
Messa, measuring.
Messer, knife.
Messerly, pocket knife.
Messias, Messiah.
Messing, brass.
Messung, measurement.
Mice, mice.
Mich, me.
Mid, middle.
Middawg, noon.
Middawg-essa, dinner.
Middlemaisich, middling.
Mile, mile.
Mileage, mileage.
Miller, miller,
Millich, milk.
Millich-hoffa, milk crock.
Milliner, milliner.
Militz, militia.
Mime, my own, mine.
Mine, mine.
Miner, mine, miner.
Mineral, mineral.
Minnut, minute.
Misbahafe, misbehave.
Mischief, mischief.
Mission, mission.
Missionary, missionary

Misht, manure.
Mistake, mistake.
Mistaken, mistaken.
Mistaka, mistaking.
Mistrow, mistrust.
Mistrowish, mistrust-
ful.
Mit, with, along.
Mitaina, embrace.
Mitdail, impart, partic-
ipate.
Mitdaila, participating.
Mittle, remedy, resource
Mitlida, compassion.
Mitwuch, Wednesday.
Mix, mix.
Mixa, mixing.
Mob, mob.
Mola, drawing.
Mollossich, molasses.
Mon, man.
Moonot, month.
Moonotlich, monthly.
Moondawg, Monday.
Mond, moon.
Mongle, want, need.
Monneer, manners.
Monneerlich, mannerly.
Monnisht, Menonite.
Monkey, monkey.
Monopoly, monopoly.
Montle, mantle.
Monument, monument.
Moof, move, remove.
Moofa, moving.
Moofment, movement.
Mook, fly.
Mooka, flies.
Moot, pluck.
Mootlose, dejected.
Mooshter, pattern.

Mooter, mother.
Mord, murder.
Morda, murdering.
Mordbrenna, arson.
Morawlish, moral.
Mork, marraw.
Morkt, market.
Morter, morter.
Mortgage, mortgage.
Morya, tomorrow.
Morya-essa, breakfast.
Mose, measurement.
Mosht, mast.
Mot, faint.
Motif, motive.
Motion, motion,
Motrotz, matress.
Mouse, mouse.
Moulda, to mould.
Moulding, moulding.
Mower, wall.
Mowra, mason work.
Mowrer, mason.
Mower-shtæ, building-
stone.
Mowl, mouth.
Mowl-ful, mouthful.
Moy, May.
Mule, mule.
Multiply, multiply.
Multiplya, multiplying
Mush, mush.
Mush-male, corn meal.
Mushkawt, nutmeg.
Mushkitter, mosquito.
Musick, music.
Musicawlish, musical.
Musleen, muslin.
Moos, must.
My, my.

N.

Nai, sew.
Naia, sewing.
Naicher, nearer.
Naichera, approximate
Naigsht, next, near.
Naitz, thread,
Nager, negro.
Namelich, namely.
Namesake, namesake.
Nardlich, northward.
Narf, nerve.
Narfa, nerves.
Narrish, crazy.
Narryats, nowhere.
Natif, native.
National, national.
Naturalize, naturalize.
Naucht, night.
Naucht-essa, supper.
Naucht-mohl, sacrament.
Nauvel, navel.
Nava, aside.
Navanonner, abreast.
Navigate, navigate.
Navigation, navigation
Navigata, navigating.
Navy, navy.
Nay, no.
Nawma, name.
Nawra, nourishing.
Nawrung, nourishment.
Naws, nose.
Naws-lecher, nostrils.
Nechtlich, nightly.
Need, clinch.
Needa, clinching.
Neera, kidneys.

Negatif, negative.
Neggle, nails.
Negociate, negociate.
Negociata, negociating
Neid, spite.
Neidish, spiteful.
Neint, ninth.
Nem, take.
Nemma, taking.
Nemohls, never.
Nesht, nest, branches.
Neshter, nests.
Net, not, nor.
Netz, net.
Netzwærk, network.
Nevvel, fog, mist.
Ni, new, in, into.
Ni-ichkeit, news.
Ni-yohr, new year.
Nidder, low.
Nidderer, lower.
Niddersht, lowest.
Niddertrechtich, baseness.
Nick-nawma, nick-name
Nimmy, never.
Nimmermæ, nevermore.
Nine, nine.
Ninetzain, nineteen.
Ninetzich, ninety.
Ninetzaint, nineteenth.
Ninetzichsht, ninetieth
Niss, nits, nuts.
Nitzlich, useful.
Nivver, across, over.
Nix, nothing.
Nixnootzich, good for nothing.

Noat, seam.
Noatwendich, necessary.
Noatwendichkeit, necessity.
Nop, knob.
Noble, noble.
Noch, near, yet, after, nor.
Nochbershoft, neighborhood.
Noch-coomer, descendant.
Nochderhond, afterwards.
Nochfulg, ensue.
Nochgevva, yielding.
Nochlessich, careless.
Nochlussa, giving away
Nochlussing, abatement, slackening.
Nockich, naked.
Nocker, knocker.
Nodle, needle.
Noddeerlich, natural.
Noddoor, nature.
Nominate, nominate.
Nominata, nominating
Nomination, nomination.
Nonsense, nonsense.
Nonsuit, nonsuit.

Noof, up.
Nook, nod.
Nooma, just, only, well.
Noomer, number.
Noomera, numbering.
Nooner, down.
Noonertzu's, downward.
Noos, nut.
Nootza, benefit, advantage.
Nord, north.
Norr, fool.
Norrheit, folly.
Noss, wet.
Nosht, bough, limb.
Notary, notary.
Note, note.
Notice, notice.
Notify, notify.
Notifya, notifying.
Notified, notified.
Notion, notion.
Nous, out.
Nous-du, eject.
Now, now.
Nuckle, knuckle.
Nuffember, november.
Nuisance, nuisance.
Nurse, nurse.
Nursa, nursing.
Nursery, nursery.

O.

O, oh.
Oabsht, fruit.
Oasht, east.
Oashter, Easter.
Obbadaik, drug store.
Obbadaiker, druggist.

Obbadit, appetite.
Obdecka, unroof.
Obdonka, discard.
Obdritt, back-house.
Obfol, leavings.
Obgakartzed, abbreviated.

Obgatzoga, skinned.
Obganooma, decreased
Obgatzared, emaciated
Obgawaned, weaned.
Obgong, egress.
Obg'shoft, abolished.
Obg'shussa, faded.
Objecta, objecting.
Objection, objection.
Obkartza, abbreviating
Obkartzung, abbreviation.
Oblawda, unload.
Obnawm, decrease.
Obnemma, decreasing.
Obsarf, observe.
Obsarfa, observing.
Obsicht, object.
Obsheed, valediction.
Obshi, abhor, detest.
Obshilich, abhorrance.
Obshoffa, abolishing.
Obshrecka, scare off.
Obshtæ, abstain.
Obshtarta, starting off.
Obshtiga, dismounting.
Obshwara, abjure.
Obshwarung, abjuration.
Obsoloot, absolute.
Obtzeega, skinning.
Obtzoog, discount.
Obtzwinga, extorting.
Obwarda, attending.
Obwartung, attendance
Obweicha, deviating.
Obwenda, averting.
Ocker, acre.
Octover, october.
Odam, breath.
Odder, or.

Oder, artery.
Offenda, offending.
Offer, offer.
Offera, offering.
Office, office.
Officer, officer.
Official, official.
Ohr, ear.
Ohra-ring, ear-ring.
Ohnmechtich, fainting.
Ole, eel.
Ola, eels.
Oll, all.
Ollai, alone.
Ollainich, alone.
Oller, all.
Olmosa, alms.
Olmitnonner, altogether.
Olsfort, constant.
Olter, age.
Omanot, somewhere.
Ombose, anvil.
Omshel, robbin.
Omt, office.
On, on, to.
Onna, down, there.
Ongsht, fear.
Onner, other.
Onnersht, otherwise.
Onshtot, instead.
Ontwart, answer.
Operate, operate.
Operation, operation.
Opinion, opinion.
Opple, apple.
Oppose, oppose.
Opposa, opposing.
Opposition, opposition.
Oppushtle, apostle.
Order, order.
Ordera, ordering.

Ordlich, middling, tolerably.

Ordnung, order.

Organize, organize.

Organiza, organizing.

Organization, organization.

Organized, organized.

Originata, originating.

Origle, organ.

Origleshpeeler, organist.

Ormæ, army.

Ormer, pauper.

Ormoot, poverty.

Ornamenta, ornamenting

Orrick, very.

Orrich, ark.

Os, as, that.

Ose, carrion.

Ous, out.

Ousawrta, degenerating.

Ousbacka, backing out

Ousbatzawla, paying out.

Ousbrooch, outbreak.

Ousdaila, distributing.

Ousdriva, exterminating.

Ousfinna, ascertaining.

Ousfleesa, emitting.

Ousfloos, emission.

Ousgadailed, divided.

Ouskara, sweeping out

Ouslaisa, picking out.

Ouslava, out living.

Ouslender, foreigner.

Ouslendish, outlandish

Ouslond, foreign land.

Ouslifta, ventilating.

Ousliftung, ventilation.

Ousgawb, expenditure.

Ousga-awrt, degenerated.

Ousgabreed, hatched out.

Ousgaholta, exempt.

Ousgaroofa, called out.

Ousg'foona, found out.

Ousg'shtorwa, died out

Ousmaucha, making out.

Ous-shpreada, spreading out.

Ous-shprecha, articulating.

Ous sicht, prospect.

Ouswendich, outside, by heart.

Ounce, ounce.

Owet, evening.

Ox, axe.

Oxle, axle.

Oy, egg.

Oyer, eggs.

Oyster, oyster.

P.

Pafement, pavement.

Page, page.

Paint, paint.

Painter, painter.

Painta, painting.

Parade, parade.

Pardone, pardon.
Pardona, pardoning.
Pardoned, pardoned.
Parfect, perfect.
Parfecta, perfecting.
Parfection, perfection.
Parform, perform.
Parforma, performing.
Parformer, performer.
Parlor, parlor.
Parshing, peaches.
Parsanelich, personal.
Parsone, person.
Partition, partition.
Party, party.
Passa, passing.
Passage, passage.
Passenger, passenger.
Paste, paste.
Pawd, path.
Pawr, pair.
Peddle, peddle.
Pedla, pedling.
Pedler, pedler.
Peepa, peeping.
Peffer, pepper.
Peffera, peppering.
Pen, fedder, pen, shtall.
Pencil, pencil.
Pesht, pest.
Peshter, pester.
Pet, pet.
Petition, petition.
Petitiona, petitioning.
Petz, pinch.
Petza, pinching.
Pew, pew.
Pie, pie.
Pick, pick.
Picka, picking.
Pickle, pickle.

Plcter, picture.
Picter frame, picture
　frame.
Pifa, whistling.
Pifer, piper, whistler.
Pile, arrow.
Pill, pill.
Pilla, pills.
Pinklich, punctual.
Pint, pint.
Pint-blech, tin cup.
Pishper, whisper.
Pishpera, whispering.
Pishtole, pistol.
Pitch, pitch.
Pitcha, pitching.
Platform, platform.
Plaudera, talking.
Plawn, plan.
Pleasa, pleasing.
Pledge, pledge.
Pledga, pledging.
Plenty, plenty.
Pleshter, plaster.
Pleshtera, plastering.
Pleshterer, plasterer.
Plesseer, pleasure.
Plesseera, pleasing.
Plesseerlich, pleasant.
Pletch, spank.
Pletcha, spanking.
Pletz, places.
Pletzlich, abrupt, sud-
　den.
Ploga, pester.
Plonk, plank.
Plons, plant.
Plonsa, planting.
Ploog, plow.
Plooga, plowing.
Ploshter, salve, plaster.

Plontawsh, plantation.
Plotz, place.
Plowm, plum.
Poetry, poetry.
Pock, pack.
Pocka, packing, wrestling.
Po-hawna, peacock.
Poke, poke.
Poka, poking.
Policy, policy.
Polish, polish.
Polisha, polishing.
Polite, polite.
Ponhaws, scrapple.
Pon, pan.
Pony, pony.
Ponna-koocha, pancake.
Poonkt, period.
Poont, pound.
Poolse, pulse,
Popular, popular.
Porpas, purpose.
Porra, preacher, minister.
Porraleit, clergy.
Porrashriftlich, clerical
Portrait, portrait.
Postpone, postpone.
Postpona, postponing.
Postponed, postponed.
Prawl, brag.
Prawla, bragging.
Prawler, bragger.
Practice, practice.
Preddich, preach.
Preddicha, preaching.
Preddicher, preacher.
Prepare, prepare.
Prepara, preparing.

Prepared, prepared.
Prentis, apprentice.
Presarf, preserve.
Presarfa, preserving.
Presarfd, preserved.
Price, price.
Prisoner, prisoner.
Principle, principle.
Proclaima, proclaiming.
Proclamation, proclamation.
Proceeda, proceeding.
Production, production.
Produsa, producing.
Professa, professing.
Professor, professor.
Promota, promoting.
Promotion, promotion.
Proof, proof.
Proofa, proving.
Propose, propose.
Proposa, proposing.
Proposition, proposition.
Prophait, prophet.
Prosecuta, prosecuting
Prosecution, prosecution.
Prosecutor, prosecutor
Protecta, protecting.
Protesht, protest.
Proteshta, protesting.
Proteshtond, protestant.
Proweer, try.
Proweera, trying.
Proweerd, tried.
Provida, providing.
Public, public.
Publish, publish.

Publisha, publishing.
Publisher, publisher.
Puffa, puffing.
Pulfer, powder.
Punch, punch.
Puncha, punching.
Punctuata, punctuating.

Push, push.
Pusha, pushing.
Pusher, pusher.
Pushta, post.
Pushtoor, posture.
Puzzle, puzzla, puzzling

Q.

Quack, quack.
Quail, vex.
Quaila, vexing.
Quality, quality.
Quantity, quantity.
Quart, quart.

Quartz, quartz.
Quell, well, spring.
Quetch, crush.
Quetcha, crushing.
Quitta, quinces.
Quittung, acquittance.

R.

Race, race.
Race-shpringa, race running.
Race-gowl, race horse.
Raffle, raffle.
Raffla, raffling.
Raft, raft.
Rafta, rafting.
Raich, reach.
Raicha, reaching.
Raif, hoop.
Raiga, rain.
Raigna, raining.
Raiga-boga, rainbow.
Raiga-wasser, rain water
Raiga-wetter, rainy weather.
Raigle, rule.
Raiglemasich, formal.
Railing, railing.

Railroad, railroad.
Rais, journey.
Raise, raise.
Raisa, raising.
Raitsel, riddle.
Rale, real
Rally, rally.
Rank, rank.
Range, range.
Rap, rap.
Rappa, rapping.
Ranka, ranking.
Rascal, rascal.
Raseen, raisin.
Rate, rate.
Ratify, ratify.
Ratifya, ratifying.
Ratification, ratification.
Ragle, rule.

Raglemasich, regular.
Rawb, rob.
Rawver, robber.
Rawva, robbing.
Rawm, cream.
Rawd, wheel.
Ravish, ravish.
Ravisha, ravishing.
Ready, ready.
Ream, ream.
Recha, rake, raking.
Rechna, cyphering.
Rechnung, account.
Recht, right.
Rechta, rights.
Rechenbooch, a r i t h -
  metic.
Rechtsmasich, rightful
Rechtshtella, vindicate
Recite, recite.
Recita, reciting.
Recollecta, recollect-
  ing.
Recommendation, r e -
  commendation.
Recommenda, recom-
  mending.
Reconsila, reconciling.
Recorda, recording.
Recorder, recorder.
Recovera, recovering.
Redder, wheels.
Redeem, redeem.
Redeema, redeeming.
Redeemed, redeemed.
Redusa, reducing.
Reeb, turnip.
Reecha, smelling.
Reeva, turnips.
Reff, rack.
Reflector, reflector.

Reform, reform.
Reforma, reforming.
Reformeerd, reformed.
Regular, regular.
Regulata, regulating.
Regulation, regulation.
Regulator, regulator.
Regeerung, g o v e r n -
  ment.
Regeera, governing.
Register, register.
Reich, rich.
Reichtume, wealth.
Rejoisa, rejoicing.
Release, release.
Releasa, releasing.
Released, released.
Relichione, religion.
Remoof, remove.
Remoofa, removing.
Remoof'd, removed.
Renewa, renewing.
Rent, rent.
Renta, renting.
Repeal, repeal.
Repeala, repealing.
Repealed, repealed.
Report, report.
Reporta, reporting.
Reporter, reporter.
Republic, republic.
Republicawner, repub-
  lican.
Reshpect, respect.
Reshpecta, respecting.
Reshpectable, respect-
  able.
Resolf, resolve.
Resolfa, resolving.
Resolution, resolution.
Resign, resign.

Resigna, resigning.
Resignation, resignation.
Retcha, back-biting.
Retcher, back-biter.
Retail, retail.
Retaila, retailing.
Retreata, retreating.
Reviva, reviving.
Revival, revival.
Revolver, revolver.
Revolva, revolving.
Revolution, revolution
Revver, river.
Reward, reward.
Rewarda, rewarding.
Ri, in, here.
Rib, rib.
Ribba, ribs.
Rice, rice.
Richtich, correct.
Rick, back.
Ricka, backing.
Rickwards, backward.
Rickstond, arrears.
Rida, riding.
Ride, ride.
Rig, rig.
Rigga, rigging.
Riggle, rail.
Riggle-waig, railway.
Rilps, belch.
Rilpsa, belching.
Rime, rhyme.
Rima, rhyming.
Rin, leak.
Rinna, leaking.
Ring, ring.
Ringa, ringing.
Rings-room, all round.
Risht, prepare.

Rishta, preparing.
Rint, heifer.
Rints-fee, cattle.
Rintsflaish, beef.
Riot, riot.
Risk, risk.
Riska, risking.
Rissate, receipt.
Ro, raw.
Road, red.
Roasht, roast.
Roat, counsel, guess.
Roata, guessing, counseling.
Roatsom, advisable.
Rohr, pipe.
Ronft, brim.
Rooder, rudder.
Roof, call.
Roofa, calling.
Roomatis, rheumatism
Roond, round.
Roontzel, wrinkle.
Roor, dysentary.
Rootch, crawl, creep.
Rootcha, crawling, creeping.
Ropple, rattle.
Roppla, rattling.
Rose, rose.
Rosa, roses.
Rosa-shtuck, rose bush.
Roshpel, rasp.
Roshpla, rasping.
Rounds, rounds, circuit.
Rous, emanate, out.
Roushend, rousing.
Rousher, rouser.
Ru, rest.
Rua, resting.

Ruf, up.
Ruich, easy, calm.
Ruineered, ruined.
Ruineera, ruining.
Ruck, coat.
Rula, ruling.
Rule, rule.
Ruler, ruler.
Rull, roll.
Rum, rum.

Run, run, brook.
Runly, brook.
Rup, pull.
Rups, muss, trouble.
Rush, rush.
Rusha, rushing.
Rusht, rust.
Rutz, snot.
Rutzich, snotty.
Rutznaws, snot-nose.

S.

Sæ, see, sea.
Sæl, soul.
Sælich, blissful.
Sælichkeit, salvation.
Sæga, blessing.
Sægna, to bless.
Safe, safe.
Safa, saving.
Saif, soap.
Saig, saw.
Saiga, sawing.
Sail, sail.
Saila, sailing.
Sailor, sailor.
Salary, salary.
Saloon, saloon.
Saluta, saluting.
Sana, saw, seen.
Sash, sash.
Satisfya, satisfying.
Satisfaction, satisfaction.
Sauch, matter.
Saucha, things, matters.
Sauft, sap, juice.
Sauwer, clean.

Sawg, say.
Sawga, saying.
Scenery, scenery.
Science, science.
Se, she, they, it.
Sechtzain, sixteen.
Sechtzich, sixty.
Sechtzaint, sixteenth.
Sechtzichsht, sixtieth.
Seck, sacks, bags.
Secretary, secretary.
Section, section.
Seech, victory.
Seecha, winning.
Seechreich, victorious.
Seed, south.
Seedlich, seutherly.
Sees, sweet.
Seeb, scive.
Seeva, sifting.
Seftich, juicy.
Seftle, jelly.
Seldens, seldom.
Select, select.
Selecta, selecting.
Selection, selection.
Sell, that.

Sellamohls, that occasion.
Selwer, self.
Selly, they, those.
Sembly, assembly.
Semblymon, assemblyman.
Senawt, senate.
Senator, senator.
Sentence, sentence.
Sentiment, sentiment.
Separata, separating.
Set, should, ought, set.
Settle, settle.
Settla, settling.
Settlement, settlement.
Setz, sit.
Setza, sitting.
Sex, six.
Sext, sixth.
Shæ, nice, neat.
Shæheit, beauty.
Shafing, shaving.
Shafe, shave.
Shafer, shepherd.
Shaft, shaft.
Shaidlich, damaging, harmful.
Shail, peel.
Shaila, peeling.
Shair, shears, scissors.
Shaira, shearing.
Shape, shape.
Share, share.
Shara, sharing.
Sharfa, sharpening.
Shartz, apron.
Shawd, a pity.
Shawda, damage, harm
Shawl, shawl.
Shawl, shell, hull.

Shawla, pealings.
Shawm, froth, foam.
Shawm, shame.
Shawmich, frothy.
Sheeb, shove, push.
Sheer, almost.
Shees, shoot.
Sheesa, shooting.
Shelf, shelf.
Sheint, seems.
Shelm, knave.
Shemt, ashamed.
Shendlich, disgraceful.
Shenk, bestow.
Shenka, donating, bestowing.
Skenkle, thigh.
Shenkung, donation.
Shep, dip.
Sheppa, dipping.
Shepper, dipper.
Shepfung, creation.
Shreef, sheriff.
Shetz, estimate.
Shetza, estimating.
Shetzung, estimation.
Shick, send.
Shicka, sending.
Shicklich, skilful, suitable.
Shicksawl, doom.
Shid, pour.
Shidda, pouring.
Shiff, ship.
Shifta, shifting.
Shild, sign, shield.
Shimmel, mould.
Shimmelich, mouldy.
Shimmel, gray (horse).
Shin, shin.
Shindle, shingle.

Shire, barn, scour.
Shira, scouring.
Shire-den, barn floor.
Shissel, dish.
Shissla, dishes.
Shittle, shake.
Shittla, shaking.
Shitza, protecting.
Shkip, skip.
Shkrape, scrape.
Shkrapa, scraping.
Shkramble, scramble.
Shkrambla, scrampling
Shklawf, slave.
Shkeem, scheme.
Shkeet, skate.
Shkeeta, skating.
Shkulduggla, putting on airs.
Shlaifa, draging.
Shlaig, whipping.
Shlager, affray.
Shlap, slap.
Shlappa, slapping.
Shlate, slate.
Shlate-pencil, slate pencil
Shlata, slating.
Shlau, cunning.
Shlaucht, slaughter.
Shlauchta, slaughtering.
Shlawg, strike.
Shlawga, striking, beating.
Shlecht, bad.
Shlechter, worse.
Shlechsht, worst.
Shleck, lick,
Shlecka, licking.
Shleesa, locking.
Shlefferich, sleepy.

Shleggle, sledge.
Shleif, grind.
Shleifa, grinding.
Shleif-shtæ, grindstone.
Shlepshlecker, sycophant.
Shlesser, locks.
Shlick, sleek.
Shlide, slide.
Shlida, sliding.
Shliffer, splinter.
Shliffle, rowdy.
Shlime, slime.
Shlip, slip.
Shlippa, slipping.
Shlipperich, slippery.
Shlissel, key.
Shlitta, sleigh.
Shlitta bawn, sleigh way.
Shlofe, sleep.
Shlofa, sleeping.
Shlong, snake.
Shlonga, snakes.
Shlook, swallow.
Shlooka, swallowing.
Shloomer, slumber.
Shloomera, slumbering.
Shloop, loop, to crawl in, hide.
Shloopa, hiding, crawling in.
Shlop, slop.
Shlop-bucket, slop-oucket.
Shlope, slope.
Shlovver, slobber.
Shlovvera, slobbering.
Shluss, lock.
Shly, sly.

Shmaichla, cajole.
Shmall, narrow.
Shmaltz, lard.
Shmart, smart.
Shmartza, pain.
Shmartzlich, painful.
Shmeer, grease, daub.
Shmeera, g r e a s i n g,
   daubing.
Shmeer-saif, soft soap.
Shmeis, throw.
Shmeisa, throwing.
Shmels, melt.
Shmelsa, melting.
Shmit, smith.
Shmoke, smoke.
Shmoka, smoking.
Shmootz, grease.
Shmootzich, greasy.
Shnai, snow.
Shnaid, snowing.
Shnai-shtorm, s n o w -
   storm.
Shnawvel, beak.
Shneck, snail.
Shnecka, snails.
Shneek, sneak.
Shneeka, sneaking.
Shnees, sneeze.
Shneesa, sneezing.
Shnell, rapid, quick.
Shnide, cut.
Shnida, cutting.
Shnider, tailor.
Shnidera, tailoring.
Shnitt, cut, slice.
Shnitz, dried apples.
Shnitz-pie, dried apple
   pie.
Shnitzla, whittling.
Shnol, buckle.

Shnolla, buckling.
Shnoor, string.
Shnoopa, cold, hay
   fever.
Shnoop-dooch, hand-
   kerchief.
Shnorrix, snore.
Shnorrixa, snoring.
Shnowfa, breathing.
Shnug, snug.
Shnuff, snuff.
Shnuffa, snuffing.
Shodda, shadow, shade
Shoe, shoe.
Shoe-bendle, s h o e -
   string.
Shoe barsht, shoe brush
Shond, shame, disgrace
Shonk, cupboard.
Shoff, work.
Shoffa, working.
Shoffdawg, working
   day.
Shoffman, workingman
Shofe, sheep.
Shofe-buck, ram.
Shofe-flaish, mutton.
Shoob-lawd, drawer.
Shoob-corrich, wheel-
   barrow.
Shool, school.
Shool-maishter, school-
   master.
Shooling, school-learn-
   ing.
Shooler, scholars.
Shool-house, school-
   nouse.
Shoold, debt.
Shooldich, indebted.
Shooldner,, debtor.

Shooldichkeit, duty.
Shoolder, shoulder.
Shooldera, shouldering
Shoonka, ham.
Shoos, shot, blast.
Shootz, shelter.
Shop, shop.
Shorf, sharp.
Shornshtæ, chimney.
Shose, lap.
Show, show.
Shower, shower.
Showfel, shovel.
Showfla, shoveling.
Shpane, chips.
Shpaiter, later.
Shpaitsht, latest.
Shpare, spare.
Shpara, sparing.
Shpawd, spade.
Shpawr, save.
Shpawra, saving.
Shpawrsom, frugal.
Shpawrsomkeit, f r u -
     gality.
Shpeck, flitch, bacon.
Shpeck-mouse, bat.
Shpeculate, speculate.
Shpeculata, speculat-
     ing.
Shpeculator, speculator.
Shpeel, play.
Shpeela, playing.
Shpeel-sauch, toys.
Shpeel-loompa, d i s h -
     cloth.
Shpees, spear.
Shpell, pin, spell.
Shpella, pins, spelling.
Shpella-kissa, pin cush-
     ion.

Shpelling-booch, spel-
     ling-book.
Shpend, spend.
Shpenda, spending.
Shpetter, mocker.
Shpiggle, mirror.
Shpike, spike.
Shpika, spiking.
Shpin, spin, spider.
Shpinna, spinning.
Shpinna-waib, cobweb.
Shpite, spite.
Shpiteful, spiteful.
Shpit-box, spittoon.
Shpitza, point.
Shpitz-bu, villain.
Shplice, splice.
Shplisa, splicing.
Shpoat, late.
Shpolta, splitting.
Shpone, chip.
Shponn, span.
Shponna, spanning.
Shpoochta, capers.
Shpook, ghost.
Shpool, spool.
Shpoonda, bung.
Shpora, spurs.
Shport, sport.
Shposs, fun.
Shpossich, funny.
Shpout, spout.
Shpow, spit.
Shpowa, spitting.
Shpraia, spreading.
Shpring, spring, run.
Shpringa, running.
Shpritz, splash, squirt.
Shpritza, s q u i r t i n g,
     sprinkling.

Shprich-wardt, adage, by-word.
Shprich-maishter, linguist.
Shproach, language.
Shprout, sprout.
Shprow, chaff.
Shpunk, spunk.
Shput, scoff, mock.
Shputta, mocking, scoffing.
Shquare, square.
Shquara, squaring.
Shquarl, squirrel.
Shquire, esquire.
Shrecka, fright.
Shrecklich, frightful.
Shribe, write.
Shriwes, writing.
Shriwer, writer.
Shriner, carpenter.
Shritt, step.
Shrowb, screw.
Shrowa, screwing.
Shrowbshtuck, vice.
Shtæ-coala, stone coal.
Shtæ, stone, stand.
Shtænich, stony.
Shtæ-brooch, stone quarry.
Shtaila, stealing.
Shtarb, die.
Shtarwa, dying.
Shtarmich, stormy.
Shtarn, star, forehead.
Shtart, start.
Shtarta, starting.
Shtarrick, strength.
Shtartza, tumbling.
Shtake, stake.
Shtall, stall.

Shtane, stone.
Shtamp, stamp.
Shtanich, stony.
Shtand, stand.
Shtate, state.
Shtawb, dust.
Shtawka, stake.
Shtauwich, dusty.
Shtawr, stare, blackbird
Shtawl, steel.
Shteak, steak.
Shteady, steady.
Shteam, steam.
Shteck-floos, croup.
Shteel, handle, chairs.
Shteddle, village.
Shtech, stab.
Shtecha, stabbing.
Shteck, (to) stick.
Shtecka, stick.
Shteef-mommy, stepmother.
Shteef-dawdy, stepfather.
Shtengle, stalk.
Shteif, stiff.
Shteiber, prop.
Shteibera, propping.
Shtemper, distemper.
Shtelsa, stilts.
Shtellung, attitude.
Shtich, piece, stitch.
Shtickly, bit.
Shtiga, mounting, ascending.
Shtill, still.
Shtiffle, boots.
Shtimm, voice, vote.
Shtimma, voting.
Shtink, stink.
Shtink-case, dutch cheese.

Shtinka, stinking.
Shtyle, style.
Shtock, stock.
Shtoll, stable.
Shtond, stand.
Shtondhoft, steadfast.
Shtom, stem, clan.
Shtoob, room.
Shtoof, stoop, step.
Shtool, chair.
Shtoom, mute.
Shtoomp, dull.
Shtoond, hour.
Shtoompa, stump.
Shtout, stout.
Shtorm, storm.
Shtore, store.
Shtore-keeper, store-keeper.
Shtore-sauch, m e r - chandise.
Shtorr, stir.
Shtorra, stirring.
Shtorrick, strong.
Shtorr-keppich, head-strong.
Shtory, story.
Shtose, jog, push.
Shtosa, pushing.
Shtraich, stroke.
Shtraifa, stripes.
Shtrail, comb.
Shtraina, streaming.
Shtrain, strain.
Shtraina, straining.
Shtrawl, ray.
Shtreck, stretch.
Shtrecka, stretching.
Shtreng, severe.
Shtreit, quarrel.
Shtreita, quarreling.

Shtrick, rope.
Shtricka, knitting.
Shtrict, strict.
Shtriggle, curry-comb.
Shtrimp, stockings.
Shtrip, strip.
Shtro, straw.
Shtrofe, punishment.
Shtrofebawr, punish-able.
Shtrome, stream.
Shtroomp, stocking.
Shtroomp-bendle, stock-ing-garter.
Shtroovelich, uncombed.
Shtrose, street.
Shtuck, (building) story.
Shtuck, cane, stick, stack.
Shtudy, study.
Shtudya, studying.
Shtudent, student.
Shtuls, proud.
Shtufft, stuff.
Shtulver, stumble.
Shtulvera, stumbling.
Shtup, stop.
Shtuppa, darning, stop-ping.
Shtupper, stopper, wad
Shtupeed, stupid.
Shtutter, stutter.
Shtuttera, stuttering.
Shtuvverich, stubborn.
Shuckla, rocking.
Shuckle, cradle, rock.
Shuckle-shtool, rock-ing-chair.
Shu, sue.
Shua, suing.
Shun, already.

Shuppa, shed.
Shware, heavy.
Shwase, sweat.
Shwarm, swarm.
Shwalm, swallow.
Shwamm, sponge.
Shwauch, weak.
Shwauchheit, weak-
ness.
Shwap, swap.
Shwappa, swapping.
Shwantz, tail.
Shwear, swear.
Shweara, swearing.
Shwechlich, weakly.
Shweffel, sulpher.
Shweffelbrenner, sul-
phur burner.
Shweshter, sister.
Shweegafodder, father-
in-law.
Shweega-mooter, moth-
er-in-law.
Shwetz, speak.
Shwetza, speaking.
Shwetzer, speaker.
Shwetzawrt, diction.
Shwetz-koonsht, elocu-
tion.
Shwift, swift.
Shwim, swim.
Shwimma, swimming.
Shwindle, swindle.
Shwindla, swindling.
Shwindler, swindler.
Shwinga, swinging.
Shwitza, sweating.
Shy, shy.
Shya, shying.
Si, being, his, its, be.
Si, hogs.

Si-ish, hoggish.
Sieri, filthy, nuisance.
Siflaish, pork.
Si-shtol, hog pen.
Si-troke, hog trougo.
Sich, one's self.
Sicher, safe.
Sicht, sight.
Sichtbawr, visible.
Sidder, since.
Side, side.
Sida-shtick, flitch.
Side-lohn, perquisite.
Siffer, drunkard.
Sigla, sealing.
Silver, silver.
Sily, pig.
Sines, his.
Sine, his.
Sinn, mind.
Sind, sin.
Sind-floot, deluge.
Sing, sing.
Singa, singing.
Sink, sink.
Sinka, sinking.
Sitz, seat.
Sitza, sitting.
Sivva, seven.
Sivvatzæ, seventeen.
Sivvatzich, seventy.
Sivvat, seventh.
Sivvatzaint, seventeenth.
Sivvatzichsht, seventieth
So, so.
Soak, soak.
Soaka, soaking.
Sober, sober.
Sock, bag, pocket.
Sock-messer, pocket-
knife.

Society, society.
Soddle, saddle.
Soddler, saddler.
Sofa, sofa.
Sogawr, even, yet.
Sohn, son.
Sole, sole.
Solid, solid.
Solicit, solicit.
Solicita, soliciting.
Solicitation, solicitation.
Sols, salt.
Solsich, salty.
Solvent, solvent.
Soma, seed.
Somla, gathering.
Somlung, assembly.
Somshdawg, Saturday.
Sond, sand.
Sondich, sandy.
Sonft, meek.
Song, song.
Sooch, seek.
Soocha, seeking.
Sookle, suck.
Sookla, sucking.
Soomer, summer.
Soondawg, sunday.
Soonsht, else.
Sorta, sorts.
Sound, sound.
Sounda, sounding.
Soup, soup.
Sour, sour.
Sow, hog.
Sowf, guzzle.
Sowfa, guzzling.
Sowferei, debauchery.
Sowf-lodle, inebriate.
Subject, subject.
Substitute, substitute.

Substituta, substituting
Subscribe, subscribe.
Subscriba, subscribing.
Subscription, subscription.
Subscriber, subscriber.
Subtracta, subtracting.
Succeeda, succeeding.
Suddich, such.
Suffera, suffering.
Suffer, suffer.
Suit, suit.
Suita, suiting.
Suldawt, soldier.
Sull, shall.
Sullawd, sallad.
Sum, sum.
Summona, snmmoning.
Summons, summon.
Supervise, supervise.
Supervisa, supervising.
Superintend, superintend.
Superintenda, superintending.
Suppose, suppose.
Supposa, supposing.
Supposition, supposition.
Support, support.
Supporta, supporting.
Sure, sure.
Suspect, suspect.
Suspecta, suspecting.
Suspicion, suspicion.
Suspenda, suspending.
Suspension, suspension
System, system.
Systemiza, systemizing

T.

Tæ, tea.
Tæ-leffle, teaspoon.
Tacks, tacks.
Tape, tape.
Tattla, tattling.
Tawd, deed.
Tawdle, censure.
Teacha, teaching.
Temperance, temperance.
Tend, tend.
Tenda, tending.
Teshtament, testament
Testimony, testimony.
Tippla, tippling.
Tit, teat.
Tittle, title.
To. tzu, aw, noch.
Tollenta, talents.
Toss, toss.
Tossa, tossing.
Town, town.
Township, township.
Tract, tract.
Traiger, carrier.
Train, train, tears.
Traina, training.
Traishta, consoling.
Traitor, traitor.
Trash, trash.
Trawg, carry.
Trawga, carrying.
Travel, travel.
Travela, traveling.
Treasury, treasury.
Treasurer, treasurer.
Treat, treat.
Treata, treating.

Treeb, cloudy, misty.
Tref, to hit.
Trenna, severing.
Trick, trick.
Trifle, trifle.
Trim, trim.
Trimma, trimming.
Troasht, consolation.
Toomp, trump.
Troompait, trumpet.
Troop, flock.
Troovel, trouble.
Troovela, troubling.
Trowb, grape.
Trow, trust.
Trowa, trusting.
Trowva, grapes.
Trowera, mourning.
Trowerich, mournful;
    sad.
Truck, truck.
Trunk, trunk.
Trustee, trustee.
Twine, twine.
Type, type.
Type setzer, type setter
Tyronn, tyrant.
Tzader, cedar.
Tzail, count.
Tzaila, counting.
Tzaicha, sign.
Tzain, ten, teeth.
Tzaint, tenth.
Tzay, tough.
Tzaya, toes.
Tzawlreich, numerous.
Tzawm, bridle.
Tzawn, tooth, cog.

Tzawma, taming.
Tzawrt, tender.
Tzeeg, pull, move.
Tzeega, pulling, moving
Tzeel, aim.
Tzeela, aiming.
Tzeit, time.
Tzeita, times.
Tzeitfertreib, passtime.
Tzeitich, ripe.
Tzeitlong, awhile.
Tzeitung, newspaper.
Tzeiga, witness.
Tzeigniss, evidence.
Tzell, cell.
Tzettle, short letter, a few lines.
Tziffer, figure.
Tzin, tin.
Tzink, zinc.
Tzitter, tremble.
Tzittera, trembling,
Tzitterly, pig feet jelly.
Tzivver, tubs.
Tzomma, together.
Tzomma-dricka, compress.
Tzomma-roofa, convene.
Tzommatzeega, concentrate.
Tzonk, scold.
Tzoonka, scolding.
Tzonkeri, brawl.
Tzoog, draft, pull.
Tzoong, tongue.
Tzooker, sugar.
Tzooker-bowl, sugar-bowl.
Tzoover, tub.
Tzorn, wrath.
Tzornich, wrathy.

Tzu, shut, to.
Tzudu, increase, add.
Tzufellich, incidental, casual.
Tzufloocht, refuge.
Tzufol, incident.
Tzufolla, devolve.
Tzufoos, afoot.
Tzufridda, satisfied.
Tzucooma, accrue.
Tzuganooma, increase.
Tzugevva, forego.
Tzukoonft, future.
Tzull, inch.
Tzull-shtuck, foot-rule.
Tzum, to it, to him.
Tzunawm, increase.
Tzunemma, increasing.
Tzurecht, aright.
Tzurick, aback.
Tzurick-handa, disgorge
Tzurick-holda, retain.
Tzushriva, ascribe.
Tzusotz, addition, annexation.
Tzuwidder, adverse.
Tzwæ, two.
Tzweifel, doubt.
Tzweifla, doubting.
Tzwelf, twelve.
Tzwelft, twelfth.
Tzwet, second.
Tzwettens, secondly.
Tzwilling, twins.
Tzwinga, compelling.
Tzwisha, between.
Tzwivvel, onion.
Tzwivvela, onions.
Tzwonsich, twenty.
Tzwonsichsht, twentieth.

U.

Ub, if whether.
Ubshun, although.
Uf, on, upon.
Uffa, stove.
Uffa-rohr, stovepipe.
Uffressa, devouring.
Ufclora, cleaning up.
Ufeera, behavior.
Ufdecka, uncovering.
Uf gevva, giving up.
Ufg'shova, postponed.
Ufg'shwolla, bloated, swollen.
Ufhalta, detaining, remaining.
Ufhaltung, detention.
Ufhara, quitting, ceasing.
Ufhava, lifting, picking up.
Uflaiga, laying on.
Ufrichta, erecting.
Ufrichtich, upright.
Ufrichtung, construction.
Ufroor, uproar.
Ufsheeva, to postpone.
Ufshoob, postponement.
Ufshleesa, unlock.
Ufshtiga, ascending.
Ufshtæ, rising up.
Ufshwella, swelling up.
Uft, often.
Uf-wecka, waking up.
Uhr, clock.
Umbrell, umbrella.
Umbringa, to kill.
Umshtond, circumstance.

Umshtenda, circumstances.
Umringa, surrounding.
Umringd, surrounded.
Umg'folla, fallen down.
Umgabortzeld, tumbled over.
Umg'shtartzd, fell down.
Umrisa, tearing down.
Umwaig, detour.
Un, and.
Unava, uneven.
Unairlich, dishonest.
Unainlich, disunited.
Unawrtich, naughty.
Unbadenkt, indiscreet.
Unbagreiflich, incomprehensible.
Unbashtimt, indefinite.
Uncle, uncle.
Uncommon, uncommon.
Undonkbawr, ungrateful.
Undeitlich, indistinct.
Unendlich, endless.
Unendeckt, undiscovered.
Unerfawra, inexperience.
Unfair, unfair.
Unfawlbawr, unfailing.
Unfol, mishap.
Unforsichtich, unregarded.
Unfriendlich, unfrendly.
Unfershamed, barefaced.
Unfershtond, senseless.

Unferdaild, undivided.
Unferdeend, unmerited.
Unfermixed, unmixed.
Unferninftich, unreasonable.
Unfersane, unprovided, unaware.
Unfersichert, unprotected.
Unfershemt, brazenfaced.
Ungabora, unborn.
Ungafair, about.
Ungadooldich, impatient.
Ungahire, monstrous, immense.
Ungalarned, illiterate.
Ungarecht, unjust.
Ungarn, dislike.
Ungadoolt, impatience
Ungawiss, uncertain.
Unglawa, disbelief.
Unglawich, credulous.
Ungleich, dissimilar.
Unglick, accident.
Unglicklich, unlucky.
Ungrawd, uneven.
Ung'soond, unwell.
Ung'shtolt, deformity.
Unhendich, unhandy.
Unite, unite.
Uniform, uniform.
Unkraut, weeds.
Unleidich, disagreeable.
Unmiglich, impossible.
Unmiglichkeit, impossibility.
Unmoneerlich, unmannerly.
Unna, under, below.

Unner, under.
Unnersht, undermost.
Unnerholta, entertaining
Unnernemma, undertaking.
Unnernemmung, enterprise.
Unnodeerlich, unnatural
Unnersheed, difference
Unnershriva, subscribing.
Unnersooch, examine.
Unnersoochung, investigation, inquiry.
Unnershrift, autograph
Unnershtiza, supporting.
Unordung, disorder.
Unproweert, untried.
Unpordi-ish, impartial.
Unrecht, injustice.
Unru, uneasiness.
Unruich, uneasy.
Uns, we, us, our.
Unser, our, ours.
Unsettle, unsettle.
Unsinn, nonsense.
Unsinnich, nonsensical
Unshicklich, improper.
Unshuldich, innocent.
Untzeitich, unripe, premature.
Untzufrida, unsatisfied
Unwillens, unwilling.
Unwohrshinelich, unlikely.
Unwohr, untrue.
Ursauch, cause.
Uvva, above, loft.
Ux, ox.
Uxa, oxen.

V.

Vacancy, vacancy.
Vacation, vacation.
Valley, valley.
Valve, valve.
Varnish, varnish.
Veil, veil.
Velvet, velvet.
Verdict, verdict.

Vest, vest.
Violata, violating.
Vote, vote.
Vota, voting.
Voter, voter.
Volunteer, volunteer.
Volunteera, volunteer-
  ing.

W.

Wær, who, is, would.
Wærdich, worthy.
Wærtlich, literal.
Wært, value, virtue.
Wært, landlord.
Wærtshouse, hotel.
Wærklich, indeed.
Wærktzeich, imple-
  ments.
Wærd, would.
Wærda-booch, vocabu-
  lary.
Wærgle-huls, rolling-
  pin.
Wærma, warming.
Wærrum, worms.
Wærmich, wormy.
Wærra, to accomplish.
Wærtick, tow.
Wahl, choice.
Wai, pain.
Waias, sore.
Waib, weave.
Waich, soft.
Waid, pasture.
Waig, road, way.

Waila, elect.
Wair, defend.
Waira, defending.
Wais, wissa.
Waiter, waiter.
Waitza, wheat.
Wandera, wandering.
Wann, when, if, wheth-
  er.
Wanka, wabble.
War, was, were.
Wara, was, were.
Ward, ward, wait.
Warda, waiting.
Wardt, word.
Wardt-for-wardt, verbat-
  um.
Warend, during.
Ware-house, ware-house.
Warm, warm.
Warn, warn.
Warnd, warned.
Warnung, warning.
Warnd, warrant.
Warsht, sausage.
Wartz, wart.

Wase, knowing.
Wass, which, what.
Wasser, water.
Wasser-amer, bucket.
Wasser- melone, water-
melon.
Wasser-soocht, dropsy.
Watch, watch.
Watcha, watching.
Watchaket, watch-chain.
Wauch, wake.
Waucha, waking.
Wauchsom, vigilent.
Wauga, wagon.
Waugner, wheelright.
Waur, ware.
Waurum, why.
Wausom, sod.
Wava, weaving.
We, how.
Wear, wear.
Weara, wearing.
Weck, wake, away, rusk
Wecka, waking.
Wechlich, weekly.
Wedder, weather.
Weeg, weigh, cradle.
Weega, weighing.
Weela, wallowing.
Weesht, nasty.
Weetich, furious, mad.
Weibshem, chimese.
Weibs-mensh, woman.
Weibs leit, women-folks.
Weida, willow.
Weil, because.
Weis, to show.
Weis, white.
Weisa, showing.
Weisla, white-washing.
Weisheit, wisdom.

Weit, far, distant.
Weiter, farther.
Weitleftich, elaborate.
Well, well, wave, which
Weller, which one.
Weller, who, which.
Welshkorn, corn.
Welshkorn-feld, corn-
field.
Welsh-hawna, turkey-
cock.
Welsh-hinkle, turkeys.
Welt, world.
Weltlich, worldly.
Wennich, few.
Wennicher, less.
Wennichsht, least.
Wesh, wash.
Wesha, washing.
Weshfraw, wash wo-
man.
Wesh-kessel, wash-boiler
Wesh-korb, wash-bas-
ket.
Wesh-kich, wash-kitchen.
Wesh-line, clothes-line
Wesh-loompa, wash-
rag.
Wesh-machine, wash-
ing-machine.
Wesh-shlissel, wash-
basin.
Wesh-tzoover, wash-tub.
Wesht, west.
Weshtlich, westward.
Weshp, wasp.
Weshpanesht, wasp-
nest.
Wessera, watering.
Wesserich, watery.
Wet, would, bet.

Wetta, betting.
Wetza, whet.
Wexle, change.
Wexla, changing.
Wicht, wick.
Wichtich, important.
Wickle, wind.
Wickla, winding.
Wide, wide.
Widfraw, widow.
Widmon, widower.
Widder, again.
Widderhola, repeating.
Widderrufa, repealing.
Wilful, wilful,
Will, will.
Willa, will.
Willens, willing.
Wilt, wild.
Wiltniss, wilderness.
Wip, whip.
Wippa, whipping.
Wiply, switch.
Wind, wind.
Windich, windy, squally
Wine, wine.
Wineglaws, wineglass.
Windle, diaper.
Wink, wink.
Winka, winking.
Winkle, square.
Winn, windlass.
Winsh, wish.
Winsha, wishing.
Winter, winter.
Wissa, knowing.
Wiss, meadow.
Wish, wipe.
Wisha, wiping.
Whiskey, whiskey.
Whisker, whisker.

Witz, wit.
Witzich, witty.
Wo, where.
Woag, scale.
Wocker, awake.
Wocka-shtæ, flintstone
Wohar, whence.
Wohl, well.
Wohn, reside.
Wohna, residing.
Wohnhoft, resident.
Wohnhouse, dwelling.
Wohnplotz, residence,
abode.
Wohnung, domicile,
dwelling.
Wohr, true.
Wohret, truth.
Wohretlich, verily.
Wohrsheinlich, likely,
probable.
Wols, roller.
Wolfish, whale.
Wonsa, bed bugs.
Woond, wound.
Wooner, wonder.
Woonera, wondering.
Woonerlich, wonder-
ful.
Woonsh, wish.
Woot, fury, rage.
Wortzel, root.
Worram, worm.
Wox, wax, grow.
Woxa, waxing, grow-
ing.
Wrangle, wrangle.
Wrapper, wrapper.
Writ, writ.
Wuch, week.
Wucha, weeks.

Wulfel, cheap.
Wulfeller, cheaper.
Wulf, wolf.
Wulk, cloud.

Wulkich, cloudy.
Wull, wool.
Wullich, woolen.

Y.

Yades, every.
Yader, each.
Yadoch, even.
Yaira, fermenting.
Yareling, yearling.
Yarelich, yearly.
Yard, yard.
Yard-shtecka, yard-measure.
Yager, hunter.
Yasus, Jesus.
Yaucht, noise.
Yaw, yes.
Yawga, hunting.
Yeamohls, evermore.
Yemmerlich, pitiful.
Yenner, January.
Yetz, present, now.
Yetzich, at present, now.

Yinger, younger.
Yingsht, youngest.
Yingler, juvenile.
Yo, yea.
Yohrtzeit, season.
Yohr, year.
Yohra, years.
Yood, jew.
Yooda, jews.
Yonuawr, January.
Yoony, june.
Yooly, july.
Yoong, young.
Yoong-fraw, virgin.
Yoosht, only, just.
Yooshtas, justice of the peace.
Yuch, yolk.
Yubilee, jubilee.

NOTES OF ERRORS.

On page 19, instead of *Brood* read *Broad*—translated *braid*.

Page 20, translation of *Bulky* read *shware*.

Page 36, translation of *Emit* read *ousfleesa*.

Page 50, *Left* translates *ferlussa* as well as *linx*.

Page 75, translation of *Tobacco* read *duwock*.

Page 76, translation of *Tye* read *binna*.

Page 81, translation of *Woman* read *weibsmensh*.

Page 84, translation of *Allæ* read *alone*.

Page 86, the English word *At* translated *drau* is out of its proper place.

Page 90, instead of *Blut-keppish* read *Blut-keppich*. Same page, instead of *Bobblemaul* read *Bobblemowl*.

Page 91, translation of *Broud* read *bride*.

EXPLANATION.

The many English words transferred into the foregoing without translation, are all in common use as part of the Pennsylvania Dutch language. In addition to those stated there are yet many more. In a number of cases we have translated English words ending with *ing* by simply using the letter *a* as the last syllable, such as

Accommodating,	*accommodata,*
Delivering,	*delivera,*

&c. In all such cases the English words are used in every other sense, as accommodate, accommodation, deliver and delivered, &c., without any change from English proper.

(TRANSLATION.—IVVERSETZUNG.)

De feela Englishe wardta transferred ins foregenglicha, sin oll in common use ols 'n dale fun der Penn. Deitsha shproach. In addition tzu denna os gevva sin, huts noch feel maner. In a noomer fun so fella hen mer Englishe wardta os mit *ing* enda ivversetzd mit 'm simple awhong fum bushtawb *a* ols der letsht syllable, so we

Accommodating,	*accommodata,*
Delivering,	*delivera,*

&c. In oll so fella sin de Englisha wardta g'used in yeader manung, so we accommodate, accommodation, deliver un delivered.

PART SECOND.

TZWETTA DALE.

The following words are generally used in the interrogative form. They constitute a prominent element in the Penn. Dutch language, and they are addressed to the second person and invariably refer to the present time.

(TRANSLATION.—IVVERSETZUNG.)

De fulgenda wardta sin for common in der form fun froga. Se sin an prominenty element in der Penn. Deitsha shproach, un se sin in yeadaw fol addressed tzu'm tzwetta parsone, un weaga der yetzich tzeit.

Agreesht?	do you agree ?
Aig'nsht	do you own
Appealsht	do you appeal
Appearsht	do you appear
Appointsht	do you appoint
Arbsht	do you inherit
Arkensht	do you confess
Arlawbsht	do you allow
Assignsht	do you assign
Bailsht	do you bail
Baleegsht	do you belie
Barawbsht	do you rob
Batreegsht	do you cheat
Batzawlsht	do you pay

Bausht?	are you building?
Beetsht	do you beat
Bocksht	are you baking
Behaifsht	do you behave
Binnsht	do you bind
Blacksht	are you blacking
Bleibsht	are you staying
Beisht	are you biting
Bluffsht	are you bluffing
Boardsht	are you boarding
Bolweersht	are you shaving
Borricksht	do you sell on trust
Boompsht	are you pumping
Brauchsht	are you using
Brawlsht	are you boasting
Brechsht	are you breaking
Breesht	are you scalding
Brensht	are you burning
Brensht	are you distilling
Bringsht	are you bringing
Brillsht	are you bellowing
Brodesht	are you frying
B'sinnsht	do you remember
Chawsht	do you chew
Calculatesht	are you calculating
Claimsht	do you claim
Clawgsht	are you complaining
Clearsht	are you clearing
Collectsht	do you collect
Condemsht	do you condemn
Confesht	do you confess
Confarmsht	do you confirm
Connectsht	do you connect
Considersht	are you considering
Consultsht	are you consulting
Contradictsht	do you contradict
Contesht	do you contest
Convictsht	do you convict
Copiesht	are you copying
Coomsht	are you coming
Corriseersht	are you courting

Cowsht?	are you masticating?
Cracksht	are you cracking
Croddlesht	are you climbing
Crowdsht	are you crowding
Curesht	do you cure
Dailsht	are you dividing
Dawfsht	are you baptising
Dealsht	are you dealing
Debatesht	are you debating
Decksht	do you cover up
Decidesht	do you decide
Declaresht	are you declaring
Defeatsht	do you defeat
Defendsht	do you defend
Definesht	are you defining
Defiesht	do you defy
Deliversht	do you deliver
Demandsht	do you demand
Denksht	do you think
Differsht	do you differ
Directsht	do you direct
Denksht	do you think
Doosht	do you
Drawmsht	are you dreaming
Drinksht	do you drink
Drooksht	are you printing
Ducktersht	are you doctoring
Editsht	are you editing
Eilsht	are you hurrying
Enjoysht	do you enjoy
Entersht	do you enter
Esht	are you eating
Examinsht	are you examining
Explainsht	are you explaining
Failsht	do you fail
Farrichsht	do you fear
Fawrsht	are you hauling
Fawrsht	are you taking a ride
Feelsht	do you feel
Ferennersht	are you altering
Ferdarbsht	are you spoiling

Fergesht?	are you forgetting?
Ferhoongersht	are you hungering
Ferkawfsht	do you sell
Ferleersht	are you losing
Ferlongsht	do you desire
Ferlusht	do you leave
Fershtaisht	do you understand
Fershprechsht	do you promise
Fersoochsht	do you taste
Ferwoonersht	do you wonder
Ferwillichsht	do you consent
Finsht	do you find
Floochsht	do you swear
Freersht	do you freeze
Freersht	are you cold or chilly
Frokeshd	do you ask
Fulksht	do you obey
Gaisht	are you going
Glawbsht	do you believe
Glawbshts	do you believe it
Grawbsht	are you digging
Gricksht	do you get
Grickshts	are you getting it
Haltsht	do you hold
Haltsht	do you stop
Haresht	do you hear
Hareshts	do you hear it
Heilsht	are you crying
Helfsht	are you helping
Henksht	do you hang
Hicklesht	are you limping
Hiresht	do you marry
Hocksht	do you chop, or cut
Husht	have you
Hushts	have you it
Hucksht	do you squat, or sit
Huffsht	do you hope
Interfeerhd	do you interfere
Insureshd	do you insure
Insultsht	do you insult
Invesht	do you invest

Ivverlaigsht ?	do you consider?
Ivversetsht	are you translating
Joinsht	do you join
Kawfsht	do you sell
Kennsht	do you know
Labesht	are you alive
Lainsht	do you lend
Lauchsht	are you laughing
Larnsht	are you learning
Lawdsht	are you loading
Lawfsht	are you walking
Leegsht	are you lying
Lusht	do you permit
Manesht	do you mean
Mauchsht	are you making
Mawlsht	are you grinding
Moofsht	are you moving
Nemsht	are you taking
Ontwardtsht	do you answer
Ordersht	do you order
Paintsht	are you painting
Picksht	are you picking
Peifsht	are you whistling
Pishpersht	are you whispering
Ploogsht	are you plowing
Preddichsht	do you preach
Preparesht	are you preparing
Proofsht	are you proving
Proweersht	are you trying
Providesht	are you providing
Renewsht	do you renew
Rentsht	are you renting
Resignsht	do you resign
Rulesht	do you rule
Sæsht	do you see
Shicksht	do you send
Shittlesht	are you shaking
Shlawgsht	are you striking
Shlawgsht	are you knocking
Shlecksht	do you lick
Shlipsht	are you slipping

Shlofesht ?	are you asleep?
Shmeersht	do you besmear
Shmeisht	are you throwing
Shmokeshd	are you smoking
Shneidsht	are you cutting
Shnowfsht	are you breathing
Shoftsht	are you working
Shpawrsht	are you saving
Shpeelsht	are you playing
Shpringsht	are you running
Shtarbsht	are you dying
Shwearsht	are you swearing
Shwetsht	are you talking
Swimsht	are you swimming
Shwindlesht	are you swindling
Singsht	do you sing
Supportsht	do you support
Tawdlesht	do you criticise
Trawgsht	do you carry
Treatsht	do you treat
Troovelsht	do you trouble
Tzailsht	are you counting
Tzeegshd	are you pulling
Tzeegshd	do you move
Unnersoochsht	do you investigate
Waisht	do you know
Waishts	do you know it
Wardsht	are you waiting
Weegsht	are you weighing
Weegshts	are you weighing it
Weisht	do you show
Weisht	do you exhibit
Weishts	do you show it
Weishts	do you exhibit it
Wexelsht	do you change
Wexelshts	are you changing it
Wickelshts	do you wind it
Winshd	do you wish
Winshds	do you wish it
Yawgsht	do you chase
Yawgshts	are you chasing it

Whilst these words or compounds are generally used in the interrogative form, there are also exceptions. For example:

AGREESHT? Do you agree? Ich sæ du agreesht mit 'm.
I see you agree with him.

CHAWSHT? Do you chew? Ich sæ du chawsht.
I see you are chewing.

DUCKTERSHT? Are you doctoring? Ich glawb du ducktershd.
I believe you are doctoring.

GAISHT? Are you going? Ich sæ du gaisht.
I see you are going.

COOMSHT? Are you coming? Ich sæ du coomsht.
I see you are coming.

GLAWBSHTS? Do you believe it? Es coomd mer fore du glawbshts net.
It seems to me you don't believe it.

HIRESHT SE? Will you marry her? Ich suspect os du se hiresht.
I suspect that you will marry her.

KAWFSHTS? Do you buy it? Ich sæ du kawfshts.
I see you are buying it.

LAWFSHT? Do you walk? Ich sæ du lawfsht.
I see you are walking.

MOOFSHT? Are you moving? Ich sæ du moofsht.
I see you are moving.

SHPRINGST? Are you running? Du springsht goot.
You run well.

WAISHTS? Do you know it? Du waishts goot ganoonk.
You know it well enough.

In almost every case this class of words are

used in a similar manner, but, as stated, they are generally in the interrogative form.

In sheer yeadam fol wærra dee closs wardta g'used uf 'm namelicha waig, awer, we **g'sawt**, se sin for common in der form fun froga.

ABBREVIATIONS.—OBKARTZUNGA.

The following are Penn. Dutch abbreviations. Many words beginning with *Ga* are abbreviated by substituting the apostrophe for the *a*, so as to produce only the consonant sound, whilst in other cases the *ga* is used. For instance :

> Ich bin gatraveled.   I have traveled.
> Ich hob 'm g'sawt.   I told him.
> De soup is gakuchd.   The soup is cooked.
> Bisht g'soond?   Are you in good health?

In a number of cases it was found difficult to determine whether to write the German *Ga* prefix, or the *g'* abbreviation.   Probably the record is as correct in this respect as it is possible to make it.

The 'm (him,) 'n (a or an) and 's (it) abbreviations are used thus :

> Ich hob 'm g'sawt.   I told him.
> Ich geb 'm anes.   I give him one.
> Mer con 'm net glauwa.   One can't believe him.
> Sell is 'n gooter opple.   That is a good apple.

Ich hob 'n ellefont g'sæ.   I saw an elephant.
Ich hob 'n aw gagookd.   I looked at him.
Ich kenn 'n net.   I know him not.
Ich con 'n leddera.   I can flog him.
Ich con 's net helfa.   I can't help it.
Du consht 's selwer sana.   You can see it for
yourself.
Yaw, 's is so.   Yes, it is so.
Ich hob 's maidle g'sæ.   I have seen the girl.

These abbreviations are not strictly necessary, but they are very convenient and constitute
one of the prominent Penn. Dutch characteristics.   All the above would be entirely correct if
written thus :

Ich hob eem g'sawt.   Ich geb eem anes.
Mer con eem net glauwa.   Sell is an gooter opple.
Ich hob an elefont gsæ.   Ich hob een aw gagookd.
Ich ken een net.   Ich con een leddera.   Ich con
es net helfa.   Du consht es selwer sana.   Yaw, es
is so.   Ich hob es maidle g'sæ.

As the abbreviations are very simple, and as
they produce the words as they are uttered, in
the natural, easy way, they are decidedly the best
in writing Penn. Dutch.

THE USE OF WORDS.

DE USE FUN WARDTA.

Acta—acting. I have seen the clown acting.
    Acting—acta. Ich hob der honswarsht sana
    acta.
Aichel—acorn. A blind hog will also find an
    acorn occasionally.
    Acorn—aichel. An blinty sow fint aw eb-
    mohls an aichel.
Arbshoft—inheritance. A large inheritance would
    be a first-rate cure for hard times.
    Inheritance—arbshoft. Au grossy arbshoft
    wær an first-raty cure for hordy tzeita.
Arwet—work. This forenoon I was hard at work.
    Work—arwet. Den formiddawg war ich
    hord on der arwet.
Awgadu—dressed. I dressed myself in my best
    clothes and went to church.
    Dressed—awgadu. Ich hob my beshty clai-
    der awgadu un bin in de kærrich gonga.
Awdale—part. With those proceedings I will
    take no part.
    Part—awdale. Mit selly proceedings nem
    ich kæ awdale.
Awganame—agreeable. A fine young lady is
    always agreeable.
    Agreeable—awganame. An finey yungy lady
    is olsfort awganame.
Awram—poor. The poor man has no home.
    Poor—awram. Der auram mon hut kæ
    haimat.

Bagrebniss—burial. Yesterday I was at the burial.

Burial—bagrebniss. Geshter war ich om bagrebniss.

Bais—angry. The lawyer talked as if he were very angry.

Angry—bais. Der lawyer hut g'shwetzd os wannar orrick bais wær.

Bakared—converted. They say a great many were converted at the camp meeting.

Converted—bakared. Se sawga es hetta sich orrick feel bakared on der camp meeting.

Barrya—bargain. I'll give you my watch for yours and five dollars in the bargain.

Bargain—barrya. Ich geb der my watch for diny un finf dawler in der barrya.

Bauch—belly. It is belly-ache that makes the baby scream.

Belly—bauch, Es is bauch wæ os's bubbely greisha maucht.

Cotzakraut—catnip. For that, there is no better remedy than catnip tea.

Catnip—cotzakraut. For sell is kæ besser mittle os cotzakraut tæ.

Crittlich—crabbed. And whenever the baby screams the old woman gets very crabbed herself.

Crabbed—crittlich. Un wann ols 's bubbely greisht don wærd aw de olt fraw orrick crittlich.

Corriseera—courting. I believe that you frequently go out courting the girls.

Courting—corriseera. Ich glawb os du uft nous gaisht de maid corriseera.

Dauch—roof. I'll put a new roof on the wood shed.

Roof—dauch. Ich du an nei dauch uf der huls shuppa.

Dawglaner—day laborer. That man is a very industrious day laborer.

Day laborer—dawglaner. Seller mon is an orrick fleisicher dawglaner.

Dawtam—date. What is the date of my note?

Date—dawtam. Was is der dawtam fun miner note?

Dawg—day. I cannot tell the exact day, as I have not the note with me.

Day—dawg. Ich con der exact dawg net sawga, for ich hob de note net by mer.

Dire—dear. I cannot afford to eat so many peanuts—they are much too dear.

Dear—dire. Ich con net afforda so feel groondnis tzu essa—se sin feel tzu dire.

Doh—here. Now just for once look here.

Here—doh. Gook now yoosht amohl doh.

Dobbich—awkward. That fellow seems to be very awkward.

Awkward—dobbich. Seller karl sheint orrick dobbich tzu si.

Doonera—thundering. Did you hear the terrible heavy thundering last night?

Thunder—doonera. Husht sell shrecklich shwær doonera g'hared de letsht naucht?

Doonkle—dark. Last night was very dark.

Dark—doonkle. De letsht naucht war 's orrick doonkle.

Ebmohls—sometimes. Sometimes I smoke cigars, but not regularly.

Sometimes—ebmohls. Ich du ebmohls cigars, shmoka awer net regularly.

Eidrook—impression. Our parson preached remarkably well on last Sunday and he made a deep impression.

Impression—eidrook. Unser porra hut ivver ous goot gapreddicht om letshta Soondawg, un ar hut aw an deefer eidrook gamaucht.

Eiwendung—objection. But yet there are many persons who make objection to that preacher, just because he is not afraid to preach the truth.

Objection—eiwendung. Es hut awer doch feel leit os eiwendung hen tzu sellam porra, yoosht weil ar sich net farricht de wohret tzu preddicha.

Essa—eating. My wife is eating apples.

Eating—essa. My fraw is om epple essa.

Essich—vinegar. Those apples are as sour as vinegar.

Vinegar—essich. Selly epple sin so sour os essich.

Fechta—fighting. That man and his wife have again been fighting like dogs and cats.

Fighting—fechta. Seller mon un si fraw waura widder om fechta we hoonda un cotza.

Feggle—birds. Winter is coming, — the birds have nearly all disappeared—gone to their southern homes.

Birds—feggle. Der winter coomd—de feggle sin sheer all disappeared—tzu era seedlieha haimata gonga.

Feicht—damp. It is said that damp weather begets rheumatism.

Damp—feicht. Es wærd ols g'sawt os feicht wetter roomatis by bringt.

Ferfolla—due. On the fifth of next month my note will be due in bank.

Due—ferfolla. Om finfta fum naighsht moonot doot my note ferfolla in der bank.

Ferlora—lost. I also used to endorse for other people and in that way I lost almost all I ever possessed.

Lost—ferlora. Ich hob aw ols endorsed for onner leit un sellerwaig hob ich sheer olles ferlora wass ich yamohls g'hot hob.

Fergess—forget. Don't forget to return that umbrella which I gave you the other day.

 Forget—fergess. Fergess net un bring widder selly umbrell tzurick os ich der gevva hob der onner dawg.

Ferrickt—deranged. That fellow acts just as if he were deranged.

 Deranged—ferrickt. Sellar karl act yoosht os wann ar ferrickt wær.

Fershrucka—frightened. He was very much frightened.

 Frightened—fershrucka. Ar war orrick fershrucka.

Fersomla—assembling. It is time to go, the people are already assembling.

 Assembling—fersomla. Es is tzeit tzu gæ, de leit du'n sich shun fersomla.

Flicka—mending. Here is that dollar for mending my shoes.

 Mending—flicka. Doh is seller dawler for my shoe flicka.

Finshterniss—eclipse. According to the almanack, we are going to have an eclipse of the sun one of these days.

Eclipse—finshterniss. According tzum collender wærra mer an soona finshterniss hawa anes fun denna dawg.

Fowla—rotting. The apples won't last long for they are rotting already.

 Rotting—fowla. De epple holta net long for se sin shun om fowla.

Froocht—grain. We can raise grain enough in this country to feed ourselves and all Europe besides.

 Grain—froocht. Mer kenna froocht genunk raisa in dem lond for uns selwer feedera un gons Europe besides.

Gabailed–bailed.   He is out of jail—one of his friends bailed him out.

Bailed—gabailed.   Ar is ous der jail—anes fun sina freind hut 'n rous gabailed.

Gaboona—bound.   The doctor bound up his sore arm.

Bound—gaboona.   Der duckter hut si waier awram tzu gaboona.

Gabreed—hatched.   Our old hen hatched out nine duck's eggs, and the young ducks now have a chicken as a step-mother.

Hatched—gabreed.   Unser olt hinkle hut nine enda oyer ousgabreed un de yungy enda hen now an hinkle ols a shteef-mommy.

Gadoold—patience.   To write such a good Penn. Dutch book takes hard work and much patience.

Patience—gadoold.   For so'n goots Penn. Deitsh booch shriva nemmts horty arwet un feel gadoold.

Gahired—married.   It is now almost thirty years since my wife and myself were married.

Married—gahired.   Es is now sheer dri-sich yohr sidder os ich un my fraw ga-hired hen

Gatri—faithful.   It is well said that a faithful man is a model among men.

Faithful—gatri.   Es is mit woret g'sawt os an gatrier mon an model unner menner is.

Gatzonkt—scolded.   When I came home at twelve o'clock, my wife scolded.

Scolded—gatzonkt.   We ich om tzwelf uhr hame cooma bin hut my fraw gatzonkt.

G'wesha—washed.   This morning I rose at six o'clock, put on my clothes and then washed myself.

Washed—g'wesha.   Den morya bin ich uf g'shtonna om sex uhr, hob my claider aw gadu un don mich g'wesha.

Geig—fiddle. After all there is no sort of instru-
mental music so enlivening as the old
fashioned fiddle.

Fiddle—geig. Om end is kæ sort inshtru-
menta musick so labehoft is de olt fash-
ionde geig.

Grexa—grunting. Half the time he is loafing
and guzzling and grunting.

Grunting—grexa. De holb tzeit doot ar loafa
un sowfa un grexa.

Harrlich—happy. He is well and happy as far
as I know.

Happy—harrlich. Ar is g'soont un harrlich
so feel os ich wase.

Hawsa—rabbits. I was out all day with gun and
dog and shot four rabbits.

Rabbits—hawsa. Ich war drous der gons
dawg mit flint un hoond un hob feer
hawsa g'shussa.

Hooshta—cough. It seems to me you have a
very dangerous cough—you'd better take
good care of yourself.

Cough—hooshta. Es coomt mer fore du
hetsht an orrick g'farelicher hooshta—
du besser gebsht goot aucht uf dich.

Hexa—witches. What is your opinion about
witches?

Witches—hexa. Wass is di opinion waega
hexa?

Ivversetza—translating. This, that I am now
writing in English and Penn. Dutch, is
what we call translating.

Translating—ivversetza. Des was ich now
shreib in English un in Penn. Deitsh is
wass mer ivversetza haist.

Kærrich—church. How many people go to
church for the purpose of exhibiting
their fine clothes?

Church—kærrich. We feel leit gane yoosht
in de kærrich for era shæna claider weisa?

Jigger—dram. That man takes regularly every morning his dram with bitters.

Dram—Jigger. Seller mon nemt olly morya regularly si drom mit bitters.

Keller—cellar. Go quickly down into the cellar and bring up a piece of butter.

Cellar—keller. Gæ g'shwint nooner in der keller un bring an shtick booter ruf.

Kinner—children. On last Sunday there were more than a hundred children in the Sunday-School.

Children—kinner. Om letshta Soondawg waura maner os a hoonert kinner in der Soondawg-School.

Klia—bran. Whoever mixes himself with bran will be eaten up by hogs.

Bran—klia. Wær sich unner de klia mixed den fressa de si.

Kup—head. Dan. Webster was a man who had a very big head—and he was no chuckle head.

Head—kup. Der Dan. Webster war an mon os an orrick grosser kup g'hot hut—un ar war kæ doom-kup.

Labe—live. I don't expect to forget my Penn. Dutch lessons as long as I live.

Live—labe. Ich expect net my Penn. Deitshe lessons tzu fergessa so long ich labe.

Lecherlich—laughable. There is no animal that is as laughable as a monkey.

Laughable—lecherlich. Es is kæ creddoor os so lecherlich is os an monkey.

Ligner—liar. What caused the muss was this: The man called the negro a liar, and then the negro knocked him down.

Liar—ligner. Wass der muss feruresauchd hut war des: Der mon hut der nager an ligner g'hasa, un don hut der nager een um g'shlawga.

Klae—small. A small article is easily read.
    Small—klae. A klæ shtick is leitcht galaisa.

Maid—girls. Nowadays we have scarcely any
    more girls, but ladies—that is more
    stylish.
    Girls—maid. Heitich dawgs huts sheer gor
    kæ maid mæ, awer ladies—sell is mæ
    stylish.

Mooka—flies. When sleigh riding there is no
    use in bothering the horse with a fly net.
    Flies—mooka. Om shlitta fawra is es for kæ
    use os mer der gowl boddert mit 'm
    mooka gawrn.

Nitzlich—useful. The study of Penn. Dutch is
    not merelv ornamental, but useful. It
    is only a question of time when it will be
    the language of the world.
    Useful—nitzlich.   De shtudy fun Penn.
    Deitsh is net yoosht for ornament, awer
    es is nitzlich. Es is aw yoosht an tzeits-
    froke wann es de shproach fun der welt
    si wærd.

Norr—fool. Everything in the world is for some
    use, but the use of a fool is not yet dis-
    covered.
    Fool—norr. Olles in der welt hut si use,
    awer de use for an norr is yoosht noch
    net ousg'foona.

Noss—wet. Every time it rains the weather be-
    comes wet.
    Wet—noss. Olly mohl os es raigent gebts
    aw noss wedder.

Nous—out. Whoever won't behave in church is
    forthwith put out of the house.
    Out—nous. Wær sich net behafed in der
    kaerrich den doot mer grawd tzum house
    nous.

Odam—breath. As long as a man draws his
    breath, so long there is hope for his life.
  Breath—odam. So long os an man si odam
    tzeegt, so long is aw huffung for si lava.

Orrick—very. Studying and reading Penn. Dutch
    goes very easily and pleasantly.
  Very—orrick. Penn. Deitsh laisa un shtudya
    gait orrick leicht, un plesseerlich.

Ouslender—foreigner. The Dutch foreigners are
    good for high German, but they must
    learn the Penn. Dutch.
  Foreigner—ouslender. De Deitshe ouslender
    sin goot om hoch Deitsh, awer Penn.
    Deitsh missa se larna.

Peffer—pepper. Liver puddings are not fit to
    eat unless they have plenty of pepper.
  Pepper—peffer. De levver wærsht sin gor
    net fit tzu essa except se hen plenty
    peffer.

Pifa—Whistling. Whistling is all right under
    certain circumstances. One who whistles
    while driving hogs or engaged cleaning
    stables may be regarded a mannerly
    man. But suppose a person would
    whistle Yankee Doodle at a funeral
    whilst they are letting down the coffin,
    what would the mourners and their
    friends think of the whistling?
  Whistling—pifa. Pifa is all recht unner g'-
    wissy umshtenda. Aner os pifed om si
    driva odder om shtol ous mishta is for
    common an monneerlicher mon. Awer
    suppose an porra dæt Yankee Doodle
    pifa on der leich, de weil se de lawd ins
    grawb lussa data—wass data de trowerer
    un era freind denka fum pifa?

Ruck—coat. To make a respectable appearance
    go to the clothing store and get yourself
    a fine new coat.

Coat—ruck. For an reshpectably appearance maucha gæ in der claider shtore un
kawf der an finer nier ruck.

Sida—silk. After all, there is nothing more beautiful to dress up a woman than fine black
silk.

Silk—sida. Om end is nix shenners for de
fraw uf dressa os finer shwartzer sida.

Sheesa—shooting. I enjoy nothing more than
going out shooting wild ducks and part-
ridges.

Shooting—sheesa. Ich du nix mæ enjoya os
nous gæ wildy enda un bottreesle sheesa.

Shlonga—snakes. There is nothing in the world
that I detest more than snakes.

Snakes—shlonga. Es is nix in der welt os
ich arger hoss os shlonga.

Shuckle-shtool—rocking-chair. For a real good
seat, give me, above all, a first-rate rock-
ing-chair.

Rocking-chair—Shuckleshtool. For'n rale
gooter sitz geb mere, fore ollem, an first-
rater shuckle-shtool.

Sow—hog. A hog is a hog, and no man of good
human sense would cast it up to a hog
on account his hogish nature.

Hog—sow. An sow is an sow, un kæ mon
fun gootam mensha fershtond daets der
sow foreshmeisa os se'n sow is.

Tæleffle—teaspoon. A teaspoon is'nt very large,
but a teaspoonful of arsenic is plenty to
get up a large funeral in the family.

Teaspoon—tæleffle. An tæleffle is net orrick
grose, awer an tæleffleful arsenic is plenty
for an grossy leich raisa in der family.

Uxa—oxen. Fat oxen afford excellent remedies
for starving people.

Oxen—uxa. Fetty uxa afforda first raty
mittle for hoongeriche leit.

Weibsleit—women. There are many handsome
    animals in the world—monkeys, ele-
    phants, kangaroos and goats, but women
    are far ahead of them all.
Women—weibsleit. Es hut feel shaney
    creddoera in der welt—monkeys,ellefonta,
    kangaroos un gais beck, awer om end
    sin de weibsleit ahead fun ena all.

COUNTING.—TZAILA.

One, two, three, four, five, six, seven, eight,
nine, ten, eleven, twelve, thirteen, fourteen, fifteen, sixteen, seventeen, eighteen, nineteen,
twenty, twenty-one, twenty-two, twenty-three,
twenty-four, twenty-five, twenty six, twenty-seven,
twenty-eight, twenty-nine, thirty, thirty-one, &c.
Forty, forty-one, &c. Fifty, fifty-one, &c. Sixty,
sixty-one, &c. Seventy, seventy-one, &c. Eighty,
eighty-one, &c. Ninety, ninety-one, &c. Hundred. Thousand. Million.

TRANSLATION.—IVVERSETZUNG.

Anes, tzwæ, dri, feer, finf, sex, sivva, aucht,
nine, tzain, elf, tzwelf, dritzain, færtzain, fooftzain,
sechtzain, sivvatzain, auchtzain, ninetzain, tzwonsich, ane-un-tzwonsich, tzæ-un-tzwonsich, dri-un-
szwonsich, feer-un-tzwonsich, finf-un-tzwonsich,
tex-un-tzwonsich, sivva-un-tzwonsich, aucht-un-
tzwansich, nine-un-tzwonsich, drisich, ane-un-
drisich, &c. Faertzich, ane-un-faertzich, &c,
Fooftzich, ane-un-fooftzich, &c. Sechtzich.

ane-un-sechtzieh, &c. Sivvatzich, ane-un-sivvat-
zich, &c.   Auchtzich, ane-un-auchtzich, &c.
Ninetzich, ane-un-ninetzich, &c. Hoonert. Daussend. Millione.

First, second, third, fourth, fifth, sixth, seventh, eighth, ninth, tenth, eleventh, twelfth, thir‾
teenth, fourteenth, fifteenth, sixteenth, seventeenth, eighteenth, nineteenth, twentieth, thirti·
eth, &c.

TRANSLATION.—IVVERSETZUNG.

Arsht, tzwett, dritt, faert, finft, sext, sivvat,
aucht, nine't, tzaint, elft, tzwelft, dritzaint, faert-
zaint, fooftzaint, sechtzaint, sivvatzaint, auchtzaint, ninetzaint, tzwonsichsht, drisichsht, &c.

MONTHS.—MOONOTA.

January,	Yonuawr;	July,	Yooly;
February,	Februawr;	August,	Augsht;
March,	Martz;	September,	September;
April,	Oppril;	October,	October;
May,	Moy;	November,	November;
June,	Yoony;	December,	Daitzember.

DAYS.—DAWGA.

Sunday,	Soondawg;	Thursday,	Doonersh-
Monday,	Moondawg;		dawg.
Tuesday,	Dinshdawg;	Friday,	Fridawg;
Wednesday,	Midwuch;	Saturday,	Somshdawg.

HOLIDAYS.--FIRE-DAWGA.

New Year,	Ni-Yohr; Thanksgiving Donk-dawg;
Easter,		Oashter; Christmas,	Crisht-dawg;
Whitsuntide, Pingsht; Fourth of July Færta Yooly

WEIGHTS.—GAWICHT.

Ton,		Ton;		Ounce,		Ounce;
Pound,		Poont;		Half ounce, Holb ounce;
Half pound, Holb poont; Quar.ounce Fartle ounce.
Quar.pound Fartle poont;

MEASURE.—MOSE.

Mile,		Mile;		Barrel,		Barl;
Half mile,	Holb mile; Bushel,	Bushel;
Quar. mile,	Fartle mile; Half bushel, Holb bushel
Yard,		Yard;		Peck,		Beck;
Foot,		Foos;		Half peck,	Holb Beck;
Inch,		Tzull;		Gallon,		Goll;
Half inch,	Holb tzull; Half gallon, Holwy goll;
Quar. inch,	Far. tzull;	Quart,		Quart;
Acre,		Ocker;		Pint,		Pint;
Half acre,	Hol. ocker; Half pint,	Holb pint;
Quar. acre,	Far. ocker; Gill,		Gill;
Hogshead,	Hoxet;		Half gill,	Holb gill.

PRACTICAL EXERCISES.

I have.   Ich hob.
He has.   Ar hut.
They have.   Se hen.
You have.   Du husht.
I can.   Ich con.
He can.   Ar con.
They can.   Se kenna.
You can.   Du consht.
I must.   Ich moos.
He must.   Ar moos.
They must.   Se missa.
You must.   Du moosht.
I walk.   Ich lawf.
He walks.   Ar lawft.
They walk.   Se lawfa.
You walk.   Du lawfsht.
I go.   Ich gæ.
He goes.   Ar gæt.
They go.   Se gæn.
You go.   Du gæsht.
I lie.   Ich leeg.
He lies.   Ar leegt.
They lie.   Se leega.
You lie.   Du leegsht.
I eat.   Ich ess.
He eats.   Ar esst.
They eat.   Se essa.
You eat.   Du esht.
I talk.   Ich shwetz.
He talks.   Ar shwetzt.
They talk.   Se shwetza.
You talk.   Du shwetsht

I look.   Ich gook.
He looks.   Ar gookt.
They look.   Se gooka.
You look.   Du gooksht.
I write.   Ich shreib.
He writes.   Ar shreibt
They write.   Se shreiva
You write.Du shreibsht
I was.   Ich war.
He was.   Ar war.
They were.   Se waura.
You was.   Du waursht
I think.   Ich denk.
He thinks.   Ar denkt.
They think.   Se denka.
You think.   Du denksht
I sing.   Ich sing.
He sings.   Ar sing'd.
They sing.   Se singa.
You sing.   Du singsht.
I do.   Ich du.
He does.   Ar du't.
They do.   Se du'n.
You do.   Du doosht.
I drink.   Ich drink.
He drinks.   Ar drinkt.
They drink.   Se drinka.
You drink.Du drinksht
I hear.   Ich hair.
He hears.   Ar haird.
They hear.   Se haira.
You hear.   Du hairsht

I don't believe that.   Ich glawb sell net.
I can do it.   Ich con 's du.
I give it up.   Ich geb 's uf.
I do not know it.   Ich wais 's net.
I took a walk.   Ich hob 'n walk g'nooma.
I walked down town.   I bin 's town nooner ga-
    luffa.
I go towards home.   Ich gæ hame tzu's.
I am going to church.   Ich gæ in de kærrich.
I am coming.   Ich bin om cooma.
I cannot say.   Ich con net sawga.
I go on the railroad.   Ich gæ uf 'm railroad.
I am going to dinner.   Ich gæ tzum middawg
    essa.
I am quite well.   Ich bin gons g'soond.
I saw my friend.   Ich hob my friend g'sæ.
I was in town.   Ich war im town.
I bought a horse.   Ich hob 'n gowl gakawft.
I need a cow.   Ich brauch an ku.
I feed the swine.   Ich feeder de si.
I want to see it.   Ich will 's sana.
I told them so.   Ich hob eena so g'sawt.
I heard that speech.   Ich hob selly speech g'hared
I hear an alarm.   Ich hair an larram.
I don't work to-day.   Ich shoff net heit.
I won't do it.   Ich will 's net du.
I won't go yet.   Ich gæ noch net.
I come this week.   Ich coom de wuch.
I want to tell him.   Ich will 's eem sawga.
I went out West.   Ich bin noch Weshta.
I was at home.   Ich war derhame.
I am at home.   Ich bin derhame.
I am going to bed.   Ich gæ ins bet.
I go to sleep now.   Ich gæ now shlofa.
Well, how goes it to-day?   Well, we gæts heit?
Are you going to town?   Gæsht in de shtadt?
What are you driving at now?   Wass treibsht
    ollaweil?
Are you all well?   Si'd eer oll g'soond?
Yes, we are all well.   Yaw, mer sin oll g'soond.
Where did you stop?   Wo husht du g'shtupt?

I must buy a new coat. Ich mus 'n nier ruck kawfa.

Did you hear him say it? Husht een 's hara sawga?

Yes, I heard it myself. Yaw, ich hob 's selwer g'hared.

Did you pay that bill? Husht selly bill betzawlt?

I paid it long ago. Ich hob 's shun long betzawlt.

Where did he come from? Wo coomd ar har?

Are you yet single? Bisht noch leddich?

Why don't you marry? Ferwass hiresht net?

Because I don't want to. Weil ich net will.

Where is the shoe store? Wo is der shoe shtore?

I need a pair of boots. Ich brauch 'n pawr shtiffle

I mean to buy a pair. Ich will a pawr kawfa.

Good boots cost money. Gooty shtiffle kushta geld.

I have nothing to do. Ich hob nix tzu du.

I'il buy a new hat. Ich kawf 'n nier hoot.

I bought a new hat. Ich hob 'n nier hoot ga- kawft.

What's the matter now? Wo faild 's now?

All's right again. Es is widder olles recht.

Did you see them? Husht se g'sana.

He died last night. Ar is de letsbt nauoht g'shtorwa

I was there myself. Ich war selwer dort.

I can't stand that. Ich con sell net shtanda.

I know nothing more. Ich wais mix mai.

On the other side. Uf der onner side.

That is what I said. Sell is wass ich g'sawt hob.

Where are you going? Wo gæsht hee?

Mind your own business. Mind di eagny bisness.

That is a very fine house down on the corner.— Sell is an orrick fines house droona uf 'm eck.

That is what the old lady told me yesterday. Sell is wass de olt fraw mer g'sawt hut geshter.

Now would be a good time to invest in lands.— Now wær 'n gooty tzeit for in lond tzu investa.

Better wait until property gets cheaper. Besser wardsht bis property wulfeller wærd.

Our merchants appear to be prospering just now.
Unser kawfleit shina glicklich tzu si olleweil.

The big circus is coming to town next week. Der
gróse circus coomd in de shtadt de naigsht
wuch.

Do you know when the animal show is coming?
Waisht wann der credoor-show coomd?

Young people travel five miles to see the circus.
Yungy leit travela finf mile der circus tzu
sana.

Elephants and monkeys are always interesting.
Ellefonta un monkeys sin olsfort interesting.

What is your opinion about monkeys, anyhow?
Wass is di opinion fun monkeys, anyhow?

Monkeys are yet considerably below human be-
ings. Monkeys sin noch ordlich weit unner
de mensha.

Not very much below some who are called men.
Net orrick weit unner a dale os se menner
haisa.

Monkeys steal, but so do many men. Monkeys
shtala, un so du'n aw feel menner.

Men lie, but I don't know as monkeys do. Menner leega, awer ich wais net os de monkeys
du'n.

Some men are hypocrites, but how about monkeys? A dale leit sin heichler, awer we mit
de monkeys?

Away with your monkeys—don't understand
them. Weck mit de monkeys—fershtae se
net.

This is a very fine horse. Des is an orrick shæ-
ner gowl.

These are very fine horses. Des sin orrick shæny
geil.

I rode to town on horseback. Ich bin ins town
garidda nf 'm gowl.

I like to read good books. Ich gleich gooty bicher
tzu laisa.

This is a very good book. Des is an orrick goots
booch.

These are very good books. Des sin orrick gooty
bicher.

This is a very fine young girl. Des is 'n orrick
fines yung maidle.

These are very fine young girls. Des sin orrick
finey yungy maid.

John is coming. home next week. Der John
coomd haim de naigsht wuch.

John was at home last week. Der John war der-
haim de letsht wuch.

John intends to travel to California. Der John
will noch California travella.

John traveled to California. Der John is nech
California gatraveled.

John has been traveling round all summer. Der
John is rumm gatraveled der gons soomer,

We have very cold weather now. Mer hen orrick
koltes wetter allaweil.

I must go to market for fresh butter. Ich moos
uf der morrick gæ for frisher bootter.

How do they sell the best butter? We ferkawfa
se der besht bootter?

What is the price of your butter? Wass is der
price fun deim bootter?

It seems to me that butter isn't good. Es coomd
mer fore seller bootter is net goot.

Are you sure that is an honest pound? Bisht
sure os sell an airliches poont is?

What will you take for the whole lot? Wass
nemmsht for de gons lot?

I sell this butter for twenty-five cents. Ich ferkawf dar bootler for finf un tzwonsich cent.

This is good butter—the very best. Dess is gooter bootter—der oller besht.

The weight is honest—you can depend on that.—
Es gawicht is airlich—du consht dich druf
ferlussa.

For twenty-three I'll sell the whole lot. For dri
un tzwonsich ferkawf ich de gons lot.

How many pounds have you? We feel poont
husht?

I have in all sixteen pounds. Ich hob in oll
    sechtzain poont.
It looks as if we would get more rain. Es gookt
    os wann mer mai raiga greega daita.
Who is that man across the way? Wær is seller
    mon ivver 'm waig.
I don't think I ever before saw that man. Ich
    denk net os ich yeamohls seller mon g'sæ
    hob.
He looks like a suspicious character. Ar gookd
    we 'n suspiciouser corrocter.
What makes you say that? Wass maucht dich
    sell sawga?
But from what do you judge? Awer fun wass
    doosht du judga?
His general appearance—his stove pipe hat. Si
    general awsæ—si shtofe pipe hoot.
And his tight pants—and his glittering breastpin.
    Un si tighty hussa—un si glitzeriche breast-
    pin.
And his waxed moustache—his fancy cane. Un
    si g'woxder mustash—si fancy shtecka.
Who is he anyhow? He needs watching. Wær
    is ar anyhow? Ar braucht watchas.
He may need watching—he may be bad. Con
    si os ar watchas braucht—ar mawg shlecht
    si.
He may be a thief, or a murderer. Ar mawg 'n
    deeb si, oddar 'n marder.
He may be even worse than that. Ar mawg aw
    shlechter si os sell.
But, who knows? Why judge before we know?
    Awer, wær wais? Waurum judga eb mer
    wissa?
He may be a wealthy humanitarian. Ar is fer-
    leicht an reicher mensha-freind.
Perhaps he is a leading capitalist. Ferleicht is
    ar an leadinger capitalisht.
Perhaps he wants to locate here. Ferleicht will
    ar doh locata.

And build a mill, a furnace or something else.
Un a meel baua, an forness, odder ebbas
soonsht.

Perhaps he is a Senator, or some Congressman.
Ar is ferleicht 'n Senator, odder 'n Congress-
mon.

Or, he may be a distinguished minister. Odder
ar mawg 'n bareemter preddicher si.

Or a great professor, or a correspondent. Odder
'n grosser professor, odder 'n correspondent.

For my part I mean to let him alone. For my
dale, ich glawb ich luss 'n gæ.

Sleighing is very good just now. Shlitta bawn is
orrick goot allaweil.

How did you like your sleigh ride? We husht
di shlitta ride gaglicha?

A good sleigh ride is always enjoyable. An
gooter shlitta ride is olsfort awganame.

Are you going to the election to-morrow? Gæsht
on de 'lection morya?

Of course I will—everybody ought to go? Uf
course will ich—yeader mon set gæ.

How do you think the election will result? We
denksht os de 'lection gæt?

I believe that the right ticket will win. Ich glawb
os 's recht ticket g'winnt.

And I believe it will be badly beaten. Un ich
glawb o 's orrick gabutta wærd.

Our district will give a large majority. Unser
district gebt an grossy majority.

I think you are greatly mistaken. Ich denk du
bisht orrick mistaken.

What makes you think that? Wass maucht
dich sell denka?

Because I hear so many talk the other way.
Weil ich so feel hare der onner waig shwetza.

Then you think our ticket will be beaten. D:n
denksht unser ticket wærd gabutta.

That is just what I firmly believe. Sell is yoosht
wass ich feshtlich glawb.

Perhaps you are going wrong yourself. Ferleicht
   gæsht du selwer letz.

No, I'm going to vote as every man should. Nay,
   ich will vota we an yeader monn vota set.

But which side do you call the right one? Awer
   welly side haisht du de recht?

Why my side is the right one, of course it is. Ei
   my side is de recht, of course is se.

What are the crop prospects this year? Wass
   sin de ous-sichta for de froocht des yohr?

Well so so; I think as a whole they are good.
   Well, so so; Ich denk, im gonsa, se sin goot.

Wheat looks very well, and so does rye. Waitza
   gookt orrick goot, un so doots korn.

Grass is not so good—it needs a good rain. Graws
   is net so goot—es faild 'm an gooter raiga.

Oats is middling, coming up to the average. Hau-
   wer is middlemaisich—coomd ruf tzum average.

Have you commenced your harvesting? Husht
   shun di arnta awg'fonga?

I think I will commence next week. Ich denk
   ich fong de naigsht woch aw.

I suppose you are done with haymaking? Ich
   fermoot du bisht færtich hoymaucha?

Not yet; we yet have about ten loads to haul in.
   Noch net; mer hen noch about tzain loads
   ei tzu fawra.

How many acres of wheat have you? We feel
   ocker waitza husht?

I have twenty-seven acres. Ich hob sivva un
   tzwonsich ocker.

And how many acres of corn? Un we feel ocker
   welshkorn?

Do you know that old Tom Jones is dead?—
   Waisht os der olt Tom Jones dote is?

I didn't know that. When did he die? Ich hob
   sell net g'wisst. Wann is ar g'shtorwa?

He died on last Thursday. Ar is g'shtorwa om
   letshta Doonershdawg.

What was the matter with him?   Wass hut 'm
g'faild?

He had an attack of billious fever.   Ar hut 'n attack fum golla fever g'hot.

Old Tom left a good deal of property.   Der olt
Tom hut ordlich feel property hinnerlussa.

Yes, I should call him worth fully fifty thousand.
Yaw, Ich dait een fullens fooftzich daussend
wært haisa.

As much as that?   So feel os sell?

Yes, all of that, and rather more.   Yaw, gons so
feel, un rather maner.

I khow of no property he owned except the farm.
I wais fun kem property os ar eagent except
de bauerei.   .

But he also has ten thousand government bonds.
Awer ar hut aw tzain daussend in government bender.

And he also has money on other securities.   Un
ar hut aw geld uf onnery securities.

Do you know whether Tom made a will?   Waisht
eb der Tom an willa g'maucht hut?

That I cannot say with with certainty.   Sell con
ich net for sure sawga.

I suppose the widow will administer.   Ich fermoot os de widfraw wærd adminishtra.

She was in town to engage a lawyer anyhow.   Se
war anyhow in der shtadt for 'n lawyer
engaga.

I suppose they will sell out some of the stock.—
Ich fermoot os se an dale fum shtock ous
ferkawfa.

What do they now pay for the best coal?   Wass
betzawla se for de beshty coala now?

I must go up to Brown's and buy a load.   Ich
moos noof ons Brown's gæ un a load kawfa.

What's the price of nut coal?   Wass is der price
fun de nut coala?

I like that kind as well as any other.   Ich gleich
selly so goot os ennich onnery.

They are more easily kindled than the larger
size. Se sin leichter aw g'shteckd os de gres-
sery.

Was you at Church on Sunday evening? Warsht
in der kærrich om Soondawg owet?

Yes, I was there, and so was my wife. Yaw, ich
war, un so war my fraw.

What do you think of the new pastor? Wass
denksht fum nia porra?

I don't like him as well as the old one. Ich
gleich 'n net so goot os der olt.

Why not, what's the matter with him? Warum
net, wass is don letz mit 'm?

Why he don't preach at all, he only reads. Ei
ar preddicht gor net, ar lais'd yoosht.

But many of the best preachers do the same.—
Awer feel fun de beshty preddicher doon 's
same.

Then why call them preachers—why not readers?
Waurum haist mer se don preddicher—ferwass net laiser?

But reading shows care, study, and industry.
Awer laisa weist auchtung, shtudy, un fleis.

That may be so, but I go in for square preaching.
Sell mawg so si, awer ich gæ ni for plain preddicha.

There is another thing about him I don't like.
Es is noch ebbas on eem os ich net gleich.

He looks as if he was very proud. Ar gookd os
wann ar orrick shtuls wær.

That's a mistake, he is very sociable. Sell is 'n
mistake, ar is orrick friendlich.

But such a waxy moustach don't suit a preacher.
Awer so'n g'woxter mustash suit kæ preddicher.

Oh, why such a mustache is just the style. Oh,
so'n mustash is yoosht der shtyle.

But what we want is more gospel and less style.
Awer wass mer wella is maner effongalium
un net so feel shtyle.

You must remember that he is yet a young man.
Du moosht aw badenka os ar noch 'n yunger
mon is.

But old enough to have plain common sense.—
Awer olt ganoonk for plainer commoner fershtond.

It seems to me you are very hard to please.
Es dinkt mich du wærsht orrick hord tzu
pleasa.

If only he'd cut off that moustache. Wann ar
yoosht seller mustash obshneida dait.

BUSINESS TALK.

BISNESS G'SHWETZ.

THE BOOK—STORE.

DER BOOCH-SHTORE.

Bookseller.—Well, what can I do for you to-day?

Booch-hondler.—Well was con ich du for dich heit?

Customer.—Have you Rauch's new book on Penn. Dutch?

Customer.—Husht 'm Rauch si ni booch uf Penn. Deitsh?

B. Just sold the last copy we had—if you'll wait ten minutes I'll have another lot.

B. Hob yoosht 's letsht copy derfu ferkawft—wann du tzæ minoota wardsht will ich an onnery lot doh hawa.

C. Accoring to that they sell rapidly.

C. According tzu sellam du'n se shtorrick ferkawfa.

B, Sell! They go off like hot buckwheat cakes. But (to clerk) just step around and order fifty more copies forthwith.

B. Ferkawfa! Se gæn ob we haisy buch-waitza koocha. Awer (tzum clarrick) shtep yoosht rumm un order fooftsich copies mainer.

C.   What's the price of the book?

    C.   Wass is der price fum booch?

B.   A dollar and a half.

    B.   A dawler un a holwer.

C.   Isn't that rather a high price?

    C.   Is sell net rather 'n hocher price?

B.   It is above the average, but it is a specialty, and when you come to see it you wouldn't do without it for five times the price. (The clerk returns with half a dozen Hand-Books, and says the remainder of the newly ordered lot will be along in the course of an hour.)

    B.   Es is uvvich 'm average, awer es is special, un wann du's amohl saisht don daitsht net ona du for finf mohl der price. (Der clarrick coomd tzurick mit a holb dootzend Hond Bicher, un sawgt os de irveriche fun der ni g'orderdy lot awcooma waerra in about a shtoond.)

C.   Well, this is a neat book, that's a fact.

    C.   Well, des is aw an shaines booch, sell in 'n fact.

B.   And who'd a thought that the Penn. Dutch contains nearly four thousand regular words, besides a thousand or more transferred from English?

    B.   Un waer hets gadenkt os de Penn. Deitsh shproah sheer feer daussend wardta het, besides a daussend mainer os yoosht ous 'm English ganooma sin ?

C.   I see its a good book, and I'll take two copies, one for myself and the other I'll send to my son-in-law in New York.

    C.   Ich sæ 's is a goots booch, un ich nem tzwæ copies, ains for mich selwer un 's onner will ich meim duchter mon in Nei Yorrick shicka.

B.   Nothing else to-day?

    B.   Nix soonsht heit?

C.   Well, let me see—yes, I want a quire of your best note paper and a package of envelopes, and, by the way—whats the price of History of the Rebellion?

B. Well, luss much sana—yaw, ich will aw an quire fum besht note bobbeer un a pock envelopes, un aw, luss sana, wass is der price fum Rebellion History?

B. Thats two and a quarter.

B. Sell is tzwæ un a fartle.

C. Say two—thats enough.

C. Sawg tzwae—sell is g'noonk.

B. Well, yes, take it. Nothing else?

B. Well, yaw, nems. Nix soonsht?

C. No, nothing else this time— oh, yes, I almost forgot—I must have a number two reader for my boy, and also a slate and slate pencil.

C. Nay, nix soonsht des mohl—oh yaw, ich het sheer fergessa, ich mus aw an number two reader hawa for my bu, un aw an shlate pencil.

B. Nothing else?

B. Nix sunsht?

C. No, that's all. Now how much does it all amount to?

C. Nay, sell is all. Now we feel maucht sell all tzomma?

B. Well, there's Rauch's Penn. Dutch, a dollar and a half a piece, three dollars; the Rebellion, two dollars; Reader, seventy-five; paper, ten; slate and pencil, say twenty-five; envelopes, ten; in all six dollars and ten cents.

B. Well, doh is's Rauch's Penn. Dutch, a dawler un a holwer's shtick, dri dawler; Rebellion, tzwæ dawler; Reader, finf un sivvatzich; boobeer, tzain; shlate un pencil, finf un tzwonsich; envelopes tzain—in oll sex dawtzain cent.

C. Say the even six dollars.

C. Sawg de ava sex dawler.

B. All right—six dollars.

B. Oll recht—sex dawler.

C. Oh, I really forgot—I must have a copy of Pilgrim's Progress for my daughter—promised her one long ngo— whats the price of that neat gilt-edged with clasps?

    C. Oh, really, ich nob fergessa—ich mus aw 'n copy fun Pilgrim's Progress hawa. Ich hobs shun long miner dochter fershprucha— wass is der price derfu—sell mit 'm gilt edge un selly clasps draw?

B. Two and a quarter.

    B. Tzwæ un a færtle.

C. Say two dollars?

    C. Sawg tzwæ dawler.

B. Well—can hardly do it, but being its you, all right.

    B. Well, ich cons hardly du, awer weil 's dich is will ich's oll recht haisa.

C. Now I am done sure, good bye!

    C. Now bin ich awer færtich sure, good bye.

B. Good bye.

    B. Good bye.

CLOTHING STORE.

CLAIDER SHTORE.

Proprietor.—Walk in, walk in—here's the place for the best and cheapest—what can I do for you —whole suit, or only coat, pants and vest?

    Proprietor.—Coom ri, coom ri—doh is der plotz fors besht un wulfelsht—wass con ich du for dich—a gonsy suit, odder yoosht an ruck, hussa un jacket?

Customer.—Indeed I hardly know—I'll just look at your pants, for that's all I need just now.

    Customer.—Ich wais g'wiss sheer net—Ich will yoosht amohl eier hussa baguoka for sell is 's ainsich os ich brauch alleweil.

P. Want them dark?

    P. Wass forriche, doonkeley?

C. Well yes, dark, but not quite black.

    C. Well, yaw, doonkle, awer net gons shwartz.

P.   Here's a pair that will just fit you—only
four dollars and a quarter; and here's a pair for
three seventy-five; and here's a pair for three
dollars.

P.   Doh sin a pawr os dich goot fitta—yoosht
feer dawler un a færtle. Uu doh sin a pawr
for dri un dri færtle, un doh an onners pawr
for dri dawler.

C.   Is'nt this stuff nearly, or entirely cotton?

C.   Is des shtuff net sheer oll bau-wull?

P.   Well no—this pair contains some cotton,
but mostly wool, and this pair is all wool and
warranted.

P.   Well nay—des pawr doh hut ebbas bau-
wull, awer der graisht dale derfu is wull, un
des doh pawr is oll wull un sell warn ich.

C.   Well, I'll give you three and a quarter but
not another cent.

C.   Well, ich geb der dri un a færtle, awer
net 'n cent mainer.

P.   Say three and a half.

P.   Sawg dri un a holwer.

C.   No, three and a quarter is all I'll do.

C.   Nay, dri un a færtle is olles os ich du.

P.   Oh, I wont stand on a quarter, so here goes,
they are yours. But now you want a vest also,
to match don't you?

P.   Oh, ich will net shtæ uf a færtle, so doh
gaits—se sin di. Awer now wid aw noch an
jacket for dertzu matcha, dusht net?

C.   What will you charge me for a vest of the
same quality of goods?

C.   Wass wid mich charga for 'n jacket
fun der same quality?

P.   Lets see; here is one—the price is two and
a quarter, and I'll put it to you at two dollars.
That's very cheap.

P.   Luss mohl sana, doh is ains, der price
is tzwæ un a færtle, un ich du's tzu der for
tzwæ dawler. C. Sell is orrick wulfel.

C. Now you do know how to charge. I can buy as good a vest as that for a dollar and a quarter.

> C. Now, du waisht we tzu charga. Ich con so'n goots vest kawfa os sell is for an dawler un a færtle.

B. Indeed you can't. Two dollars is the lowest possible price for which it can be sold without loss. The fact is, it costs me just one dollar and ninety cents.

> B. Du consht gawiss net. Tzwæ dawler is 's niddersht os ich nemma con defore ona tzu ferleera. De facht is, 's kusht mich yusht ea dawler un ninetzich cent.

C. Well, I don't care what it cost you—I'll take it at one seventy-five.

> C. Well, ich geb nix drum wass es dich gakusht nut—ich nems for ain dawler un finf un sivvatzich cent.

P. As times are rather hard just now you can have it at that. Now let me show you a coat, I'm sure you need one.

> P. Weil de tzeita rather hord sin yoosht nems. Now luss mich der amohl an ruck weisa, for ich bin sure os du aner brauchsht.

C. But I can't well afford it just now.

> C. Awer ich con 's net goot afforda olleweil.

P. Here's one very cheap—same quality of goods for nine and a half.

> P. Doh is ainer orrick wulfel—same quality fun shtuff, for nine un a holwer.

C. Even if I wanted a coat, I would'nt give you more than about seven and a half for it.

> C. Wann ich aw an ruck wet dait ich der net mæ gerva derfore os sivva un a holwer.

P. But you do want one, and I'll let you have it for nine dollars.

> P. Awer du doosht ane braucha un ich geb der den doh for nine dawler.

C. Whats the use of talking—I say I don't want any coat just now, and even if I did, I would'nt go a cent above eight dollars no how.

C. Wass is de use derfu tzu shwetza? Ich sawg ich will kenner olleweil, un wann ich aw ainer wet dait ich kæ cent haicher gæ os aucht dawler.

P. Say eight seventy-five.

P. Sawg aucht finf un sivvatzich.

C. I tell you again I don't need a coat just now.

C. Ich sawg noch amohl ich brauch kæ ruck ollaweil.

P. Just to see how well it will become you— suppose you try it on.

P. Yoosht tzu sana we goot ar dich bacoomt, suppose du proweersht 'n amohl aw.

C. Whats the use of trying it on when I don't mean coat business?

C. Wass is de use for 'n aw proweera wan nich doch net uf der ruck bisness mainung bin?

P. Oh, well, just try it on any how. (C. tries it on) now thats what I call a first rate fit—perfectly faultless. Here's the glass, look and see for yourself.

P. Oh, well, proweer'n yoosht aw any how (C. proweert'n aw) now sell is wass ich an first rater fit hais—parfectly failer fri. Doh is 'n glaws, gook 'n amohl aw un sæ for dich selwer.

C. Well, (looking at it before the glass) it is a pretty good fit thats a fact, but then as I said already, I don't need a coat—I'll—let me see— whats the lowest you'll take for it?

C. Well, (fore 'm glaws) es is 'n ordlich gooty fit, sell is 'n fact, awer we shun amohl g'sawt, ich brauch kæ ruck—ich—luss mich sana— wass is 's niddersht os du nemsht derfore?

P.   I said eight seventy-five, but as it becomes you so admirably you may keep it for eight and a half.

P.   Ich hob aucht finf on sivatzich g'sawt, awer weil ar deer so goot bacoomd mawgsht 'n b'holta for aucht un a holwer.

C.   Well, I guess I might as well take it. Have you any suspenders ?

C.   Well, ich denk ich dait 'n yoosht so goot nemma.   Husht aw gallases ?

P.   Yes, here's a fine variety—these are twenty-five cents, these thirty-five, and this lot sixty.

P.   Yaw, doh is 'n finey sort—de doh sin finf un tzwonsich cent, de doh finf un drisich, un selly onner lot sechtzich.

C.   I'll take a pair of these at thirty-five.

C.   Ich nem a pawr fun denna on finf un drisich.

P.   Any thing else ?

P.   Ennich ebbas soonsht ?

C.   Yes, a box of No. 15 paper collars.

C.   Yaw, 'n box No. 15 bobbeerny collars.

P.   We also have some very good and cheap underclothing.

P.   Mer hen aw orrick gooty un wulfelly unnerclaider.

C.   But I positively want nothing in that line.

C.   Awer ich will positeefly nix in seller line.

P.   Here are some very excellent undershirts at seventy-five, and drawers at the same.

P.   Doh sin ivver ous gootyunner hemmer for finf un sirvatzich cent, un drawers om same.

C.   Well give me a pair of each.

C.   Well, geb mer a pawr fun yadam.

P.   Now you want stockings—here's some for twenty cents a pair.

P·   Now, du wid aw shtrimp—doh sin for finf un tzwonsich cent 's pawr.

C. Give me about three pair.

    C. Geb mer about dri pawr.

P. Nothing else?

    P. Nix soonsht?

C. That is all. Now how much is the whole bill?

    C. Nay, sell is oll. Now we feel maucht de gons bill.

P. (Noting down and adding up) seventeen dollars and fifty-five cents, the cheapest out fit ever sold.

    P. (Doot olles tzomma adda) sivvatzain dawler un finf un fooftsich cent, de wulfelsht out fit os yeamohls ferkawft is warra.

Customer settles up, and bids farewell.

    Der customer settled uf un sawgt farrywell.

THE DRUG STORE.—DE OBBADAIK.

Invalid.—Have you any thing to cure rheumatism?

    Invalid.—Husht eunich ebbas os roomatis cured?

Druggist.—The very best remedy in the world —its Jones' unfailing herb remedy, positively curing every complaint from whooping cough down to square tooth ache.

    Obbadaiker.—'S very besht in der welt—'m Jones si unfailbawry kreiter mittle possiteefly cured olly menshlichy complaints fum blo hooshta aw bis nunner tzu shquare tzaw-wai.

I. And how do you sell that stuff?

    I. Un we ferkawfsht sell shtuft?

D. One dollar a bottle.

    D. Ain dawler de buttle.

I. Well, I'll take a bottle.

    I. Well, ich nem a buttle.

D. Any thing else?

    D. Ennich ebbas soonsht?

I. Why yes—the old woman wants a box of the celebrated Swiss pills—I believe you keep them.

    I. Ei yaw—de olt fraw will a box fun de
bareemta Shweitzer pilla—ich glawb der halta
fun sella?

D. Yes, we keep them until we sell them.   Here
is a box.   You will find directions on the wrapper.
One dose from three to five, and if that fails to operate then take the box.

    D. Yaw, mer holta se bis mer se ferkawfa.
Doh is an box derfu.   Du finnsht de directions
uf 'm wrapper.   Ea dose fun dri bis finf, un
wann sell failed tzu shoffa don nem de box.

The invalid paid for his remedies and left.

    Der invalid hut si duckter shtuft batzawlt
un is uf un ob.

THE DOCTOR.—DER DUCKTER.

Doctor in sick room.—Well, what seems to be
the matter with Annie?

    Duckter in der kronka shtoob.—Well, wass
is letz mit der Annie?

Mother at bed side.—Indeed I dont know what
is the matter.   She was ailing all of yesterday
and last night, with severe headache and feverish,
and it seems to me also that she has a swelling of
the neck.

    Mooter om side fum bet.—Eei ich wais g'wiss
net wo's failed.   Se hut gaclaug'd geshter der
gons dawg un aw de letsht naucht, hut kup-
wæ un fever, un es coomd mer aw fore era
hols wær g'shwulla.

D. (Feeling pulse) Yes, she seems to be a little
feverish.   Annie, just let me see your tongue.
Yes, that's it.   Has Annie been eating anything
this morning?

    D. (Feeld der pools) Yaw, se sheind a wen-
nich feverish tzu si.   Annie, weis mer amohl
di tzoong.   Yaw. so is 's.   Hut de Annie ebbas
g'essa den morya?

M. No, not a mouthful except two soft boiled
eggs, a piece of toast well buttered and a piece of
steak about half as big as my hand.   She drank

two cups of coffee, however.

M. Nay, net a mowlful except tzwæ waich gakuchty oyer, a shtick toast goot gabooterd un a shtick flaish net holb so gross os my hond. Se hut aw tzwæ cuplin coffee gadroonka.

D. Oh then her case may not necessarily be a serious one. At all events I think we'll oon get her over this attack.

D. Oh don is era case doch net g'fairlich. Anyhow ich donk mer wærra se bol ivver den attack bringa.

M. I hope so, for I dont know what I'd do if Annie would die—it would set me crazy.

M. Ich will so huffa, for ich wais net wass ich du dait wann de Annie shtarwa set—es dait mer narrich maucha.

D. Don't be uneasy—she'll be all right in a day or two—no danger at all.

D. Si net unruish— se coomd oll recht in a dawg odder tzwæ— gor kæ g'fore.

M. What is it that's the matter with—it is'nt what they call congestion of the brain, is it?

M. Wass is es os era failed—is 's net wass se de congestian fum gaharn haisa?

D. No indeed—nothing of that kind—its only a case of overtasking the stomach and a slight cold, causing some nervous agitation, with a little mental prostration.

D. Nay, nay, nix fun der awrt—es is yoosht an ivverlawdung fum mawga un a wennich kalt os an narfishe unru feroorsaucht mit a wennich gameets fershwecherung.

M. But doctor, Annie is very sick—seriously sick, and I'm sure she needs medicine.

M. Awer duckter, de Annie is orrick kronk —g'fairlich kronk, un ich bin sure os se meditzeen hawa moos.

D. Well yes, of course, its as I say—she's sick, but what I mean is she is not in that sort of condition as to cause the least alarm.

D. Well yaw, of course, es is we ich sawg, se is kronk, awer wass ich mane is os se net in so a condition is os enniche unru feroor-saucha set.

M. May be its what they call diphtheria—oh ; I do hope she'll get over it.

M. Ferleicht is 's wass se diphtheria haisa. Oh ! ich du huffa se coomd drivve .

D. No diphtheria at all, and in fact nothing se-rious of any kind.   Fact is I can't name any par-ticular complaint, because there is none other than as I stated—slightly indisposed.

D. Gor kæ diphtheria, un in fact gor nix g'fairlichs fun ennicher awrt.   De fact is ich con kæ particularer nawma fun kronkheit gevva weil es kæ realy kronkheit is, awer yoosht a wennich ung'soondichkeit.

M. Then you are not going to give her any medicine, are you? If you won't, I'll have to send for Doctor Smith, because I'm as certain as I live that Annie is seriously sick.

M. Demnoch wid era kæ meditzeen gevva; wann net shick ich for der Duckter Shmit, for ich bin so sure os ich læb os de Annie g'fairlich kronk is.

D. Well, you may send for Doctor Smith if you will, and if you do, he will fully agree with me that there is nothing serious the matter with Annie.

D. Well, du mawgsht for der Duckter Shmit shicka wana du wit, un wann du doosht don wærd ar aw fullens agreea mit mer os gor nix g'fairliches mit der Annie is.

M. Well I,ll take your word for it, but, then I'm sure she needs some medicine.

M. Well, ich will don di wardt derfore nemma, awer, ich bin sure os se doch medi-tzeen hawa mus.

D. Oh yes, of course she does and I mean to give her just what she needs, and if you'll let me have a piece of paper I'll prepare some powders—the the very thing that will bring her all right inside of twenty-four hours.

D. Oh yaw, of course, un ich will aw gevva yoosht wass se braucht, un wann du mer 'n shtick bobbeer gebsht will ich etlich pilferlin prepara for se; un selly bringa se rous in wennicher os feer un tzwonsich shtoond

The Doctor prepared the powders, and directed one to be taken in sugar every two hours, and as he left the room, Annie's mother began to suspect that after all she may have been needlessly alarmed.

Der Duckter hut de pilferlin prepared un g'orderd anes ei tzu gevva olly tzwæ shtoond, un we ar tzu der shtoob nous is, hut der Annie era mooter suspect os om end hut se kæ ursauch g'hot for nnrooich tzu si.

DRY GOODS.

Clerk.—How do you do to-day mam. Can I be of any service to you?

Clarrick.—We mauchts heit. Con ich ebbas du for dich?

Lady.—I want to see some of your best black silks.

Lady.—Ich will amohl eier beshter shwartza sida sana.

C. Yes 'm. Just please step this way. Here are the best goods ever produced—perfectly faultless. Here is a piece at a dollar; and here at one and a quarter; this at one dollar sixty and here still better at one eighty.

C. Yaw. Si so goot un shtep den waig. Doh sin de beshty goods os yeamohls g'maucht sin warra, parfect un failer-fri. Doh is 'n shtick on a dawler; un doh on anes un a færtle; nu des doh a dawler un sechtzich, un doh ols noch besser for an dawler un auchtzich.

L. Sure that this is the best?

L. Sure os des 's besht is?

C. Rely on it, this is the very best that the lead-

ing houses of New York and Philadelphia can
furnish. There is nothing any where to surpass
these goods.

C. Ferluss dich druf, des is 's very besht os
mer kawfa con in de leading heiser in Nei
Yorrick odder Philadelphia. Es sin gor kæ
goods os de doh beata kenna.

L. It looks well—you are sure its the best? Mrs.
Jenkins has a dress that seemed to me unsurpassed, and I want none below that grade.

L. Es gookt shæ—bisht sure os des 's besht
is os tzu hawa is? De Mrs. Jenkins hut 'n
dress os mer ivvertrefflich fore ccomd un ich
will nix os net uf coomd tzu eras.

C. Why Mrs. Jenkins' dress to which you refer
is from this very piece, and you say truly, it is
unsurpassed.

C. Ei der Mrs. Senkins era dress is fun dem
very same shtick, un du husht recht wann
du sawgsht 's is ivvertrefflich.

L. Then you have none to beat this, have you?

L. Demnoch husht nix os des beata con?

C. Well, let me see, here is a piece of figured
goods, equal as to quailty and as a matter of taste
I incline to think it is richer in consequence of
the figure.

C. Well, luss mich sana—doh is 'n shtick
os g'figgerd is, un es is yoosht 'n froke fun
taste eb 's shenner is; ich denk de figger gebt
dem a shenners awsai.

L. What's the price of it?

L. Wass is der price fum dem?

C. Well, the price of this is two ten—just twenty-
five cents per yard more.

C. Well, der price fun dem is tzwæ dawler
un tzæ cent—yusht finf un tzwonsich cent de
yord mainer.

L. Its higher priced, then, is it?

L. Don is des doh haicher in price?

C. Yes, twenty-five cents higher, and I think it

worth fully that much more.

C. Yaw, finf un tzwonsich cent haicher, un ich denk es is aw fullens so feel mai wært.

L. I don't know but that it is, and I think it looks yet richer than Mrs. Jenkins'—don't you think so too?

L. Ich wase net eb 's net so is, un ich denk es gookt noch reicher os der Mrs. Jenkins eras—denksht net aw so?

C. Oh certainly, its richer and better.

C. Yaw gawiss, es is reicher un besser.

L. Well, I'll take—let me see—eighteen yards —and you may fill the necessary trimmings, and send it up to No. 945, Quality street. The bill you'll send to my husband, Mr. Swelling at his office, No. 28 Finawe Avenue.

L. Well, ich nemn—luss mohl san'a auchtzain yard, un du mawgsht de trimmings adda, un shicks nuf tzu nummer nine hoonert un finf un færtzich (945) Quality shtrose. De bill shicksht tzu meim monn on siner office, nummer aucht un tzwonsich (28) Finawe avenue.

FURNITURE STORE.

Housekeeper.—I want to look at some of your parlor chairs.

Housekeeper.—Ich will amohl eir parlor shteelbagooka.

Proprietor.—Just please follow me—we have a splendid lot and I think I can suit you. Here they are, as you see, a splendid assortment.

Proprietor.—Yusht si so goot un lawf mit —mer hen a splendity lot an ich denk ich con dich suita. Doh sin se, un du sæsht os es an finey sortment is.

H. What's the price of this set, including rocking chair?

H. Wass is der price fun dara set, mit 'm shuckle shtool?

P. I'll sell you that set at twenty-six dollars—

you couldn't select a finer set than that.

P. Ich ferkawf der selley for sex un tzwon-sich dawler—du consht narryats kæ finery set os selly finna.

H. And whats the price of these.

H. Un wass is der price fun denna?

P. They are a little cheaper—twenty-two.

P. De sin a wennich wulfeller—tzwæ un tzwonsich.

H. And these?

H. Un dee?

P. These are the same price. Now, here is a set, the best we have and you can't get a finer set than this one any where. I'll sell them to you for thirty-four—rocker and stool included.

P. Dee sin der same price. Now, doh is 'n set, de beshty os mer hen, un du consht nar-ryats kæ finery set finna os dee sin, gook wo du wit. Selly ferkawf ich for feer un drisich, der rocker un shtool gane mit.

I. Is'nt the price rather high?

H. Is sell net rather hoch?

P. It seems high, but not when you come to con-sider that they are the best you can buy any where, they are not too high.

P. Es sheint hoch tzu si, awer wann du con-siddersht os es de beshty sin os mer kawfa con, don sin se om end net tzu hoch.

H. If you'll take thirty dollars I,ll take them.

H. Wan du's drisich dawler nemsht don nem ich se.

P. Say thirty-two—split the difference.

P. Sawg tzwæ un drisich—shplit der differ-ei,ce.

H. Is that the best you can do?

H. Is sell 's best os'd du consht?

P. That is the very best I can do. You see the most valuable goods, though in the end the cheap-est, do cost more and run into cash, and for that we must keep the figures down as low as possible, and thirty-two dollars is as low as I can make it. The fact is, it cuts off almost the entire profit.

P. Sell is' s besht os ich du con. Du waisht de beshty goods sin om end de wulfelshty, awer es is wohr, se runna haicher ins geld, un des is de ursauch os mer de figgers so weit os miglich droona halta missa, un tzwæ un drisich is so nidder os ich 's maucha con. De fact is es du't der pruffit sheer gor all ous wisha.

H. How soon can you send them down.

H. We bol kensht se nooner shicka?

P. I can send them down inside of an hour.

P. Ich con snooner shicka inside fun a shtoond.

H. Well, I'll take 'em. Just please make me a bill and receipt it. Here's two twenties—forty dollars.

H. Well, ich nem se. Si so goot un mauch 'n bill derfu un du se risseeta. Doh sin tzwæ tzwonsich dawler nota—færtzich dawler.

P. Lets see, I must give you eight dollars change--here is five, and one is six, and one is seven and one more makes eight. Much obliged to you. Here's the receipt. I'll have 'em down inside of half an hour.

P. Luss mohl sana—ich mus der aucht dawler wexel gevva—doh sin, finf, un anes maucht sex, un anes sivva, un noch anes aucht. Donk der aw. Doh is de risseet. Ich shick se nooner inside fun a holwy shtoond.

H. All right. Good day.

H. All recht. Good bye.

P. Good day. Call soon again.

P. Good bye. Coom bol widder.

GROCERY.

Grocer.—And what can we do for you this time?

Grocer.—Un wass kenna mer du for dich desmohl?

Customer.—I want two pounds of roasted coffee.

    Customer.—Ich het garn tzwæ poont g'-roashter coffee.

G. What price—here is some for twenty-five, here thirty, and this, the best at thirty-five.

    G. Weller price—doh is for finf un tzwonsich, doh drisich, un dar doh, der besht, for finf un drisich.

C. Give me the thirty five.

    C. Geb mer fum finf un drisich.

G. What else?

    G. Wass noch?

C. Three pounds of your ten cent sugar.

    C. Dri poont tzain cent tzooker.

G. And what else?

    G. Un wass noch?

C. Have you any country soap?

    C. Husht aw haim g'mauchty saif?

G. We have, and of the very best quality.

    G. Ich hob, un fun der oller besht quality.

C. Give me three pounds, and also two boxes of matches, a quart of salt and a half pound of the best green tea.

    C. Geb mer dri poont, un aw tzwe box matches, a quart sols un a holb poont fum beshta greena tæ.

G. Any thing else to-day?

    G. Ennich ebbes soonsht heit?

C. Well, let me see, how do you sell these dried peaches?

    C. Well, luss mohl sana, we ferkawfsht de drookny parshing?

G. These we sell at ten cents per quart, or thirty-five cents per half peck.

    G. De ferkawfa mer on tzæ cent de quart, odder for finf un drisich cent de holb beck.

C. Sure they are the best?

    C. Sure os se de beshty sin?

G. I'll insure them to be the very best.

    G. Ich insures os se de very beshty sin.

C. Well let me have a half peck.   And coming

to think I want about two pounds of cheese, and
also a good mackarel and a package of clear
starch.

    C. Well luss mich an holb beck hawa. Un
now denk ich draw, ich will aw about tzwæ
poont kais, un aw 'n gooter mackrel un a
pock shtarrick.

G. Nothing else?

    G, Nix soonsht?

C. I believe that's all. How much does that
make?

    C. Ich glawb sell is olles. We feel mauchts?
The grocer foots up and the customer squares
the bill and left with a good basket full.

    Der grocer doots uf tzaila un der customer
shquared de account un traveled ob mit seim
korrab ful.

THE HOTEL.

Landlord.—Well, also in town. When did you
arrive?

    Landlord.—Well, aw in der shtadt. Wann
bisht aw cooma?

Guest.—Just came in.

    Gosht.—Bin yoosht cooma.

L. Take a seat—up at the stove. Fine day. All
well at home?

    L. Nem a sitz—doh on der uffa. Finer
dawg. Seid er all g'soond derhame?

L. We have had remarkably fine weather, considering the time of year.

    L. Mer hen ivver ous shainas wedder g'hot,
considering de yohrstzeit.

G. Yes, the weather is very fine, but we need
rain, as the streams are getting low and millers'
find some difficuly on account of low water.

    G. Yaw, 's wedder is orrick fine, awer mer
setta raiga hawa weil 's wasser awfongs nidder wærd, un de miller finna difficulty weaga
'm nidder wasser.

L. Did you come in afoot?

    L. Bisht ri galuffa?

G. No, I drove as far as the bridge and there I tied the horse and walked across, and so did'nt have to pay the toll.

G. Nay, ich bin g'fawra so weit os on de brick un dort hob ich der gowl awgaboona un bin rivver g'luffa un seller wæg hob ich kæ bricka geld tzawla braucha.

The Landlord did'nt seem to be very favorably impressed with his bridge dodging customer, and found it convenient to attend to the wants of one who had just arrived with a carpet bag.

Der wæert hu net g'sheint orrick favorably impressed tzu si mit seim brika dodge customer, un ar huts noatwendich g'foona for tzu aim tenda os yusht aw cooma is mit 'm a carpet bag in der hond.

THE LAWYER.

Lawyer. Well sir—let me see, Mr. Mack, I believe?

Lawyer.—Well, luss mich sana, ich glawb du bisht der Mr. Mack?

Client.—Yes, Mack is my name.

Client.—Yaw, Mack is my nawma.

L. You reside up in the valley I believe?

L. Du wohnsht druvva in der valley, net so?

C. Yes, I have lived there for now nearly ten years, and I just came down to-day to see you about some business.

C. Yaw, dort hob ich shun sheer tzain yohr g'wohnt, un ich bin heit yoosht rooner cooma for tzu sana weaga a wennich bisness.

L. Well, Mr. Mack, what's the nature of the business?

L. Well, Mr. Mack, was is de noddoor fun der bisness?

C. Why its about settling up my father-in-law's estate.

C. Ei es is weaga meim shweega fodder siner eshtate settla.

L. When did he die?

L. Wann is ar g'shtorwa?

C. He died week before last.

C. De woch for der letsht is ar g'shtorwa.

L. Leave much property?

L. Hut ar feel property hinnerlussa?

C. Well yes, he left his farm, and some bonds and notes, and a good deal of stock on the farm.

C. Well yaw, ar hut si baueri, un bender, un notes un aw an ordlich grosser shtock uf der baueri.

L. And who is going to administer?

L. Un wær will adminishtra?

C. That's what I want you to see about.

C. Sell is evva weaga wass os ich dich sana will.

L. Is the widow living?

L. Læbt de widfraw noch?

C. No, she died two years ago.

L. Nay, se is g'shtorwa for tzwæ yohr.

L. Your wife is living is she?

L. Di fraw læbt noch, net so?

C. Yes, she and her sister and one brother—that's all the family.

C. Yaw, se du't, nn aw era shweshter un brooder—sell is de gons family.

L. Has he any debts on his property?

L. Sin enniche shoolda uf 'm property?

C. Oh, well, he has some debts, but not a great many.

C. Oh, well, ar hut shoolda, awer net orrick feel.

L. And you want to administer, I suppose?

L. Un ich fermoot os du selwer adminishtra wid?

C. Well yes, that's my intention, but may be Sam my brother-in-law thinks he ought to do the same.

C. Well yaw, sell is my obsicht, awer der Sam, my shwoger will ferleicht aw sell du.

L. Did you talk to him about it?

L. Husht shun mit eem g'shwetzd derweaga?

C. I did, and he said he thought we should both administer.

C. Ich hob, un ar hut g'maned mer setta oll tzwæ administera.

L. Well, Mr. Mack, your best way is in the first place to pay me a retainer of twenty dollars, and that will enable me to act professionally in the matter.

L. Well, Mr. Mack, di beshter waig is im arshta plotz mer amohl an retainer fun tzwonsich dawler gevva, un sell gebt mer d'no an professional recht der my roat tzu gev.va.

C. Retainer!—Let's see, that, I suppose, means a lawyer's fee?

C. Retainer!—Luss mohl sæ, sell mained denk ich, au lawyer's fee?

L. Exactly so. Being only the first instalment we call it a retainer—to retain me in the case.

L. Exactly so. Es is der arsht inshtalment, os mer 'n retainer haisa—for mich im case retaina.

C. Yes, now I understand. Well, here is twenty dollars. Now, what next?

C. Yaw, now fershtæ ich 's. Well, doh sin de tzwonsich dawler. Now, wass naigsht?

L. Well, from all you have told me, my advice is that you come again and bring Sam, your brother-in-law with you, and then we'll consult him and proceed to business.

L. Well, fun ollem os du mer sawgsht is my advice os du widder coomsht un bringsht der Sam, di shwoger, for mitnonner consulta un on de bisness gæ.

C. Then that's all we can do to-day?

C. Don is des olles wass heit tzu du is?

L. That's all. But you can come again to-morrow, or next day.

L. Sell is olles. Ower coom morrya, odder de naigsht dawg.

C. Well yes, say next day.

    C. Well yaw, der naigsht dawg.

This ended the first professional interview in regard to Mr. Mack's father-in- law's estate.

    Sell war 's end fum arshta professional g'shpraich weaga 'm Mr. Mack seim shweega fodder siner eshtate.

PROGRESS OF PENN. DUTCH LITERATURE.

The late Rev. Henry Harbaugh, D. D., a native of Franklin County, Pa., a prominent Reformed minister, was the author of a number of Penn. Dutch poems. His best production was "Shool House on der Creek," which has been extensively published in different newspapers. Rev. Harbangh's productions have all been republished, since his death, in a neat volume of a hundred and twenty-one pages, which book may be obtained at the Reformed Church Publication House at Philadelphia.

Mr. Harbaugh adhered strictly to the German orthography, whilst we adhere to the English, for reasons already stated.

Mr. Tobias Witner, residing in the vicinity of Buffalo, N. Y. is also a good writer of the new-born language, and he has made some very able productions.

Some years ago, Mr. E. M. Eberman wrote a number of humerous articles for a paper then published at South Bethlehem, but his orthography was a mixture of English and German, and he therefore lacked uniformity, though his productions were very humerous. A number of the German papers devote a portion of their space to Penn. Dutch, and all, as far as we know, adhere to the German spelling. Among these are the Allentown *Republikaner*, the Lebanon *Pennsylvanier*, Easton *Demokrat*, Bucks County *Express*, and Doylestown *Morgen Stern*. The Penn. Dutch writers for English papers generally use the English, as we do, but they are mostly very irregular in their spelling.

In 1874, Mrs. P. E. Gibbons published a book of about 300 pages, entitled "Pennsylvania Dutch," but it only gives some of the peculiarities of the Penn. Dutch people, and makes no attempt to produce the language except here and there a mere sentence, and in these efforts the writer utterly fails. For instance, " buggy fawra " (buggy riding) she writes " Buggy fawry," and "wait a bit" she translates "halty bissel" instead of "halt a bissel " as it should be written. Also "Good evening " she translates " Gutenobit " instead of " Good 'n owet." In her comments on the peculiarities of the English spoken by people of the Penn. Dutch regions, Mrs. Gibbons is more successful.

Prof. S. S. Haldeman of the University of Pennsylvania, has written a very able essay on Pennsylvania Dutch, which was published by the Philological society of London, and may also be obtained at the Reformed Publication House, at Philadelphia. In said production, Prof. H. gives a number of extracts from Harbaugh, Witmer, Rauch and others. But the book does not pretend to be a record of the language, but only descriptive. His spelling is also German.

Miss Rachael Bahn, of York County, Pa., is another successful writer of Penn. Dutch, and she has contributed several very good productions of poetry.

Mr. Zimmerman, of the *Times* and *Dispatch*, at Reading, Pa., has published a number of translations of English and Scotch poetry. Whilst he has done it remarkably well, they lack the necessary Penn. Dutch spirit to gain popularity.

It is admitted by all, that the author of this book has had much more experience in writing Penn. Dutch than any other individual living. His " Pit Schwefflbruner " letters were commenced in 1868, and then published in the political campaign paper called " Father Abraham," at Lancaster, and they gained a very large circulation. He has since then, at different times, supplied several papers with similar productions. In September 1878, he commenced publishing *The Carbon County Democrat*, at Mauch Chunk, Pa., with a letter·from "Pit" regularly every week, and being himself the publisher of said paper, the letters will be continued.

The following are specimen extracts from the productions of some of the writers referred to with translations:

From Harbaugh's "Shool House on Der Creek":

(German Orthography as it came from the pen of the author.)

> Heit is 's 'xæctly zwansig Johr,
>   Dass ich bin owwe naus;
> Naw bin ich widder lewig z'rick,
>   Un schteh am Schulhaus an d'r Krick,
> Juscht neekscht an's Dady's Haus.
>
> Ich bin in hunnert Heiser g'west,
>   Vun Maerbelstee un Brick,
> Un alles was sie hen, de Leit
> Dhet ich verschwappe eenig zeit
>   For's Schulhaus on der Krick.
>
> Wer mied deheem is, un will fort,
>   So luss ihn numme geh'—
> Ich sag ihm awwer vorne naus
> Es is all Humbuk owwe draus,
>   Un er werd's selwert seh'!
>
>   *   *   *   *
>
> Doh bin ich gange in die Schul
>   Wo ich noch war gans klee';
> Dort war der Meeschter in seim Schtuhl,
> Dort war sei wip, un dort sei Ruhl,—
>   Ich kann's noch Alles seh.
>
>   *   *   *   *

Mit all wass mer so sawga Kann,
    War's doch en guti Schul ;
Du finnscht keen Meeschter so, geh such—
Der seifre kann darch's ganze Buch,
    Un schkippt keen eeni Ruhl

    *   *   *   *

De kleene Maed hen Ring geschpielt
    Uf sllam Waasum da
Wann grosse Maed sin in der Ring—
'S is doch en wunnervolles Ding !—
    Sin grose Buwe ah !

Die Grose hen de Grose taggt,
    Die Kleene all vermisst!
Wie sin se g'schprunge ab un uf,
Wer g'wunne hot, verloss dich druf,
    Hot dichdiglich gekisst !

THE SAME AS WE WRITE IT, ENGLISH ORTHOGRAPHY.

Heit ishs exactly tzwonsich yohr
    Os ich bin uvva nous ;
Now bin ich widder levvich tzrick,
Un shtæ om shool house on der creek
    Yoosht naigsht ons dawdy's house.

Ich bin in hoonert heiser g'west
    Fun marble-shtæ un brick,
Un olles wass se hen, de leit,
Date ich fershwappa ennich tzeit
    For's school-house on der creek.

Wær meed derhame is, un will faurt,
    So luss een nooma gæ—
Ich sawg 'eem awer forna nous
Es is all humbug uvva drous
    Un ar wærds selwer sæ !

    *   *   *   *

Doh bin ich gonga in de shool
 We ich noch war gons klæ
Dort war der maishter in seim shtool,
Dort war si wip, un dort si rule—
 Ich con 's noch olles sæ.
  * * * *

Mit olles os mer sawga con
 War 's doch an gooty shool;
Du finnsht kæ maishter so, gæ, sooch
Dar cyphera con dorrich 's gonsa booch
 Un shkipt ken eany rule.
  * * * *

De klaney maid hen ring gashpeeld
 Uf sellam wausam doh;
Wann grosse maid sin in der ring
'S war doch 'n woonerfulles ding!
 Sin grosse boowa aw!

De grosse hen als grosse tag'd,
 De klaney all fermisst!
Wass sin se g'shproonga, ob un uf—
Wær g'woona hut, ferluss dich druf,
 Hut aw si share gakisst!

The following is a translation of the same extracts, as it appears in "Harbaugh's Harfe."

To-day it is just twenty years,
 Since I began to roam;
Now, safely back, I stand once more,
Before the quaint old school-house door,
 Close by my father's home.

I've been in hundred houses since
 Of marble built and brick;
Though grander far, their aim they miss,
To lure my hearts old love from this
 Old school-house at the creek.

Let those who dream of happier scenes,
    Go forth those scenes to find;
They'll learn what many have confessed,
That with our home our heart's true rest
    Is ever left behind.

     *   *   *   *

'Twas, here I first attended school
    Wen I was very small;
There was the Master on his stool,
There was his whip, and there his rule—
    I seem to see it all.

     *   *   *   *

With all the drawbacks, that was still,
    A well conducted school;
For master such, in vain you look,
Who cyphers through and through the book,
    And never skips a rule!

     *   *   *   *

The little girls, of ring most fond
    Their giggling circle drew;
When large girls joined in the ring
Now is it not a curious thing?
    The large boys did it too!

The large ones always tagged the large—
    The small ones always missed!
Then for the prize began the race;
The one that s caught, has now to face
    The music, and be kissed!

ANOTHER TRANSLATION.

As in our judgment, the foregoing translation
fails to convey an idea as to the genuine Pennsylvania Dutch spirit of the original, we have
translated the same extracts into "Dutchified,"
or broken English, as follows:

To-day it vas joost dwendy years
    Ven I out vesht dit go;
Un now I's back, so nice, un shlick
Un here's der shkool house on de creek
    Joost close by daddy's house.

I haf in hundred houses been,
    Of marble, shtones un brick;
But all of dem vat I dit see,
I'd shwap 'm off on any day,
    For 'd sokool-house on der creek.

Ven one don't vant to shtay at home,
    So joost you led him go;
But I can dell him—un I know besht—
It is all hoombug out in 'd vesht
    Un he vill find as dat is'h so!

        *   *   *   *

Yes, here's der blase I vent in 'd shkool,
    Ven I vas so quite shmall;
Dare vas der masder, on his shtool,
Dare vas his vip, un dare his rule
    Me dinks I see 'm all.

Mit all der drawbacks, any how,
    It vas a first rate shkool;
You find no masder so, go, look,
Vat cyphers trough and trough der book
    Mitout he shkip one single rule.

        *   *   *   *

De leedle garls in ring dit blay,
    On dis same grass batch here;
Ven beeger garls dit go in 'd ring—
It vas a very funny ding—
    Der beeg boys sure vas alvays dare,

Der beeg ones alvays beeg one tag'd
   Der leedle ones vas alvays misst;
Un den dey run so round un round,
Un ven he catch 'm I'll pe bound
   Dare vas som garls vot much got kiss'd.

EXTRACTS FROM HARBAUGH'S "HAMEWEH."

   English Orthography and translation.

We gleich ich selly bobbla bame !
Se shtane we breder doh;
Dort uf 'm gibble—g'wiss ich labe,
Huckt ollaweil 'n shtawr;
D'r gibble beegt sich, gook we's gownsht—
Ar habe'd sich awer fesht,
Ich sæ si roaty fliggle plain
Wann ar si feddra wesht;
Will wetta os si frawly hut
Uf sellam bawn 'n nesht.

TRANSLATION.—IVVERSETZUNG.

How well I love those poplar trees,
That stand like brothers there!
And on the top—sure as I live,
A black-bird perches now.
The top is bending—how it swings,
But still the bird holds fast,
How plain I see his scarlet wings
When he his feathers dressed!
I'll bet you, on that very tree
His wifie has a nest.

   It will be seen that in order to read the late
Dr. Harbauch's "Shool House on der Creek," and
his other poems as published in "Harbaugh's
Harfe" (Harbaugh's Harp) it is necessary to have
the benefit of a German education.   Here are a
few specimens of his German way of spelling
some of the words and names occuring in his productions:

Office—" Affis"; Orrick goot— (very good) "arg
gut"; Deer (door) "Dhier"; Jack (name)
Dschaeck"; General Jackson " Dscheneral Jeck-
schen "; Jim (name) "Dschim "; Juryman (Juryman) "Dschuryman"; Agent, "Edschent" Managed, "Maenedscht"; Nesht, (nest) "Nescht"
Notion, " Noschen "; Shnug, (snug) " Schnock "
Sbquire, (Esquire) "Schqueier.

Extract from Prof. Tobias Witmer's Penn.
Dutch Poem entitled : "Garboorts dawg, on my
Olty." (Birth day—To my old Woman.")

(Our own spelling.)

Oh was is shenner uf der welt
Os blimlin roat un weis?
Un blo, un gail, im arbla feld—
Wass sin de doch so neis!
Ich wais noch goot in seller tzeit
Hob ich nix leevers du,
Os in de wissa, long un breit
So blimlin g'soocht we du.
Doch is 's shun a longy tzeit
Os ich dort in dem feld,
De blimlin g'soocht, uf long un breit
Un uf di bosom g'shpelld.
Der hend amohl a gardle g'hot,
Di shweshterly un du ;
Ich hobs prepared, mit hock un shpawd
De blooma ni tzu du ;
Un wu ich hob im grossa shwail
De kee dort hinna g'soocht,
De lady shlippers, weis un gail
Hob ich mit hame gabrucht,
Un hob se in sell gartle plonst
By naucht im mondes licht,
Der hends net g'wist; bis yoosht at once'd
Hend eers gagest 's war mich.

TRANSLATION.--VIVVERSETZUNG.

Oh what is finer in the world
Than flowrets red and white?
And blue and yellow in the field

How beautiful and bright!
I know yet well that in that time
Nought would I rather do;
Than in the meadows, long and wide,
Such flowrets seek as you;
Yet it is quite a lengthened time
Since I in yonder field,
Sought out the flowers far and wide
And on thy bosom pinned.
You also had a garden bed—
You and your sister fair,
Which I prepared with hoe and spade,
To plant the flowers there;
And when I in the ample vale
The cattle there had sought,
The lady-slippers, gold and pale,
With me I homeward brought,
And in that garden bed at night
I set them when the moon was light;
You did not know who it could be,
But all at once you guessed—t'was me.

From a poem by Miss Rachel Bahn, of York, Pa.

Well, any how, wann's fre-yohr coomd,
Bin ich gapleased first-rate;
Die luft's so fair un awganame,
De rose so leeblich weht.
Now geha my gedonka nuf
Wu's immer fre-yohr is,
Wu's kæ feren'ring gevva du't
Wu's harrlich is gawiss.

TRANSLATION.—IVVERSETZUNg.

Well, any how, when spring times comes,
Then I am pleased first-rate;
So fair and soft the breezes blow,
So lovely is the rose,
'Tis then my thoughts are raised on high,
Where spring forever blooms,
Where change can never more be felt,
But glory shines around.

QUOTATIONS FROM SHAKESPEARE.

The following are extracts from Shakespeare.—
1. Brutas on the death of Cæsar; **2.** From Richard the III, and 3. From Hamlet—the latter being a burlesque rather than a translation :

ON THE DEATH OF CÆSAR.

BRUTAS GOES INTO THE ROSTRUM.

Bru. Romans, mit-barger un freinda! Har mich now aw; seid shtill, so os eer oll hara kent; glawbt meer uf my air, un wann eer reshpect hen for my air don glawbt eer aw wass ich sawg; blamed mich in eirm goota fershtond, awer luss aw eier fershtond wocker bleiva so os eer besser judga kent. Wann aner in dar fersommlung is os 'n gooter freind tzu'm Cæsar war, tzu eem sawg ich os ar ken besserer freind tzu'm war os ich selwer. Wann seller freind froked un wissa will ferwoss os der Brutas uf g'shtonna is geaga der Cæsar, don is des my ontwardt : Os ich der Cæsar net wennicher gaglicha hob, awer os ich Rome maner gaglicha hob. Wær 's eich leever wann der Cæsar lava date un eer all shklawfa, os der Cæsar dode un eer all freie menner? Weil der Cæsar my freind war du ich my traina fergeesa for een ; we ar glicklich war huts meer plesseer gevva ; ar war 'n brawfer mon, un ich air 'n, awer weil ar ambitious war, hob ich 'm si lava ganooma. Un now, wo is aner so mean os ar willens wær 'n bondsmon tzu si? Wann so aner doh is, luss 'n rous shwetza. Is aner doh os net 'n Roman is? Is aner doh os net seim lond der fore-tzoog gebt? Wann so aner doh is, luss 'n rous shwetza —so aner, of course, du ich net suita. Ich wart for 'n ontwardt !

FROM KING RICHARD III—ACT 1. SCENE 1.

GLOSTER.—Now is der winter fun unser unru
Glorreich g'maucht by der sun fun Yorrick;
Un all de wulka os ivver unserm house waura,
Sin deef in de sæ ni fergrawa.
Now sin unser kep badeck'd mit seeg's krentza,
Unser g'woreny g'ware uf g'hunka for monu-
    menta ;
Unser larms tzeita gachanged tzu plesseer meet-
    ings ;
Unser longy marcha tzu awganamey walks.
Shrecklicher greek hut si g'sicht fershennert,
Un now, onshtot os mer uf shteiga in der soddle
For de sæla fun unser geagner tzu fergelshtera,
Capera mer so doh room mit de ladies.
Awer ich ich bin net g'shaped for so shports un
    tricks—
Bin net g'maucht for shpiggle glesser corris-
    seera—
Bin kroom, obgakartz'd, ous proportion,
Un ous gooty noddoor's g'shtolt batroga—
Bin ous shape gamaucht, un fore meiner tzeit
In de welt cooma—net holwer g'finished—
Lawm un shep, so weesht un ous der fashion,
Os de hoond on mich gowtza wann ich se yoosht
    aw gook.
Un now, in so shtilly freedens tzeita
Hob ich nix tzu du os meer aw shtate—
Except ols my shodda bagooka, in der sun,
Un considera ivver my eagny ung'shtolt.
Dawrum, weil ich gor net der mon bin
For mich ob gevva mit so'shtock we weibsleit,
Will ich ebbas soonsht proweera—der rascal acta,
Un all de freedens plesseera uf brecha.
Plans hob ich g'laigd for 'n ufroor raisa
Tzwisha meim bruder Clarence un 'm Kanich—
Se amohl uf hetza geaga nonner—in doder hos ;
Un wann der Kanich Edward so true is os ich
    falsh bin
Don wærd der Clarence aw amohl uf g'used.
*   *   *   *

ACT V.—SCENE IV.

CATESBY—Hilf, my Hærr fun Norfolk, hilf, hilf!
Der Kanich act mæ woonerlich os 'n mensh.—
Farricht sich for nemond—gebt nix um g'fore;
Si gowl is dode, un now fecht ar olles tzu foos,
Un soocht der Richmond. for dode un lava—
Hilf, hilf, my Hærr, odder der dawg is ferlora!

ENTER KING RICHARD.

K. RICH. 'N gowl! 'N gowl! my kanichreich for
'n gowl!

CATE.—Tzurick, my Hærr, ich helf der tzu 'm
a gowl.

K. RICH.—Shklawf! Ich hob my lava uf gapohst
Un ich luss 's now druf aw cooma;
Wann aw sex Richmond's im feld sin,
Finf hob ich shun dode g'maucht, onshtot een,
'N gowl, 'n gowl! my kanichreich for 'n gowl!

  *   *   *   *

RICHMOND.—Lobe Gott un eier g'wehr; lobe tzu
unser seechreiche freind;
Der dawg is unser, der blootich hoond is dode!

FROM HAMLET.

ACT I.—SCENE V.—RE-ENTER GHOST AND HAMLET.

HAM.—Wo wid mich onna nemma? Shtwetz, ich
gæ nimmy weider.

GHOST.—Now mind mich;

HAM.—Ich will.

GHOST.—My shtoond is sheer gor cooma
Os ich tzurick mus, in de shweffel's flomma,
Muss ich mich widder uf gevva.

HAM.—Oh! du ormas shpook!

GHOST.—Pity mich net, awer geb mer now di ora,
For ich will der amohl ebbas sawga.

HAM.—Shwetz rous, for ich will 's now aw hara.

GHOST.—Un wann du 's haresht don nemsht aw
satisfaction.

HAM. Well, wass is 's? Rous mit!

GHOST. Ich bin deim dawdy si shpook;
G'sentenced for a tzeit long rumm lawfa
nauchts,

Un im dawg fesht shtecka im fire,
Bis de shlechty saucha os ich gadu hob in
  meina noddoor's dawga.
Ous gabrenn'd un ous g'loxeerd sin.
Awer, ich darraf der now net sawga
Wass de secrets fun meim g'fengniss sin.
Ich kent der 'n shtory derfu fertzaila,
So os 's garingshta wardt
Deer di sale uf reisa dait; di yoong's bloot
  kalt freera;
Die tzwæ awga ous 'm kup rous gooka
  maucha we fireiche shtarna,
Un di hohr uf 'm kup grawd nuf shtella,
We dicky, shteify si-barshta.
Awer ich darraf 's net du
Os ich 's sawg tzu ora fun flaish un bloot.
Un now, hurrich! hurrich!
Wann du yeamohls ebbas fun deim dawdy
  gadenkt husht!
HAM.—Oh, Himmel!
GHOST.—Un now nem aw satisfaction for si mord.
HAM.—Du sawgsht doch net mord?
GHOST.—Yo, ich sawgs, un 's arricksht is, 'n weesh-
  ter, unnoddeerlicher mord—
HAM.—Well don, rous mit, luss mich now olles
  wissa,
  Un ferluss dich druf os ich aw satisfaction
  nem.
GHOST.—Ich sæ du bisht ready,
  Un wann du's derbei lussa daitsht
  Wærsht net maner wært os ferfowlts un-
  kraut.
  Now Hamlet, horrich wass ich der sawg;
  Es war ous gevva os ich g'shlofa het in meim
  bomgorda.
  Un os 'n shlong on mich gacroddled wær,
  Un het mich dote gabissa.
  Sell war de shtory im gonsa lond,
  Awer de very shlong os di dawdy dote gabis-
  sa hut,

Trawgt ollaweil deim dawdy si crone uf 'm
kup !

HAM.—Oh, by meiner sale—demnoch war 's my
Uncle !

GHOST.—Yaw, 's war—der weesht ketzer—
An dreckicher un falsher dihenker,
Hut sich d'no aw gamaucht by meiner fraw
—di eagny mommy,
Un hut se g'hired un tzu sich g'nooma.
Awer du de mommy net blama—
Luss se mit fridda—se is evva doch di mom-
my—
Awer ich con nimmy lenger bleiva—
De naucht is sheer om end, un dawges licht
is om cooma,
Un ich muss ob, un tzurick, tzurick !
Yusht noch ea wardt maner :
We ich sellamohls dort g'shlofa hob—
'S war so about midda im nummidawg,
Is my eagner bruder—di uncle
On mich nuf g'shneeked cooma
Un hut 'n gons buttly ful gift ous g'lared in
my ore,
Un sell hut mich ob g'fixed, un ich bin aw
grawd druf g'shnopt,
Un mit all meina sinda nous g'shtept in de
onner welt
Unprepared un unbakared !
Now mind, du moosht satisfaction nemma,
So farry well.   Fergess mich net.
Farry well, farry well ! [Exit Ghost.]

HAM.—Awer now will ich aw de shwarnote krega
Wann ich net aw satisfaction nem,
Un now doh gaits.   Hole mich der shinner,
Wann 's net desmohl 'n gons g'wittrich gros-
ser rumpus gebt doh im shteddle !

EXTRACT FROM SCRIPTURE.

STORY OF THE PRODIGAL SON.—Luke XV.

An g'wisser mon hut tzwæ boova g'hot.
Un der yingsht fun ena hut g'sawt tzu seim dawdy,

Dawdy, geb mer 's dale fun der arbshaft os
tzu meer folt.   Un ar hut si living unner ena
ferdaild.

Un net feel dawga nochderh ond, hut der yingsht
sohn olles tzomma g'sommelt un is gonga
weit in 'n onner lond, un dort hut ar si sauch
fershwent mit shlechts lava.

Un we ar olles g'shpent hut sin orrick hordy tzeita
ivver 's lond cooma, un ar war d'no in grossy
note.

Un ar is gonga un hut sich ferdingt tzu 'm a eiwohner fun sellam lond ; un seller hut 'n nous
g'shickt for si tzu feedera in de felder.

Un ar hut hut selwer nix tzu essa g'hot os 's food-
er wo se de si mit g'feederd hen ; un nemond
hut 'm ebbas gevva.

Un we ar tzu sich selwer cooma is hut ar g'sawt :
We feel fun mein dawdy si gadingty leit hen
brode ganunk un noch ivverich, un ich du
doh hoonger leida.

Ich will uf un tzu mein dawdy gæ un will tzu eem
sawga, Dawdy, ich hob mich fersindich'd
geaga Himmel un fore deer.

Un ich bin 's nimmy wært di sohn tzu sei : mauch
mich we anes fun dina gadingty.

Un ar is uf, un tzu seim Dawdy gonga.   Awer we
ar noch weit ob war hut si Dawdy een g'sana,
un hut mitleida mit 'm g'hot, un is g'shproong-
a, un hut 'n um der hols grickt, un hut 'n
gabuss'd.

Un der sohn hut g'sawt, Dawdy, ich hob mich
fersindich'd geaga Himmel, un fore dina awga,
un ich bin 's net wært di sohn tzu sei.

Awer der Dawdy hut g'sawt tzu sina gadingty leit,
bring der besht ruck un du 'n eem aw ; un du
'n ring on si finger, un shoe uf si fees.

Un bring 's fetshd colb, un shlauchts, un luss uns
essa, un looshtich si.

For my sohn war dode, un is widder levvich ; ar
war ferlora, un is g'foona, un se hen aw g'fong-
a looshtich tzu wærra.

Now, der eldsht sohn war im feld; un we ar
naigsht ons house cooma is hut ar g'hared os
se music hen, un donsa.

Un ar hut anes fun de deener g'froked was des
olles maned?

Un ar hut 'm g'sawt, dei bruder is cooma; un dei
Dawdy hut 's fet colb g'shlaucht, weil ar safe
un sound aw cooma is.

Un ar war bais, un hut net ni gæ wella, dawrum
is si Dawdy nous, un hut 'n gacoaxed.

Un in ontwardt hut ar tzu seim dawdy g'sawt,
Doh de feela yohr hob ich der gadeend, un
hob nee net di rules gabrucha; un doch husht
du mer nee net amohl 'n yung gais'l gevva os
ich plesseer maucha kent mit mina freinda.

Awer so bol os dar doh sohn aw cooma is, wo 's
sauch os du 'm gevva husht ferhous'd hut
mit lava unner shlechty weibsleit, d'no husht
's fet colb g'shlaucht for 'n.

Un ar hut tzu 'm g'sawt, sohn, du warsht olsfordt
by mer, un olles os ich hob is di.

Es war recht os mer looshtich un fro warra sin;
for dei bruder war dode, un is widder levvich;
un war ferlora un is g'foona.

THE TREE IS KNOWN BY ITS FRUIT.
FROM MATT. VII, 13TH TO 20TH.

Gæ ni dorrich 's enga doar, for gross is 's doar,
un braid is der waig os tzu ruination feerd, un feel
huts os seller waig gane.

Weil de deer eng is un der waig shmall os in 's
lava feerd sin wennich os 's finna.

Heet eich fore falshy profaita wo in shofe's
claidung cooma, un innerlich hoongeriche welf
sin.

Eer mist se kenna by era frichta. Du'n leit
trow-wa somla fun dorna, odder feiga fun dishtle
shteck?

An yeader gooter bawn produced yoosht gooty
froocht. Awer 'n shlechter bawm produced
shlechty froocht.

An gooter bawm con kæ shlechty froocht produsa, un 'n shlechter bawm con kæ gooty froocht
produsa.

An yeader bawm os kæ gooty froocht produced
wærd um g'hocke'd un ins fire g'shmissa.

Dawrum, by era froocht mist er se kenna.

THE LORD'S PRAYER.

'M HÆRR SI GABAIT.

Unser Fodder, du os im Himmel bisht. G'aird
is di nawma. Di kanichreich coom'd. Di willa
sul gadu wærra uf der ard so we im Himmel. Geb
uns heit unser daiglich brode. Fergeb uns unser
shoolda, so we mer unser shooldner fergevva. Un
luss uns net ferfeer'd wærra in shlechtes, awer
heet uns geaga ungoot. For di is 's kanichreich,
un de gawalt, un all de air for immer, Awmen.

SPELLING REFORM.

Years ago, Prof. Witmer (specimens of his
Penn. Dutch are herein given) endeavored to per-
suade the author of THE HAND BOOK to adopt a
mode of spelling which he contends would be
more simple and practical than any other system
ever proposed, and that it would answer the wants
of English and German as well as Penn. Dutch.
After considering the matter, and making a few
trials, we are almost persuaded that he is correct.
His system is simply to have each vowal to represent its own proper sound and no other, and
this would need the addition of one vowel, making six instead of five—the vowels to represent
the sounds:

ʊ————aw		i————e
a————ah		o————o
e————a		u————u

The "aw" we here represent by an "a" up
side down (ʊ.) The difference between the long
and short sounds is made by single and double
vowels—as it and iit, or bot (but) and boot (boat.)

To illustrate, we now propose to write this sentence according to the new system as advocated
by Prof. Witmer, thus:

Tu illostreet wii nuu propoos tu wrait this sen-
tens accʊrding tu thi nuu sistem as advoceted bai
Prof. Witmer, thus:

Eben so gut kann man deitsch schreiben—so
wohl als pennsylvanisch deitsch oder English—
eins so gut als dasz andere.

Eben so guut kʊnn mʊn daitsh shraiben—so
wool ʊls pennsilvʊnish daitsh odar english—ains
so guut ʊls dʊs ʊndere.

Up im Pennsylvania Deitsh wær's yoosht so
goot. De fact is, wann se 'mWitmer si plan aw
nemma data don kents gor kæ mistakes gevva im
Deitsh, English odder Pennsylvania Deitsh shreiva
—for 's wær all unner der same rule, un Je leit
kenta anes so goot lasa os 's onner.

Un im Pennsilveenia Daitsh war 's yusht so
guut. Di fact is wen sii 'm Witmer sai plan v
nema deeta den kents ger kee misteeks geva im
Daitsh,English odder Pennsilvenia Daitsh shraiwa,
fer 's war el unnar dar seem ruul, un de lait kenta
eens so guut leesa es 's ennar.

PIT SCHWEFFELBRENNER.

The following is an extract from one of the humerous letters from " Pit Schweffelbrenner," giving his plan for a narrow guage Railway and other scientific subjects, which we copy from a recent number of the CARBON COUNTY DEMOCRAT:

MISTER DROOKER:—Sidder os ich selly phonograph shwetz machine g'sana hob doh fergonga hob ich an gonsy set neie gadonka in meim kup shtecka. Un es is kæ mistake in seller machine. Es is net feel gresser os der Bevvy era closeringer, un es hut aw 'n handle, so uf 'n awrt os we 'n booterfos. Ich hob shun uft leit hara sawga os se now 'n ding hen os wann mer ni shwetzt odder peift, os mer de wardta un oll de sounds ei shparra con, un se enniche tzeit nochderhond rous lussa—so os de machine shwetzt. Awer now hob ich 's selwer g'sæ, un mit mina eagny ora hob ich de wardta selwer hara ous der machine rous cooma.

Un now bin ich aw g'satisfied os gor nix in der gonsa weld unmiglich is. My mind is now aw uf gamaucht os ich mich noch dem entirely ob geb mit science. Now gæ ich ni for inventions un du se all patenta un d'no ferkawf ich de County rights un mauch geld g'nunk for 'n grose sondshtainich house baua un a pawr match geil holta un der Bevvy 'n first-rater neier dress kawfa besides.

Ich hob now shun an plan for 'n neier patent narrow guage Railroad—aner os yusht holwer so feel kusht os 'n braid guage double track. Yusht ea riggle is my plan. Du denksht awer mer con kæ train runna uf so'm a single track, awer ich hob 'n plan os 's du't.

My plan is os der head engineer sich forna uf de ingine shtellt mit so'm a longer pole un du't de gons train sellerwæg balansa—so uf 'n awrt os we der circus mon os uf 'm tight g'shponnta

shtrick uf un ob lawft. Un we shtarricker os de
train runnd uf meim patent single track, we safer
os 's is, for es is yusht wann de cars shtill shtane
os se umfolla kenna. Of course my plan is os mer
de cars uf yader side shteibert wann de train ols
shtupt on de stations, un wann mer ob shtart
nemmt mer de shteiber aweck un der mon mit
'm longa pole gait widder on's balansa, der Con-
ducter gebt's wardt allaboard, un d'no widder uf
un ob we'n hoonert horse power g'witter shtorm.

Ich hob aw'n plan for 'n Raliroad os mer de
train's runna con barrick nuf un nooner ona
engine—gons entirely fun selwer. Of course,
ennicher norr wase os barrick nooner gaits anyhow fun selwer. Awer barrick nuff runna fun
selwer is'n onner ding. Awer ich hob der plan
un nem aw'n patent rous derfore. Der plan is os
ich de hinnera redder feel gresser mauch os de
fuddera, un sell du't d'no's gawicht fum car fun
hinna ahead pusha un es fershtæt sich fun selwer
os's de fuddera redder forna weck dreibt un de
hinnera aw d'no hinna noch tzeegd.

Ich con der awer sawga os 's gons ferdeihenkert
feel kup arwet g'nooma hut eb os ich uf den plan
cooma bin.

Un so bol os ich my patent Railroad cars
amohl im gong hob sin aw de locomotiff's ous
g'shpeelt. Ich hob im sin company un Shtate
rights fum patent tzu ferkawfa. Du consht 'm
head mon fum Lehigh Valley Railroad dort in
Mauch Chunk sawga os ich willens bin ena's
patent recht tzu gevva for about fooftzich daussend dawler, un os se mer'n breef shreiva sulla
un mich's grawd wissa lussa eb se's nemma odder
net.

Ich hob aw'n plan for 'n neie sort patent
hinkle soup kucha—an soup os ame feel geld
shpawrd in denna hordty tzeita. Der plan is des:
Mer grickt 'n shanes fettas hinkle un nemmts
tzu'm photograph mon un lust's obnemma. D'no

wann mer hinkle soup maucht du't mer evva
yusht about tzwæ quart wasser in der eisa hoffa,
'n holb pint bona, about finf grumbeera in klaney
shticker shneida, un plenty peffer un sols dertzu.
Wann de soup om kucha is d'no muss mer der
eisa-hoffa uf decka un 's photograph picter fum
hinkle a kortz shtickly uvva drau henka un a
reflecter so uf fixa os 's de reflection fum picter
gawd in der hoffa ni runnd, un sell gebt der soup
d'no aw der flavor fum hinkle yusht exactly so
goot os wann's gons hinkle mit kup, fees un
shwons in de soup ni gakucht wær. Mit ame
photograph picter fum a fetta hinkle con mer
soup kucha olly dawg for'n gonses yohr.

De Bevvy glawbt awer net os mer raly gooty
hinkle soup maucha con mitout mer du't's hinkle
selwer in de soup ni kucha. Awer de lelt hen aw
net gaglawbt os mer'n machine maucha con os'n
levviche mensha shproach shwetzt we seller
phonograph. Awer sell hob ich selver g'sana.
Un now will ich de boardlng heiser un hotels
amohl larna wulfelly hinkle soup kucha. Un
ich insures aw os de soup yusht so goot wærd os
de wo mer grickt in de boarding heiser in der shtadt.

Ich bin aw om considera for 'n patent waeg ous
finna so os de boilers uf de shteam boats net
ferbursta kenna. My plan is for 's wasser kucha
uf forna nous uf 'm lond eb os 's boat ob shtart,
un wann's fartich gakucht is du't mer's in de
shteam ingine ni runna un d'no is gor kæ g'fore os
's an explosion gebt.

ANOTHER SPECIMEN.

From another letter by Pit Schweffelbrenner, published in the same paper, we copy the following on the subject of chewing tobacco in Church; domestic affairs, &c.

De letsht wuch war my breef aw amohl interesting, for maner os a dootzend hen mer g'sawt os se gor nix ous g'fuoona hetta fum welshkorn plousa un huckle-baira picka im midda winter wann se's net selwer g'sana hetta uf shwartz un wise in der Tzeitung.

Well, ennicher norr con saucha nooner shreiva os olly leit wissa. Awer 's nemt 'n shmarter mon for de leit saucha sawga os se gor net wissa.

Un now, weil ich so goot gadu hob will ich der noch and frishy lot news items shicka.

De hinkle neshter sin plenty, awer de hinkle un de oyer sin rawr. Im olt Solaklupper seim shtol is shtro g'nunk for finf hoonert hinkle nesh ter, awer ar hut nix os ea hawna, dri hinkle un ea olty clook, un selly shtane all drooka ollaweil.

Om Soondawg war ich un de Bevvy in der Kærrich. Der porra hut yusht about goot gapreddichd. Der subject war ebbas fum Crishtuffel Columbus, un ar hut aw an allusion g'maucht tzum Pushtle Paulus we ar unser lond frei g'maucht hut im dreisich yaireicha greek. De Kærrich war orrick g'crowd, for as war 'n party dort fum Clobboardshteddle un se sin im shlidda cooma. We de foreshtayer awer drau gonga sin for de collection uf nemma sin se sheer all uf un nous gonga. Aner hut awer doch ebbas gadu for de Kærrich —ar hut about 'n holb poont ous gacowder chawduwock, mit maner os'n pint frishy bree uf 'm budda g'lust for de benefit fum shweeper.

In der Kærrich is 'n first rater plotz for ame si
chaw duwock goot enjoya.   A dale leit sin awer
so shtarns particular os se 'n fuss maucha wann
aner chaw duwock bree uf der dudda shpowt in
der Kærrich, un bahawpta sell wær shlechty monneer.   Awer mer muss nix um so leit gevva. Der
chaw duwock woxt for de benefit fum fulk.   Un
wo is 'n besserer plotz for 'n grose mowl ful goot
enjoya os in der Kærrich?   Un es maucht aw nix
ous eb 'n carpet uf 'm budda is odder net.   Wan
kæ carpet is, ei don duts anyhow kæ shawda, for
de bree hut ols 'n gonsy wuch tzeit for shæ ins
huls ni drickla, un es du't der floor aw protecta,
for huls os goot ei g'soked is mit chaw duwock
bree dut ne net ferfowla, un es fertreibt aw de wær-
ram.   Es is wohr, es du't der floor a wennich
fleckich gooka maucha, awer wær sell net garn
sana will moos evva in an onnery direction gooka.
Anyhow, se hen kæ bisness der floor tzu watcha
un inshpecta, de weil os der porra on der arwet
is om Gottes deensht.   Un wann an carpet uf 'm
floor is don du't chaw duwock bree aw kæ shawda,
for 's carpet dut de bree all uf soaka, un sellerwæg is der floor entirely protect.

Unser shteddle is now aw om improofa, un
sell is 'n sign os widder amohl gooty tzeita cooma.
Doh will ich der 'n lisht gevva fun de hawpt im-
profments :

Der Kitzelderfer hut 'n neie deer maucha lussa
on seim shtol, un a nei dauch uf si huls-shuppa.

Der olt Solaklupper hut im sin a nier si-shtall
baua naigsht free-yohr, mit a hinkle shtall im
tzwetta shtuck.   Der ainsich difficulty mit 'm
Solaklupper is weaga de shtamps.

De Betz Schnitzler, 'm Henner si fraw, bleibt
now aw widder omohl a while derhame.   Es is 'n
bu, un der Henner hut forgeshter owet aw amohl
de rounds g'shtand ons Kitzelderfer's.   Es hut 'n
a dawler un a holwer gakusht, un de Bevvy sawgt
sell het grawd amohl 'm bubbelly a pawr frocks

un hemdlin un socks gakawft. Om naigsht Soondawg wella se's klæ dingly dawfa lussa, un ich
hob'n Henner g'sawt os wann ar's Pit haist, odder Pitty, don kawf ich 'm aw an neier frock os 'n
fartle dawler de yard kusht.

Wann de tzeita net bol besser wærra doh im
shteddle don gæ ich in a neie bisness im free-yohr
—an frenology office shtarta for de- leit era kep
feela un ena explaina wass drin shteckt. Aner
os 's kep feela fershtæt con olles explaina so goot
un so wohr os 'n wohr-sawger. A dale leit hen
orrick feel benevolence, un ideality un venera-
tion un so sauch in era kep. Ich hob 'n booch
os olles explained. Wann ich in de bisness ni gæ
don charge ich net maner os 'n holwer dawler for
'n kup examina—weibsleit for holb price. Un
sellerwæg con ich easy tzwelf dawler der dawg
ferdeena, providing ich grick de customers.

De Bevvy is g'soond ollaweil, un se lust dich
greesa. Se is a wennich woonerfitzich eb du noch
leddich bisht odder net? Se sawgt wann du noch
kæ fraw husht glawbt se os du 'n gooty chance
shtæ daitsht by der Sally Ann Braidfoos, abbor-
dich now· sidder os se 'n neie set tzain grickt hut
fum tzaw duckter. Se gooktnow tzwansich yohr
vinger, un de Bevvy bahawpt se dait yusht suita
for an editors fraw, weil se so ivver ous monneerlich un gadooldich is. Now consht der hint nemma. For particulars, roof aw by der Bevvy.

A POLITICAL EXTRACT.

Pit and Bevvy disagree politically, and this is the way he attempts to get ahead of his better half, being another extract from THE CARBON COUNTY DEMOCRAT :

Om letshta Moondawg owet war ich on der meeting, all der waig druvva in Yommerstown, un wann de Bevvy 's g'wist het os ich dort war don hets widder amohl 'n rumpus gevva. Awer des mohl hob ich se g'foold, for ich hob se weis gamaucht os ich ommanot soonsht onna gonga waer for ousfinna eb ich net krumbeera kawfa kent for de huckshter bisness shtarta. Ich will now aw mentiona os wann du ebber waisht os garn krumbeera ferkawfa will for a fartle dawler de bushel, os ich ready bin 'm se ob tzu kawfa un 'm my note gevva for 's cash. In der krumbeera bisness is geld tzu maucha, providing mer con se kawfa uf borricks un ferkawfa for cash.

Es war'n gons boomerawlish grosser crowd dort —awer, somehow, es is mer fore cooma os der graisht dale fun ena uf der letza side waura.

Awer de speecha waura yoosht about goot. Der arsht os der lead g'nooma hut war 'n Englisher —any how ar hut English g'shwetzt un hut denna karls amohl Hail Columby gevva. Ar hut ena g'sawt fum Shmidt—wass 'n gooter, frümmer un crishtlicher mon os ar is, un os mer all mitnonner for 'n vota setta weil ar olsfort gooty coompany halt. Sell is aw so. Ich kenn 'n goot. Ar coom'd aw ebmohls ons Kitzelderfers, un dort is de coompany olsfort first-rate—so leit os we ich un der Olt Solaklupper un der Benshy Bixmiller un der Sammy Schnitzler un so karls. Un waer der Shmidt bakannt is we ich bin mus aw confessa os ar nemond nix in der waig laigd. Anyhow ich vote for 'n—except im fol os de Bevvy troovel maucht derweaga.

CLOSING REMARKS.

Whilst the author has found several rather provoking typographical errors in the preceeding pages, he flatters himself that, all things considered, his work has been done quite as well as could be expected, and he is more strongly convinced than ever before that his effort will be recognized as a gratifying success, especially so in view of the fact that it is a comprehensive and valuable original record of a language spoken by some millions of American people who are noted for many very commendable characteristics. It is quite safe to say that a more industrious, honest, or substancial people than the Penn. Dutch cannot be found in this or in any other country on the globe. As agriculturalists they are certainly unsurpassed. The well known fact that, as a general rule, the very richest soil of Pennsylvania—such as the counties of Lancaster, Berks, Lebanon, Lehigh, Northampton, York, Cumberland, and the best and richest parts of Adams, Bucks, Montgomery, Snyder, Union, Northumberland and Dauphin, are occupied mainly by our people and their descendants, seems to go very far to prove the superior sagacity of the early Penn. Dutch settlers of these rich and beautiful agriculturial regions.

We also venture to say that the percentage of Penn. Dutch people who become inmates of penitentiaries and alms houses is remarkably small, notwithstanding the fact that their average of educational advantages is considerably smaller than that of our English speaking people.

It is also a fact that among the leading merchants and manufacturers of the large cities and towns—especially of Philadelphia, the Penn. Dutch element is largely represented, and that, as a general rule, they are men of the highest order of integrity. And when they find their way to high political positions in the state or nation, they generally compare favorably with any other class.

When such old school Penn. Dutchmen as Heister, Snyder, Schultz, Wolf, Ritner, Shunk, and Hartranft filled the highest state office, all the people, of every political faith, were well satisfied that the executive chair was occupied by strictly honest and competent men.

Professor Haldeman's treatise on Penn. Dutch has already been referred to in the foregoing pages. Preceeding the same, we find an explanatory notice, by Prof. Alexander J. Ellis, of Kensington, England, from which we extract the following:

" While I was engaged with the third part of my *Early English Pronunciation*, Prof. Haldeman sent me a reprint of some humerous letters by Rauch, entitled : ' Pennsylvania Deitsh ; De Campain Breefa fum Pit Schweffelbrenner.' Perceiving, at once, the analogy between this debased German with English intermixture, and Chaucer's debased Anglo-Saxon with Norman intermixture, I requested, and obtained such further information as enabled me to give an account of this singular modern reproduction of the manner in which our English language itself was built up, and insert it in the introduction to my chapter on Chaucer's pronunciation. But, I felt it would be a loss to Philology if this curious living example of a mixture of languages were dismissed with such a cursory notice, and I therefore requested Prof. Haldeman, who by birth and residence, philological and phonetic knowledge, was so well fitted for the task, to draw up a more extended notice, as a paper to be read before the Philological Society of London. Hence arose the following little treatise of which, I, for my own part, can only regret the brevity. But the Philological Society having recently exhausted most of its resources by undertaking the publication of several extra volumes, was unable to issue another of such length, and hence the present essay appears independently.   *   *   *

Sufficient importance does not seem to have been hitherto attached to watching the growth and change of *living languages*. We have devoted our philological energies to the study of dead tongues which we could not pronounce, and have therefore been compelled to compare by letters rather than by sounds, and which we know only in the form impressed upon them by the scholars of various times. The form in which they were originally written is for ever concealed. The form in which they appear in the earliest manuscripts has practically never been published, but has to be painfully collected from a mass of various readings. The form we know is a critical, conjectural form, patched up by men distinguished for scholarship, but for the most part entirely ignorant of the laws which govern the changes of speech. The very orthography is medieval. We are thus enabled to see as little of the real genesis of language, in form, in sound, in gramatical and logical construction, in short, in the real pith of philological investigation—the relation of thought to speech-sounds—as the study of a full grown salmon would enable us to judge of the marvelous development of that beautiful fish. Such studies as the present, will, I hope, serve among others to stimulate exertion *in the new* direction. We cannot learn life by *studying fossils alone*."

These very encouraging words from Mr. Ellis finally removed all doubt as to the expediency of publishing this volume. Penn. Dutch is " a living language " and it is no longer without a record, though an imperfect one. It is a beginning, and others, much more able and better fitted, will take up the subject and greatly improve upon this effort.

Should this little enterprise receive sufficient encouragement, moral and financial, it is probable that we will in the near future venture upon another and a more extensive effort to treat the public to Penn. Dutch literature. Be this as it may, we will continue regularly to write and publish our "Pit Schweffelbrenner" letters in our own paper, The *Carbon County Democrat*, published at Mauch Chunk, Pa. The author writes for no other paper. Whilst said letters are humerous, they also incidentally afford much practical instruction in Penn. Dutch.

THE

Carbon County

DEMOCRAT.

Pit Schweffelbrenner.

PUBLISHED every SATURDAY,

—AT—

MAUCH CHUNK, PA.,

—BY—

E. H. RAUCH.

Price of Subscription,   -   - $1.50.

The Carbon County Democrat

**is the only paper containing the regular
Pennsylvania Dutch productions by
PIT SCHWEFFELBRENNER.**

*Metalmark Books is a joint imprint of The Pennsylvania State University
Press and the Office of Digital Scholarly Publishing at The Pennsylvania State
University Libraries. The facsimile editions published under this
imprint are reproductions of out-of-print, public domain works that hold
a significant place in Pennsylvania's rich literary and cultural past.
Metalmark editions are primarily reproduced from the University Libraries'
extensive Pennsylvania collections and in cooperation with other
state libraries. These volumes are available to the public for viewing online
and can be ordered as print-on-demand paperbacks.*

LIBRARY OF CONGRESS CATALOGING-IN-PUBLICATION DATA

Rauch, E. H. (Edward H.), 1826–1902
Rauch's Pennsylvania Dutch hand-book : a book for instruction = Rauch's
Pennsylvania deitsh hond-booch : en booch for inshtructa / by E. H. Rauch.
p.   cm.
Summary: "A dictionary and guide to the language of the Pennsylvania
Germans. Includes English–Pennsylvania German and Pennsylvania
German–English translations, along with a phrase book and bilingual sections
on conducting business in various settings. Concludes with translated excerpts
of poetry, Bible verses, and Shakespeare"—Provided by publisher.
Originally published: Rauch's Pennsylvania Dutch hand-book : a book for
instruction, 1879.
ISBN 978-0-271-04883-3 (pbk. : alk. paper)
1. Pennsylvania German dialect—Dictionaries.
2. Pennsylvania German dialect—Conversation and phrase books.
3. English language—Dictionaries—German.
4. German language—Dictionaries—English.
I. Title.
II. Title: Pennsylvania Dutch hand-book = Pennsylvania deitsh hond-booch.

PF5936.R3 2011
437'.9748—dc22
2010053197

Printed in the United States of America
Reprinted 2011 by The Pennsylvania State University Press
University Park, PA 16802-1003